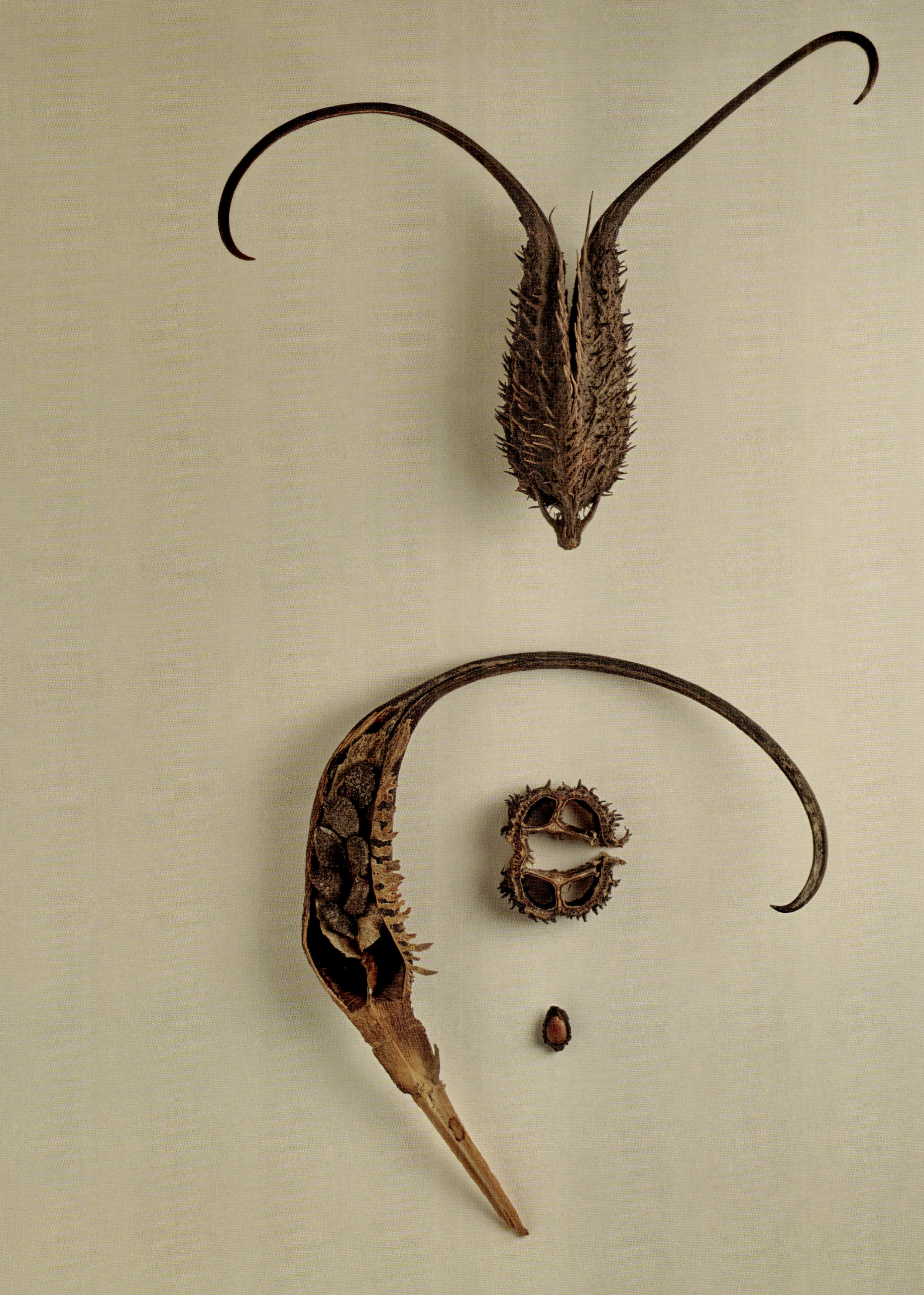

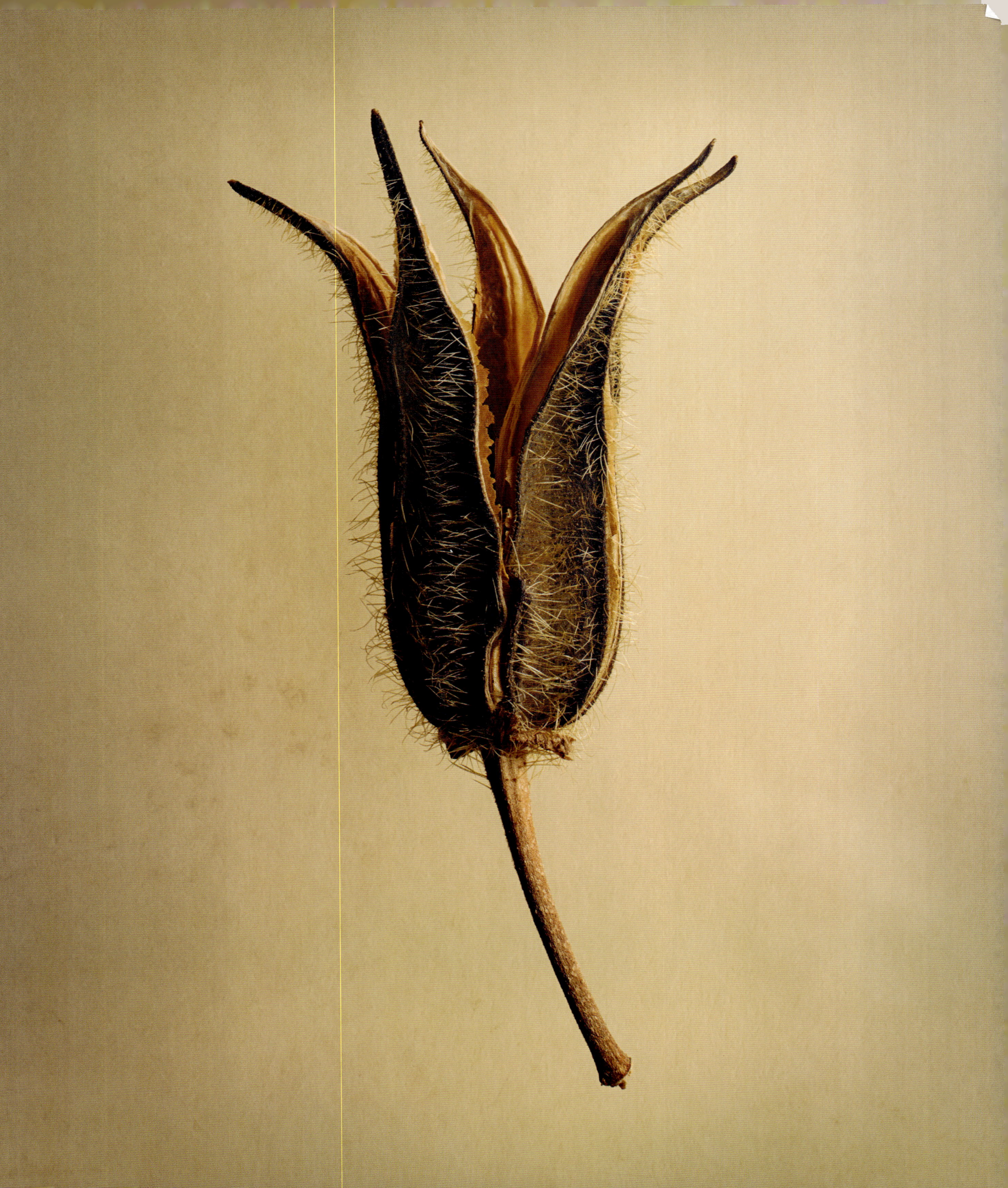

THE HIDDEN BEAUTY OF

SEEDS
&
FRUITS

The Botanical Photography of

LEVON BISS

ABRAMS, NEW YORK

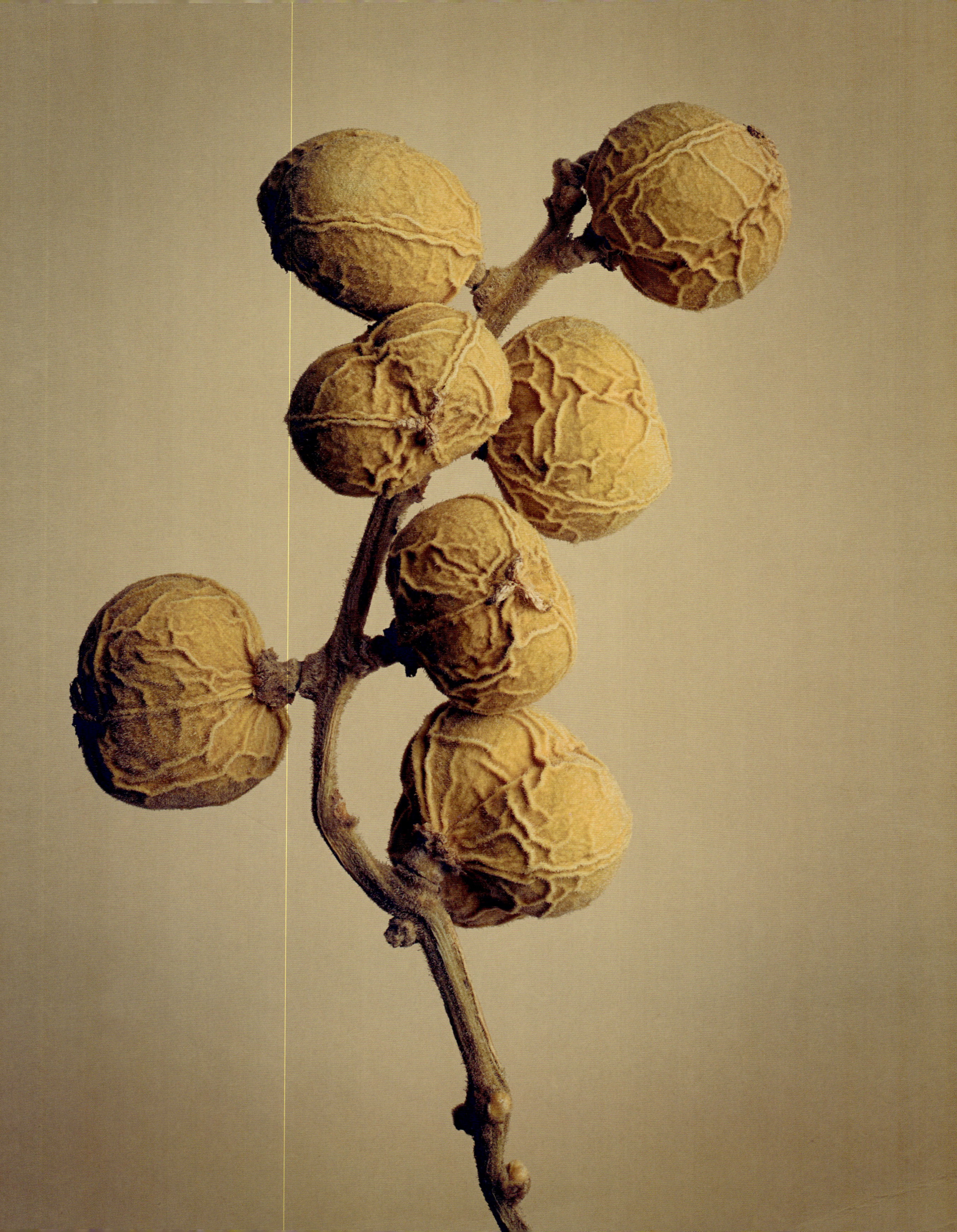

FOREWORD DAVID HARRIS

The herbarium at the Royal Botanic Garden Edinburgh (RBGE) houses more than three million specimens of dried plants collected from all over the world, covering a period of over three hundred years. And it continues to grow—we are currently adding new specimens, collected by our staff, students, and international colleagues, at a rate of about ten thousand per year.

Throughout its long history, scientists have used the RBGE herbarium collection to help them interpret the diversity of plants and fungi. Crops, poisonous plants, garden plants, medicinal plants, tiny herbs, giant rain-forest trees—all kinds of plants and fungi can be found here. Herbaria such as the one in Edinburgh, by acting as "libraries" of plant material, have been crucial in helping us to determine which plants grow where and how we can differentiate them.

The scientific documentation of the natural history of the world started as part of the Enlightenment project in the eighteenth century. In Scotland, botanists had almost all been men, while women and people from other countries who were involved in the work very rarely had their contributions recorded on the labels or in the literature. In parallel, there are items in the herbarium that reflect a historical, colonial approach to the global exploration, acquisition, and exploitation of the world's natural resources. It is key that we remain aware of the circumstances in which some specimens were collected; at the same time, it is critically important that the valuable resources within the collections are available and used as a global resource. Although our modern botanical community is very different from how it was three hundred years ago, it is only by acknowledging the past that we are able to continue to push for more respect and inclusion.

Now, faced with the twin challenges of climate change and the biodiversity crisis, researchers are using herbarium specimens in new ways to understand and address these threats to our planet. For example, old herbarium specimens from Scotland, which pre-date the Industrial Revolution, provide a "snapshot" of the environment before human activities started to have a major impact on it. Plants absorb pollutants from air and water, and these can remain in the dried specimens. Therefore, by analyzing herbarium specimens, we can track rises and falls in levels of pollutants from a time when they were hardly produced. To give another example, by examining herbarium records of the time of first flowering over two hundred years, we can track plants' response to changing global temperatures. We can also use herbarium records to track plant migration, and use the information to predict how plants will respond to climate change in the future.

Over the past ten years, we have digitized a sixth of the collection by capturing high-resolution technical images of the specimens, each accompanied by a ruler (for scale) and a color chart, and making them freely available on the Internet. This has enabled researchers from anywhere in the world to virtually examine the physical material held in the cupboards here in Edinburgh, and to download the images and relevant collection data. This is one of a number of international programs that allow access to the information needed by those working to halt biodiversity loss.

Information from herbarium specimens is used to help determine the conservation status of plant species, which are included in the *International Union for Conservation of Nature (IUCN) Red List of Threatened Species*. This is an essential source of information on the extinction risk of individual plant, animal, and fungus species, and as such, informs global efforts to conserve biodiversity. Based on comprehensive assessments of wild populations, thousands of plants have been assigned to categories such as Vulnerable or Endangered, or, in the worst cases, Extinct.

Most herbarium specimens have been pressed flat and affixed to a standard-size piece of card called an herbarium sheet. Once the specimen has been prepared, the sheet is placed in a folder. Multiple folders are then stored flat on shelves in specially designed cupboards. Some specimens, however, are too bulky to fit on an herbarium sheet; instead, they are stored in boxes and bags of different sizes. Together, these specimens are called the carpological collection, because they consist almost entirely of fruits and seeds.

When I visited the *Microsculpture* exhibition at Inverleith House Gallery last year, I was struck by the intensity of the jewel-like hues of the insect portraits of Levon Biss. Therefore, when the possibility of interesting him in taking photographs of the carpological collection was suggested, I was unsure whether he would find enough color in the specimens, despite their huge variety of form. However, when he first visited the herbarium and took his first tour of the carpological collection, we realized that this idea could come to fruition.

It was gratifying to witness his engagement with the specimens: he examined the collection with a remarkable intensity, his eye moving from one item to the next, always focused, occasionally asking a short question. We have shown many people around the herbarium, and I can tell from their reaction whether they are genuinely interested. With Levon, I knew within a few seconds that he was hooked!

The next time I saw him, he was working in the herbarium with his camera, with the exact same focus we see so often on the faces of the scientists who examine these collections. It is this fascination that we hope to share.

We were also asked to provide common names in English for all the plants. This was a slight problem for us: our role is to provide scientific names, as we know that even in Scotland common names can be contentious. In the spirit of co-operation and with the understanding that some people find scientific names in Latin names a barrier to their appreciation of plants, we have done our best to provide English common names, following Levon's request. However, some plants do not have an English name, and so if we found names in other languages, we used them. Readers should be aware that in some languages, there can be more than one name for the same plant, and we are not equipped to choose between the names, or even between which languages should be represented. We have made some arbitrary choices of common names to serve up what could be seen as exemplar names. Some names we even translated directly from Latin into English. If you want to find out anything more about the plants, we suggest you search using the scientific names.

Here, at the intersection between art and science, we find beauty. It is my hope that these photographs will inspire people to engage more with plants for a better future for us all.

David Harris, Herbarium Curator
June 2020

FOREWORD LESLEY SCOTT

It has been a pleasure and a privilege to meet and work with Levon Biss, to be able to introduce him to the RBGE herbarium collection, to witness his meticulous photographic process, and to share in the wonder of creating these fascinating images.

Visitors to the herbarium are usually taxonomists from around the world who examine our plant specimens to further their research. They are interested in the morphological characters, which are the features they can examine, to determine identification of the correct scientific name. They also scrutinize the label information to record the date on which the specimen was collected and the specific location where it was found.

Working alongside Levon, we used the collection in an entirely different way. The experience was thoroughly rewarding, both in terms of the scale of the project and for having the chance to be truly involved in locating the best source material for the beautiful images he created. Over a period of six months, we examined the entire carpological collection of around 3,500 specimens. Opening cabinet after cabinet, we sifted carefully through the boxes in the drawers within, looking for interesting textures, distinct shapes, or unique evolutionary features that Levon knew would be astonishing when shot through the precision of his camera setup.

These extraordinarily detailed images capture a varied range of surface details, and we are given a tantalizing glimpse of seeds still nestled in their fruits. Some of the images show the mechanisms plants use to achieve seed dispersal, displaying papery wings and other lightweight structures that aid flight. Others show the remnants of pulpy material that would have attracted birds and mammals to take the fruit, later depositing the seeds far away from the parent plant and thus giving them a fighting chance of germination and survival. We can also see where seeds have been attached and the scars that remain.

The species represented here reflect over one hundred years of botanical collecting and span the globe—from Chile to Congo, from Turkey to Indonesia—and include species from areas of the world where our scientists are currently carrying out fieldwork and collaborating fully with local botanical organizations. They also showcase the RBGE-cultivated collection: dried samples of the fruits grown from wild-origin seed and cared for in our living collection.

It has been a fantastic opportunity for us to craft the stories around these images, conveying information on the amazing process of seed dispersal and the different uses that humans have found for plant material.

Some of the plants in this collection are described as "endemic." In botany, this word is used in a different way from medicine. When referring to a plant, "endemic" means that the wild species only occurs in one geographic area—it might be a country, or an island. It does not occur naturally anywhere else in the world.

Some of the plants featured in these pages were and continue to be used as traditional medicines. The uses described are often based on an understanding of the world that have been very different from the scientists who recorded them, and the remedies may not have been assessed for efficacy and safety.

Herbarium collections are a crucial resource for botanical science, but as this book reveals, Levon has made it accessible to a far wider audience than just the scientific community. We hope you enjoy taking this journey with us through the world of plants.

Lesley Scott
Assistant Herbarium Curator

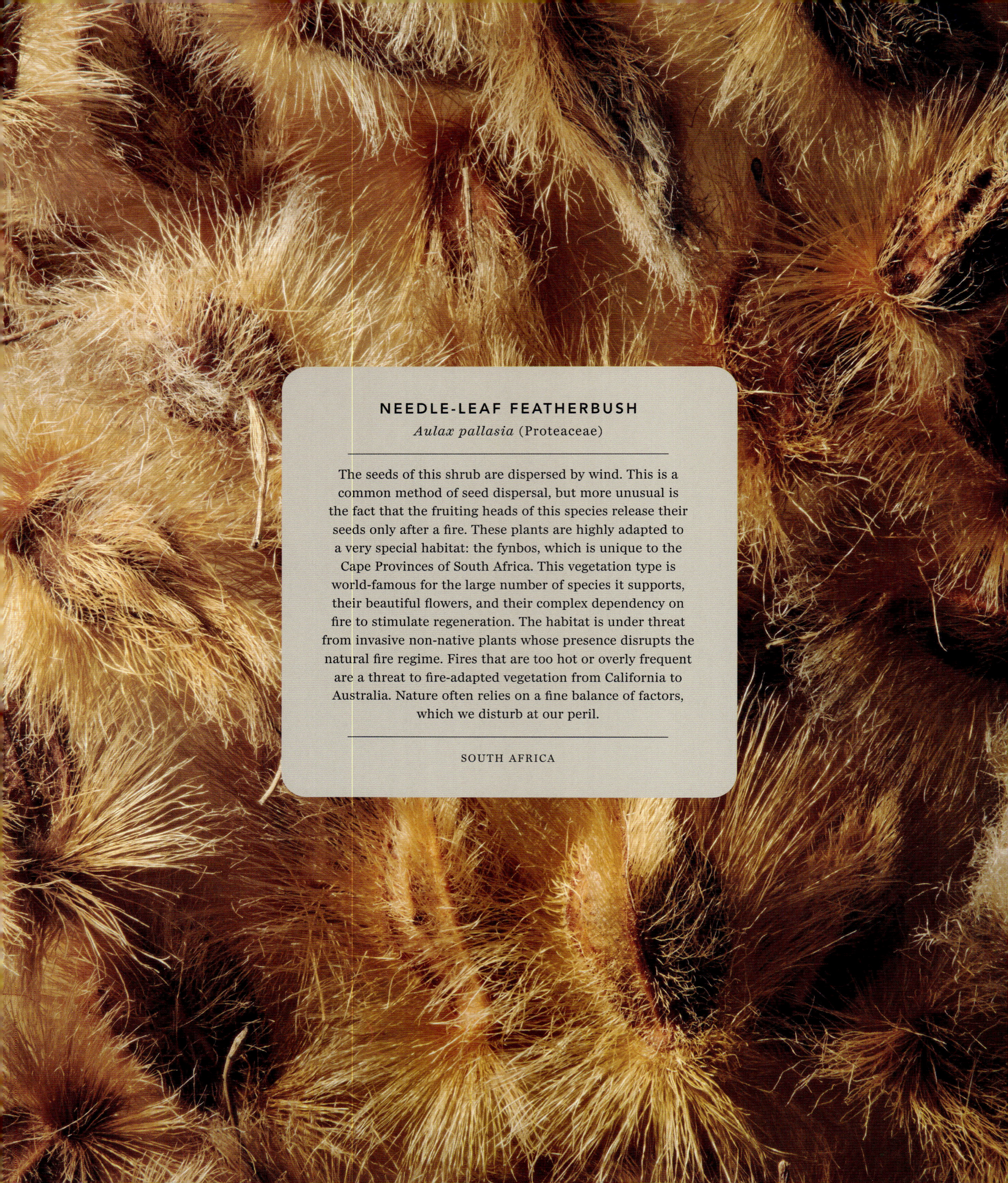

NEEDLE-LEAF FEATHERBUSH

Aulax pallasia (Proteaceae)

The seeds of this shrub are dispersed by wind. This is a
common method of seed dispersal, but more unusual is
the fact that the fruiting heads of this species release their
seeds only after a fire. These plants are highly adapted to
a very special habitat: the fynbos, which is unique to the
Cape Provinces of South Africa. This vegetation type is
world-famous for the large number of species it supports,
their beautiful flowers, and their complex dependency on
fire to stimulate regeneration. The habitat is under threat
from invasive non-native plants whose presence disrupts the
natural fire regime. Fires that are too hot or overly frequent
are a threat to fire-adapted vegetation from California to
Australia. Nature often relies on a fine balance of factors,
which we disturb at our peril.

SOUTH AFRICA

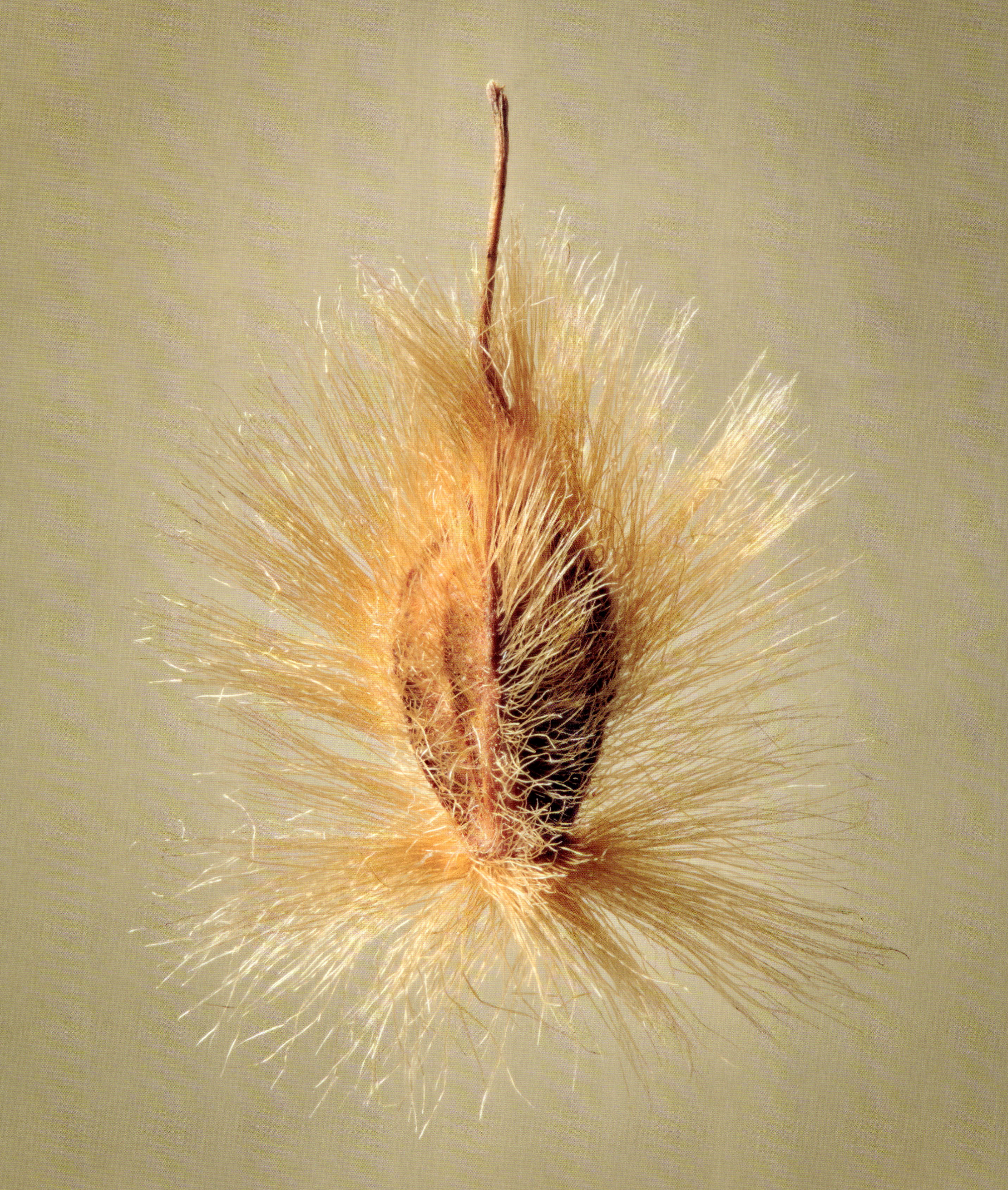

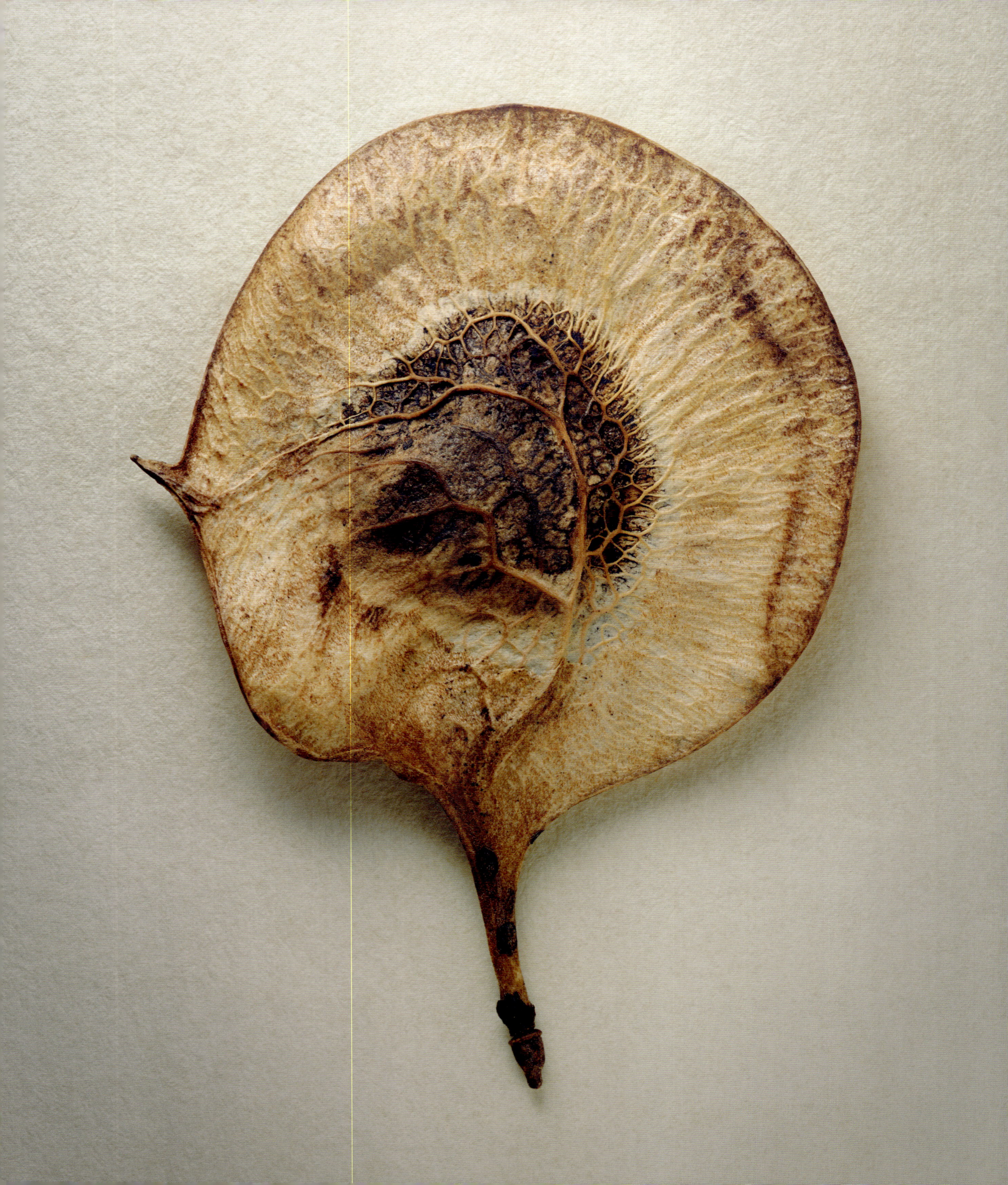

BURMESE ROSEWOOD

Pterocarpus indicus (Fabaceae)

OPPOSITE: Unusually for a member of the legume family, the seeds of this large tree are not contained in pea pod–like fruit. Instead, they are found in disc-shaped samaras whose papery margins aid wind dispersal. The flowers of *Pterocarpus indicus* are a source of nectar for honey, and infusions of its leaves are used as shampoo. Its wood is prized for making furniture and musical instruments; importantly, it is resistant to attack by termites. Rosewood, the catchall name for beautiful woods from a variety of *Pterocarpus* and *Dalbergia* species from different countries across the tropics, is the most widely traded wildlife commodity in the world, and much of it is illegally sourced.

MYANMAR

CASTOR OIL PLANT

Ricinus communis (Euphorbiaceae)

OVERLEAF LEFT: The seeds of this large herbaceous plant are extremely poisonous owing to the ricin they contain. Ricin is one of the world's most toxic substances, and one for which no antidote exists. At one end of each seed is a yellowish-white, wart-like organ called the caruncle, which is attractive to ants. The ants carry the seeds to their underground nests, where they remove the caruncles for feeding to their larvae. They have no use for the seeds themselves, so these are discarded on piles of the colony's waste outside the nests. The waste provides a rich substrate for germination. In seeds that retain the caruncle, it may function to absorb and store water for transfer to the seed in the early stages of germination. The seeds look like ticks, hence the genus name (*ricinus* is Latin for "tick").

RBGE CULTIVATED

BLUEBERRY ASH

Elaeocarpus reticulatus (Elaeocarpaceae)

OVERLEAF RIGHT: This tree is an endemic Australian species found along the eastern coast from Queensland south to Tasmania. Its bell-shaped flowers are white or pale pink with frilly edges, giving rise to its more fanciful common name: "fairy petticoats." The beauty and licorice-like scent of the flowers, coupled with the vivid blue color of the fruits that arise from them, make this species a popular ornamental plant. The fruits also appeal to the male satin bowerbird (*Ptilonorhynchus violaceus*), which favors blue objects for decorating the entrance to its elaborate nest. This group image shows fruits at various stages of ripeness.

AUSTRALIA

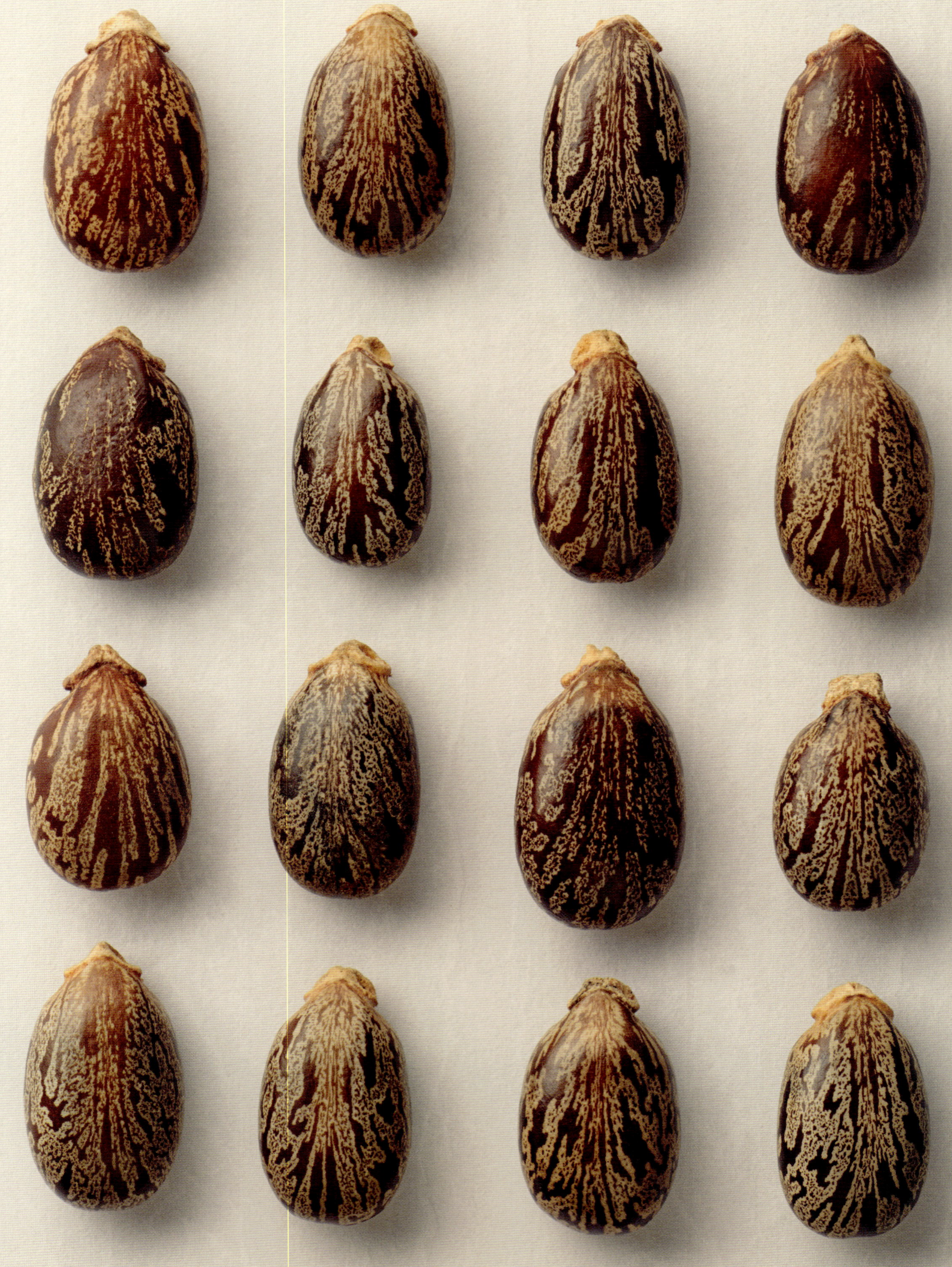

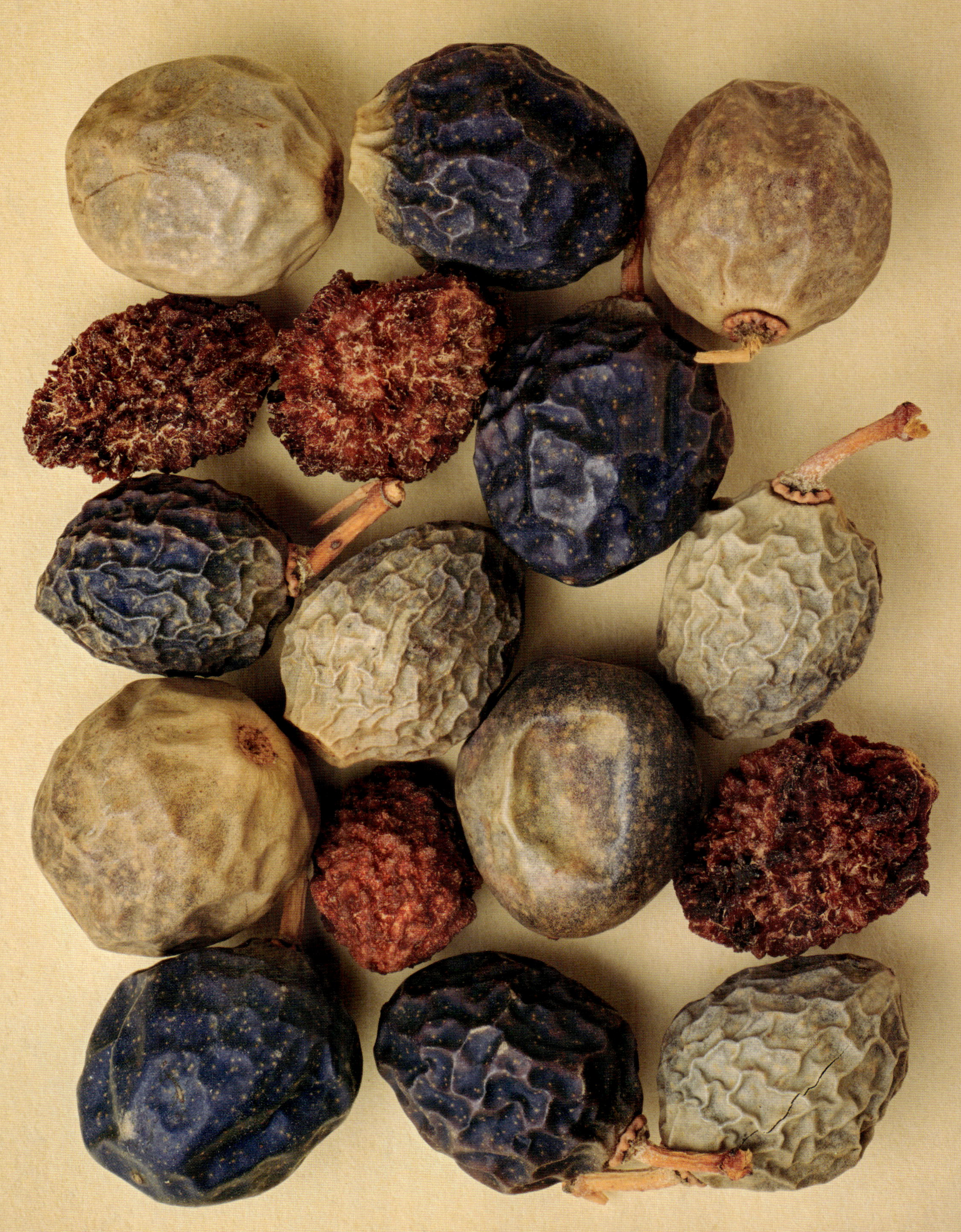

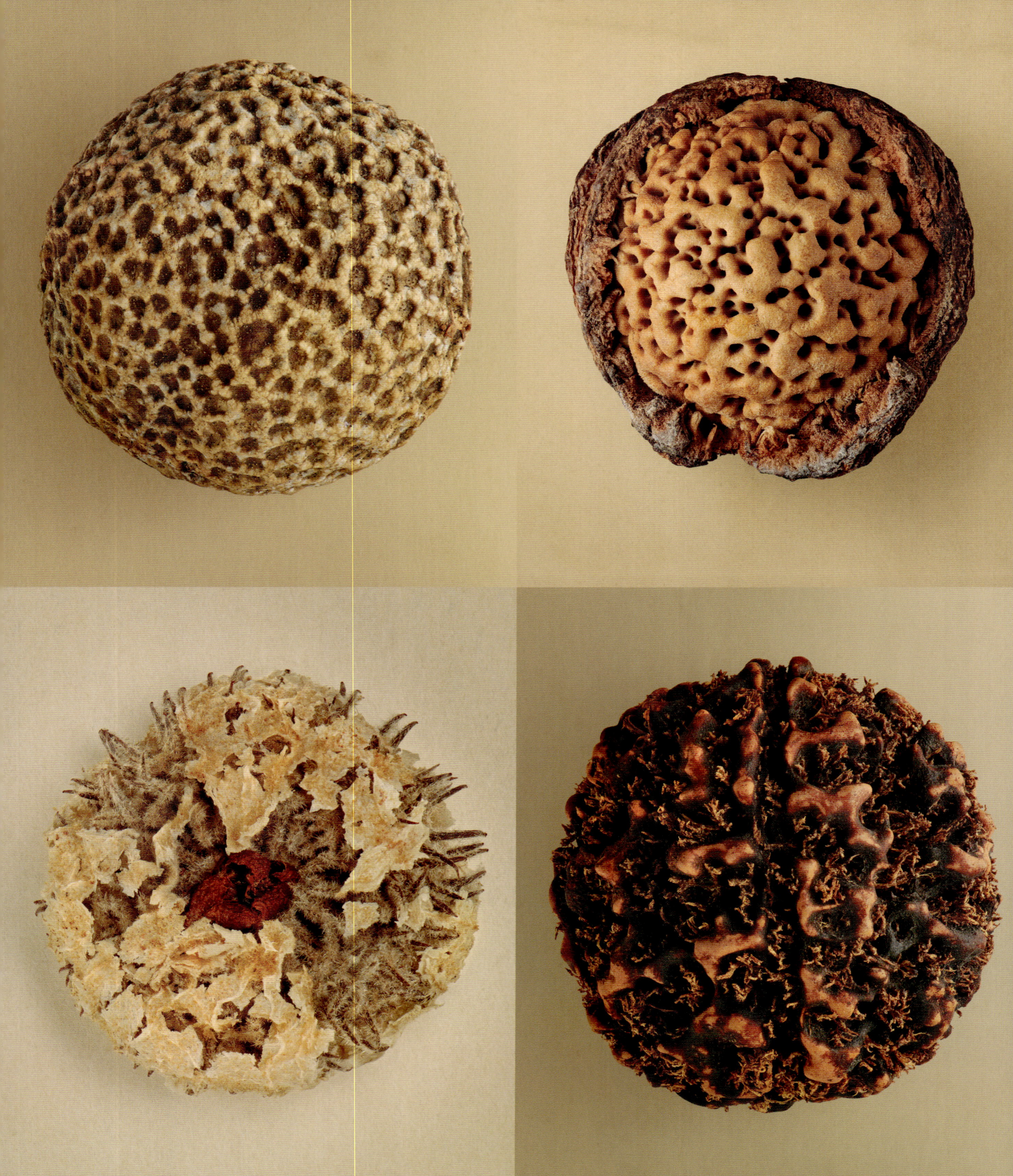

BLUEBERRY ASH

Elaeocarpus reticulatus (Elaeocarpaceae)

TOP LEFT: Endemic to the eastern coast of Australia, the specimen in this image shows a worn and weathered stone which has had the soft flesh and blue outer skin removed or they have rotted away. The seed will still be safely inside, but it is unlikely to germinate in this condition.

AUSTRALIA

SANDALWOOD

Santalum sp. (Santalaceae)

TOP RIGHT: The only information on the label for this specimen is *"Santalum* sp."; there are no collection details to aid identification to species level. It may be *Santalum album*, commonly known as aromatic sandalwood. This semiparasitic tree grows to 26 feet (8 m) in height and is famed for its fragrant timber. Its fruit is a single-seeded drupe with an attractively pitted woody inner wall. This specimen retains much of its outer coat, but it is shrivelled from drying. In the living plant, this part of the fruit is fleshy and dark purple, presumably to attract birds for seed dispersal.

INDIA

LIFESAVER BURR

Sida platycalyx (Malvaceae)

BOTTOM LEFT: This low-growing shrub is called the lifesaver burr because the outer rings of its fruit, when mature, resemble life buoys. The appearance of these rings has also given rise to the colloquial name "teddy bears' bums." The fruit is a burr; its rough outer layer is made up of numerous spines that enable it to attach to any animals with which it comes into contact. The fruit is indehiscent, meaning that it does not split open at maturity. Instead, the extremes of temperature change in the plant's desert habitat cause the fruit to break apart into sections. The papery material on the exterior is all that remains of the parts of the plant that protected the fruit during ripening.

AUSTRALIA

OIL FRUIT

Elaeocarpus sp. (Elaeocarpaceae)

BOTTOM RIGHT: This genus comprises around 480 recognized species of trees and shrubs. Its name comes from the Greek for "olive fruited." The elaborately textured *Elaeocarpus* seeds are often used in organic jewelry, such as the garlands of prayer beads (*rudraksha*) that have special significance in Hinduism. The specimen depicted here was collected in Australia, which is home to thirty to forty *Elaeocarpus* species. It has yet to be identified, but may be *Elaeocarpus angustifolius* ("blue quandong"), which is widespread in that country.

AUSTRALIA

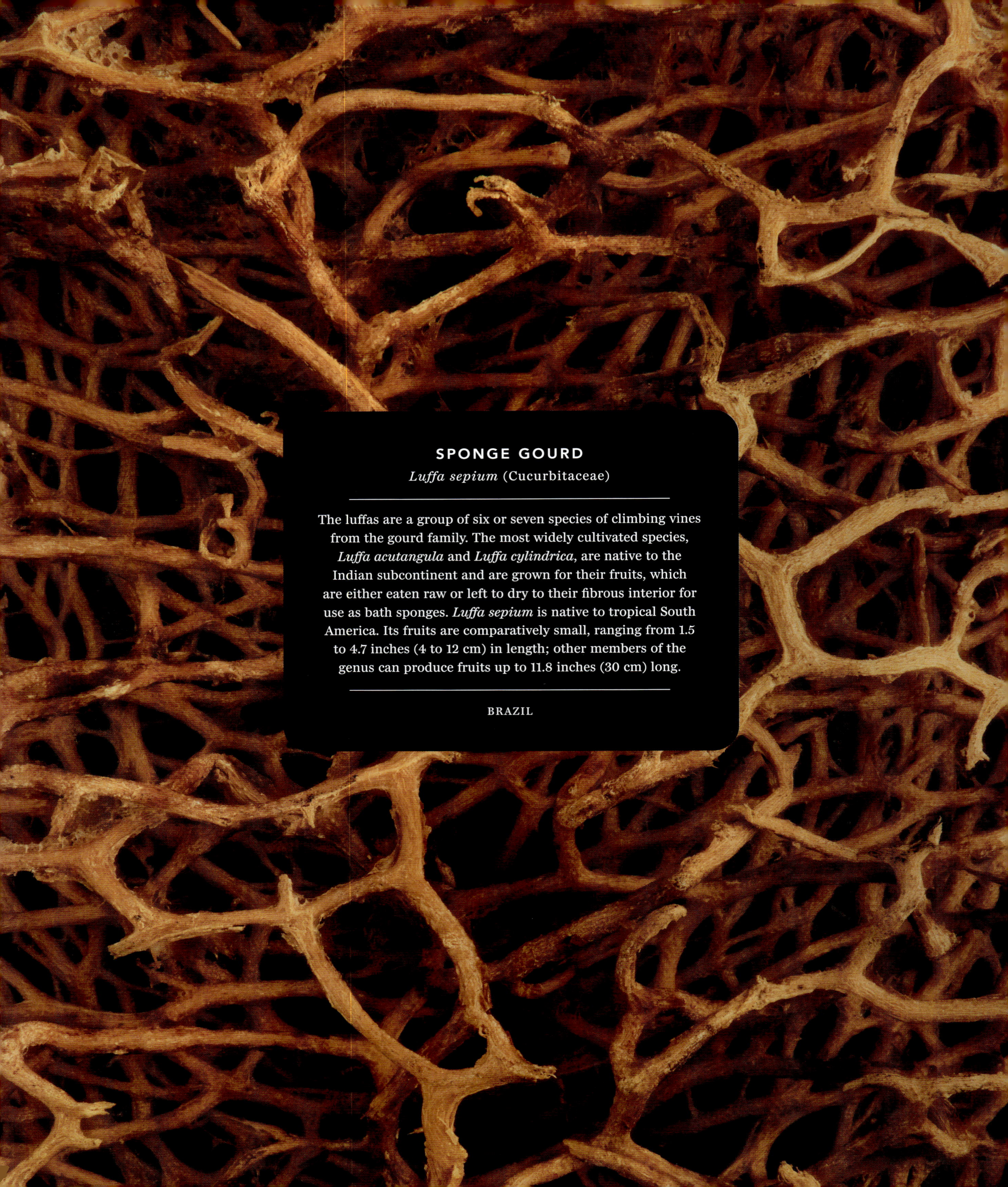

SPONGE GOURD

Luffa sepium (Cucurbitaceae)

The luffas are a group of six or seven species of climbing vines
from the gourd family. The most widely cultivated species,
Luffa acutangula and *Luffa cylindrica*, are native to the
Indian subcontinent and are grown for their fruits, which
are either eaten raw or left to dry to their fibrous interior for
use as bath sponges. *Luffa sepium* is native to tropical South
America. Its fruits are comparatively small, ranging from 1.5
to 4.7 inches (4 to 12 cm) in length; other members of the
genus can produce fruits up to 11.8 inches (30 cm) long.

BRAZIL

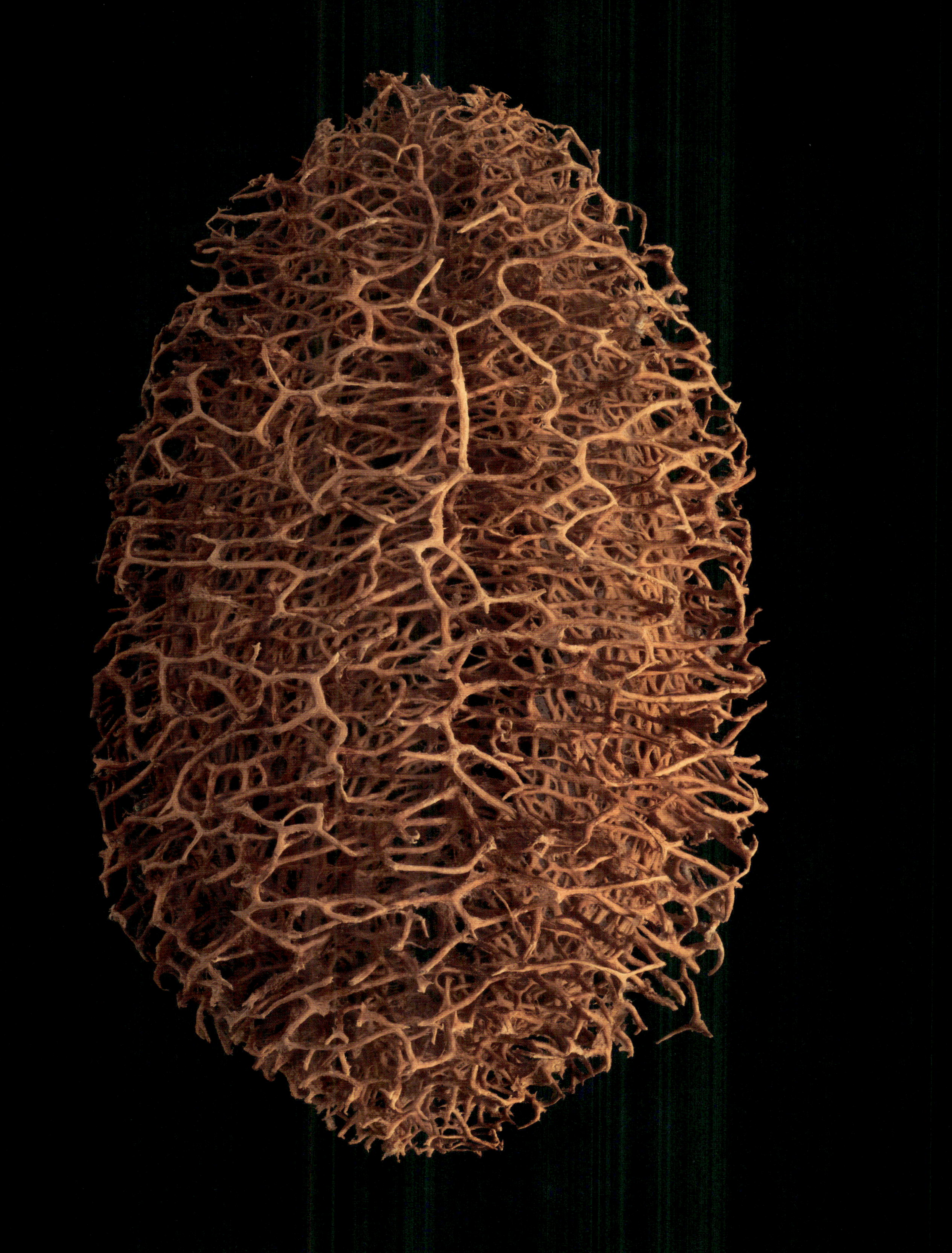

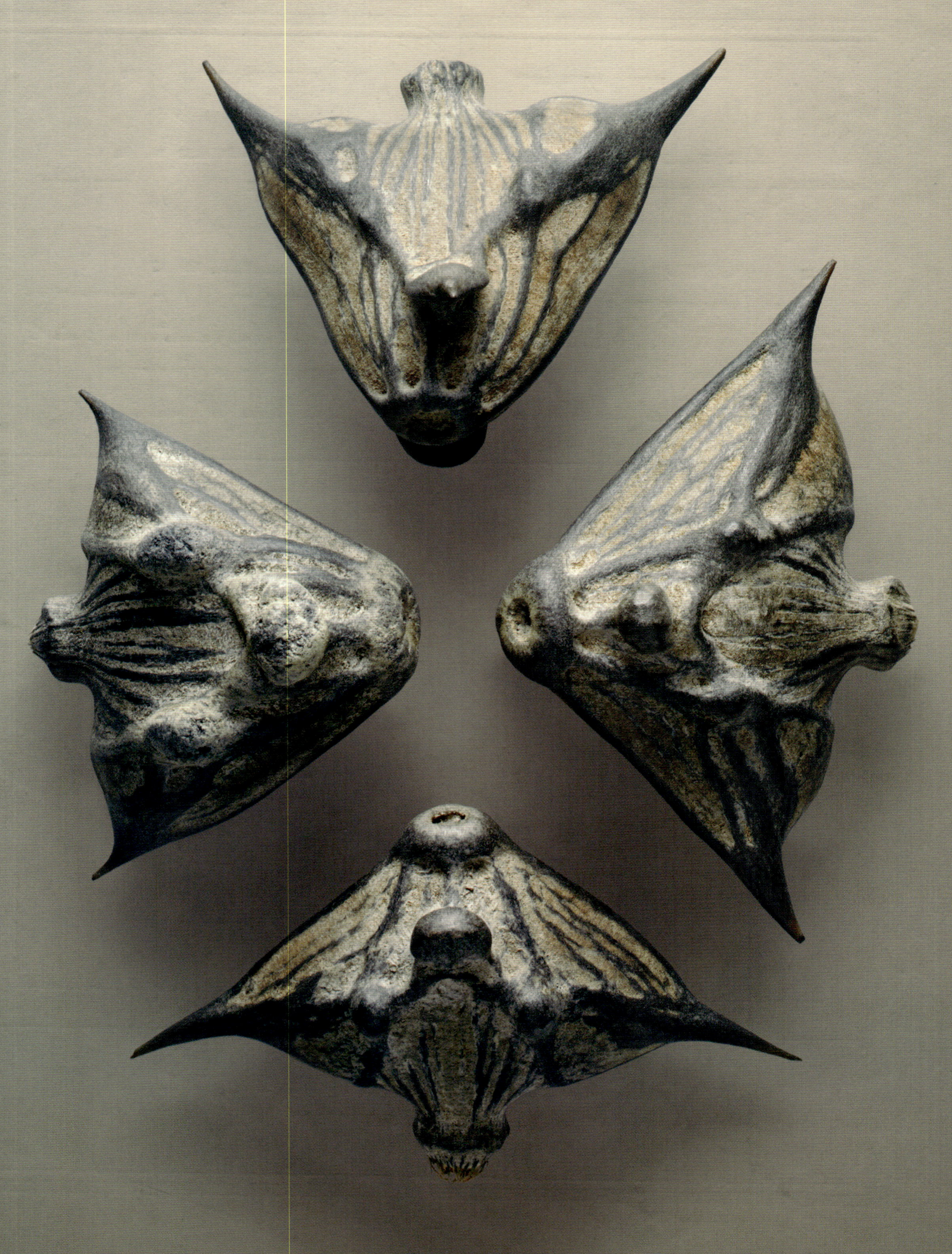

TWO-SPINED SINGHARA NUT

Trapa natans var. *bispinosa* (Lythraceae)

OPPOSITE: The fruit of the water chestnut is edible. As a useful source of starch and fat, it can be dried and ground into flour. It is therefore widely cultivated in the tropics, and in India it is called "singhara." It also has the name "water caltrops," because its single-seeded fruits resemble the spiky metal devices scattered on the ground to pierce the hooves of an enemy's horse in medieval times. The spines develop from two or more of the four corners of the fruit. The form with two spines was described in 1815 by William Roxburgh from a specimen from India and given the name *Trapa bispinosa*. It is now recognized as a variety.

INDIA

MELEMBU

Pterocymbium tinctorium (Malvaceae)

OVERLEAF LEFT: This is a large tree growing up to 164 feet (50 m) tall, often with a silvery smooth bark with warty projections. The distinctive shape of the fruit gives the genus its name, *Pterocymbium* (Greek for "winged boot"). The wing of the fruit is red on the outside and green-gold on the inside when fresh, becoming brown then black and papery when dry and ready for the seeds to be released for wind dispersal. The single-seeded fruits usually hang in clumps of five. The bark is a source of fiber for rope making. It is also used in dyeing cloth; the specific epithet, *tinctorium*, reflects this.

MALAYSIA

BIRTHWORT

Aristolochia sp. (Aristolochiaceae)

OVERLEAF RIGHT: The Aristolochiaceae are a family of herbaceous or woody climbers or shrubs. Both the family name (Greek for "best for childbirth") and the common name ("birthworts") refer to the fact that, from the classical to the late medieval period, women drank the juice from the stems to stimulate uterine contractions and help expel the placenta. However, modern research has shown that the roots and stems contain high levels of aristolochic acid, which is carcinogenic and damages the kidneys. The genus *Aristolochia* is distributed throughout the tropics and subtropics. Their flowers emit a smell to attract pollinating insects such as carrion flies, which are then trapped by hairs inside the floral tube. They are released only when the hairs wither at the end of the day, by which time they are covered in pollen and ready to visit another flower. The specimen shown here is an unopened fruit.

USA

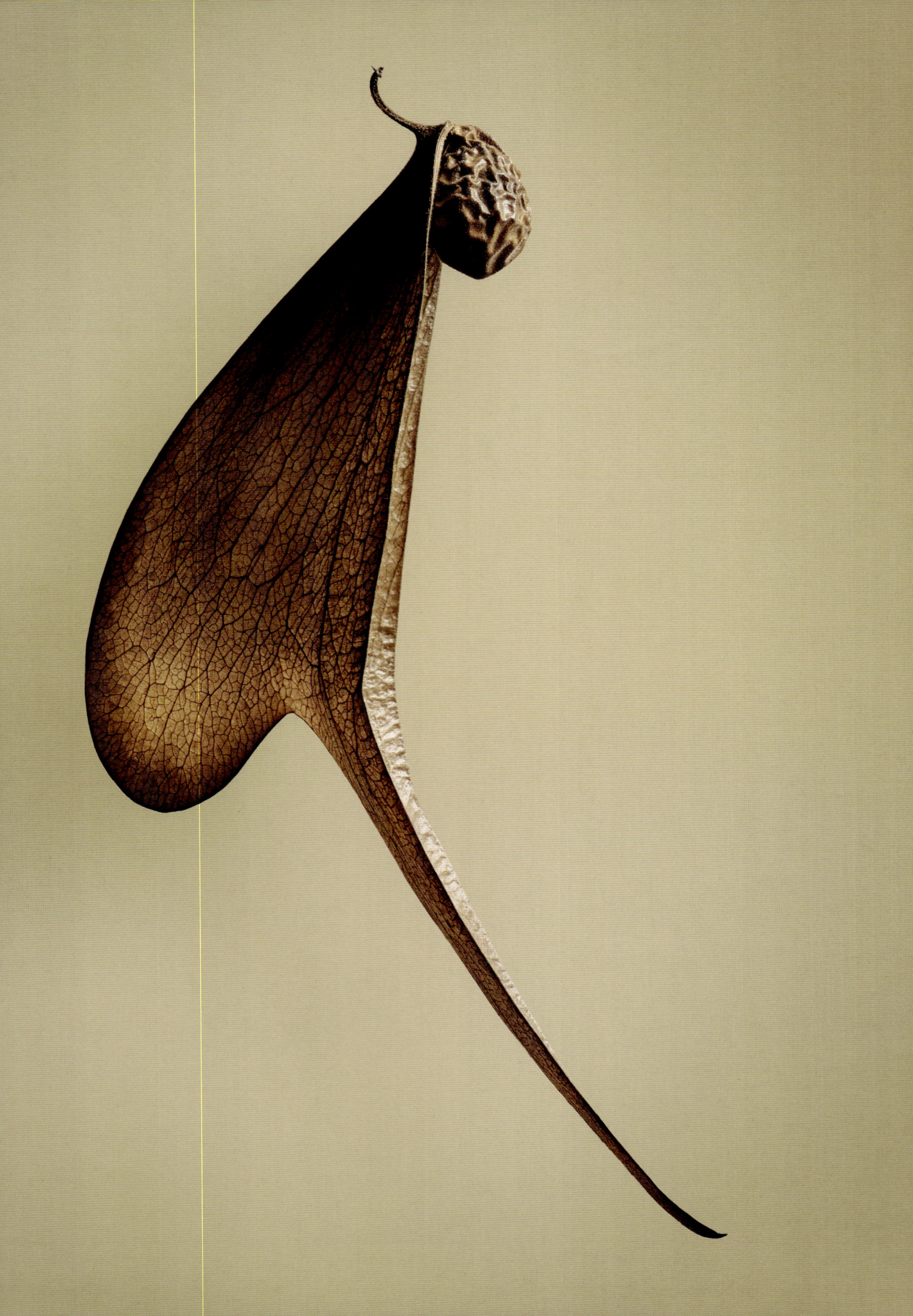

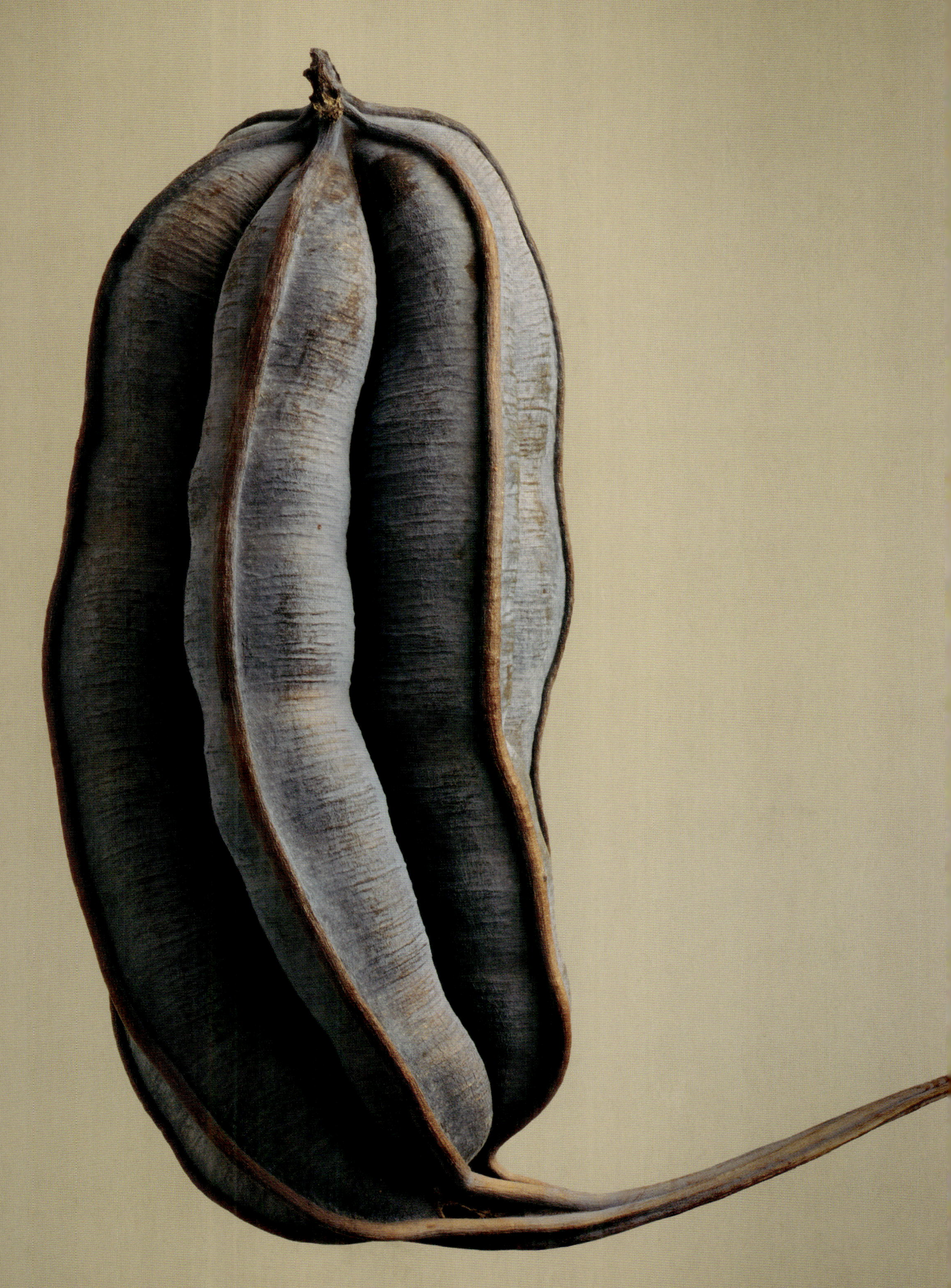

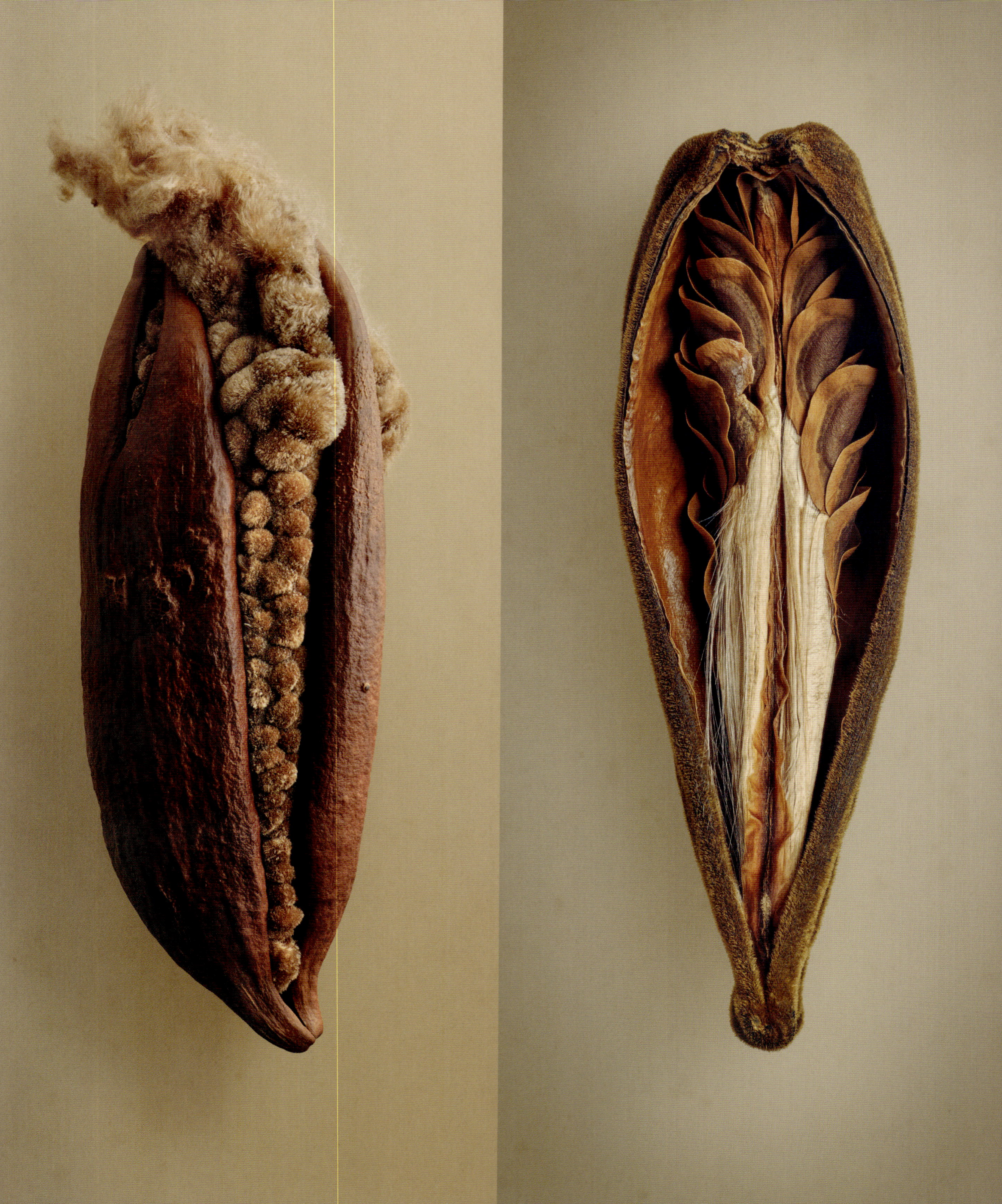

WORLD TREE

Ceiba sp. (Malvaceae)

OPPOSITE LEFT: *Ceiba* is a genus of trees growing throughout the tropical Americas. They usually exceed 98 feet (30 m) in height. In pre-Colombian Central America, the Mayan civilization revered the *Ceiba* as the "World Tree": the roots existing in the underworld, the trunk in our middle world, and the branches reaching toward or supporting the upper world. The mature *Ceiba* tree is an impressive sight, with its enormous buttress roots extending many feet up and out from the smooth, straight trunk. *Ceiba* trees are commonly found growing at the center of Mayan villages throughout Central America.

PERU

WOOLLY DYEING ROSEBAY

Wrightia arborea (Apocynaceae)

OPPOSITE RIGHT AND DETAIL ON OVERLEAF LEFT: This deciduous tree, with its distinctive rounded crown, grows to 66 feet (20 m) tall and is in the same family as the ornamentals frangipani and oleander. It has long, paired fruits (up to 8 inches/20 cm) containing large seeds with wispy hairs to aid their dispersal by the wind. The bark and roots are traditionally used as an antidote against snakebites and scorpion stings, as well as for treating kidney and menstrual complaints. A dye derived from the seeds, roots, and leaves is used to add color to clothes, and the light, soft wood is used to make pencils and packaging. Its native range is India and the Himalayas across southern China and south to Peninsular Malaysia.

MALAYSIA

YANGUA

Cybistax antisyphilitica (Bignoniaceae)

OVERLEAF RIGHT: A small tree typical of the savannas and dry forests of South America, this species has had a huge variety of uses ascribed to it. German botanist Carl Friedrich Philipp von Martius recorded its use by the peoples of the Amazon region to treat syphilis, hence the scientific name. The wood is reported to be used for building boats and is also soaked in water to produce a blue dye for "purifying" the blood in traditional medicine. *Cybistax antisyphilitica* has an inconspicuous appearance but can be recognized by its green flowers (extremely unusual for the plant family Bignoniaceae) and oblong fruits with twelve prominent longitudinal ribs. Packed inside each fruit are winged seeds.

BOLIVIA

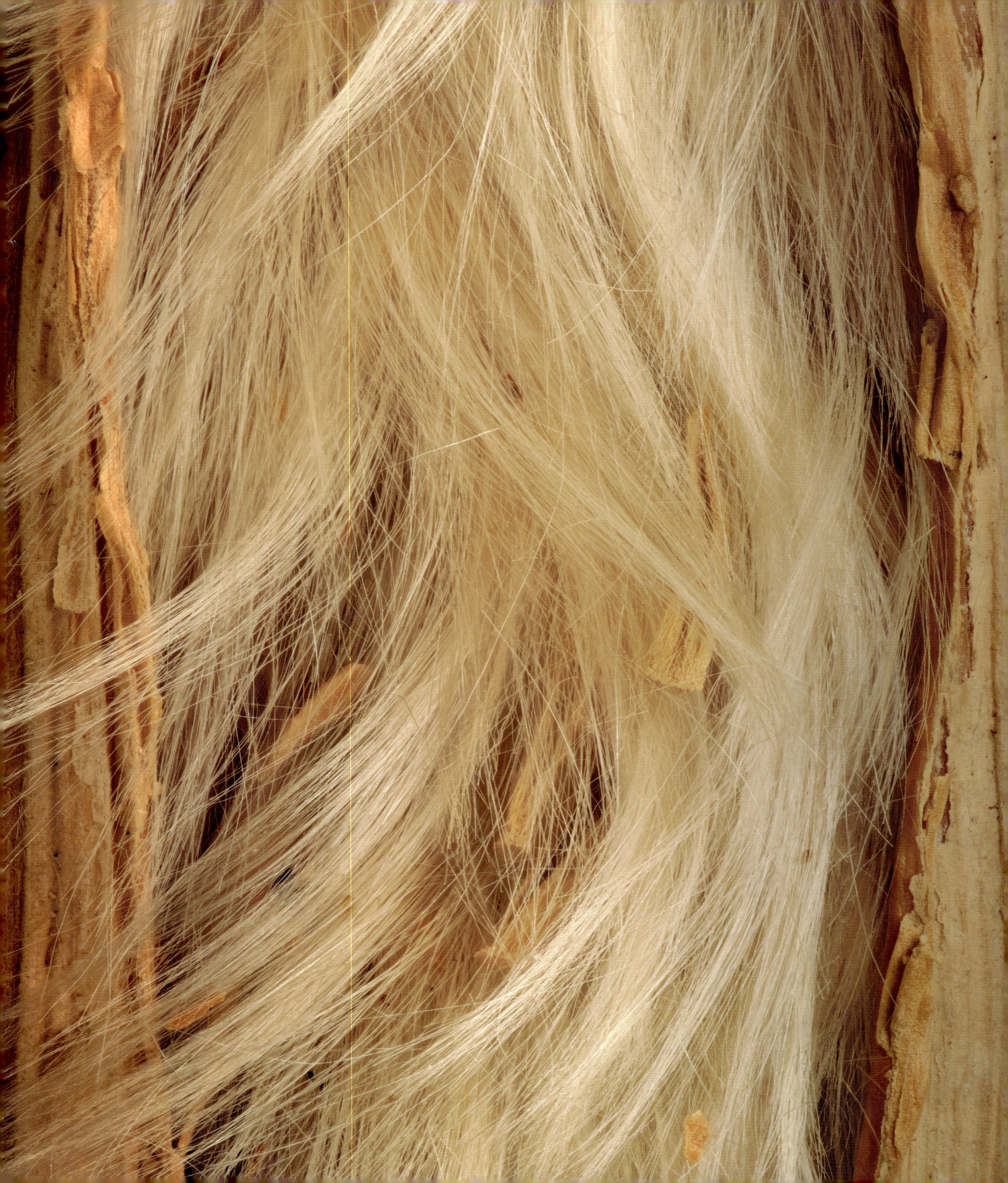

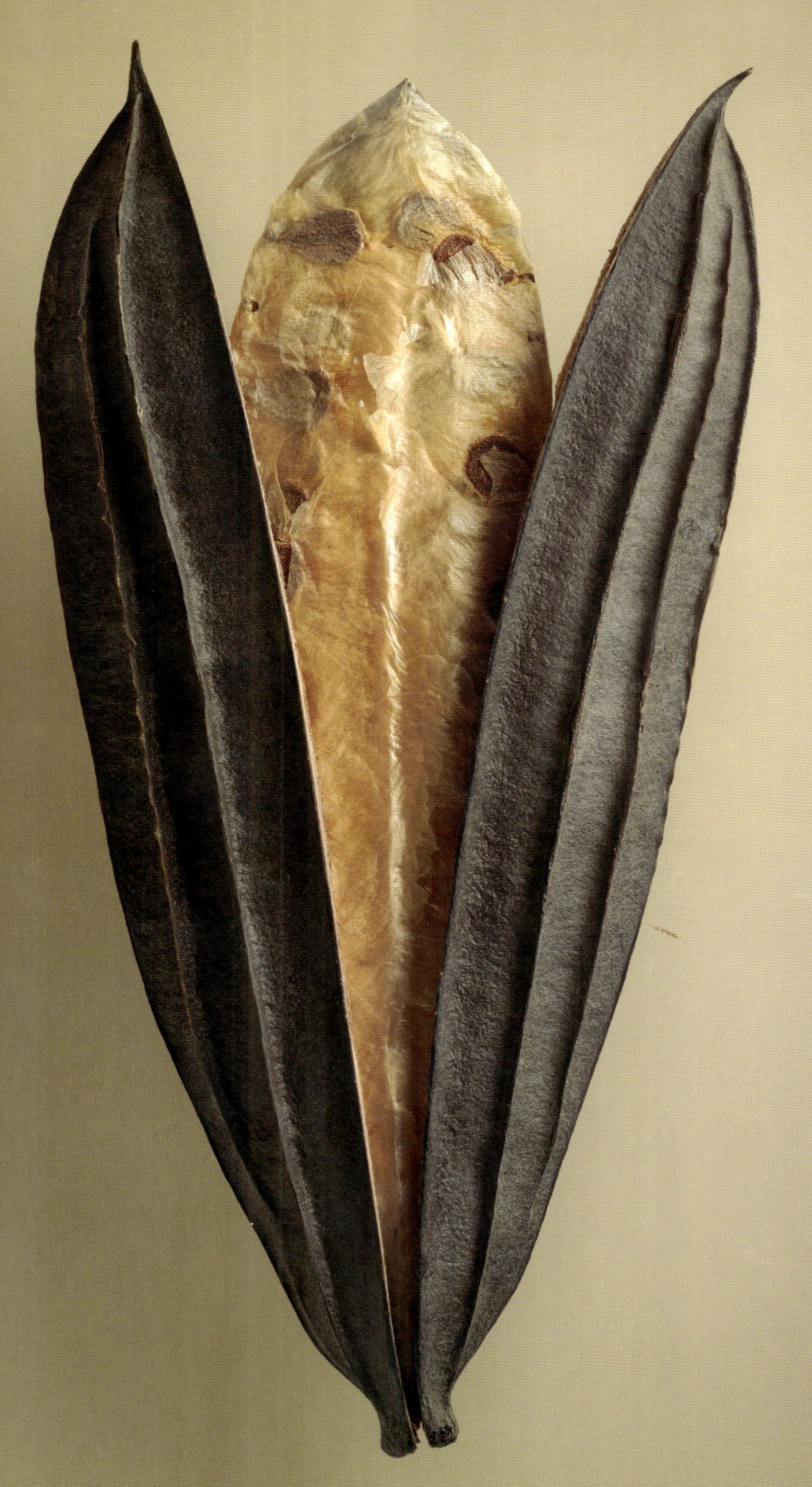

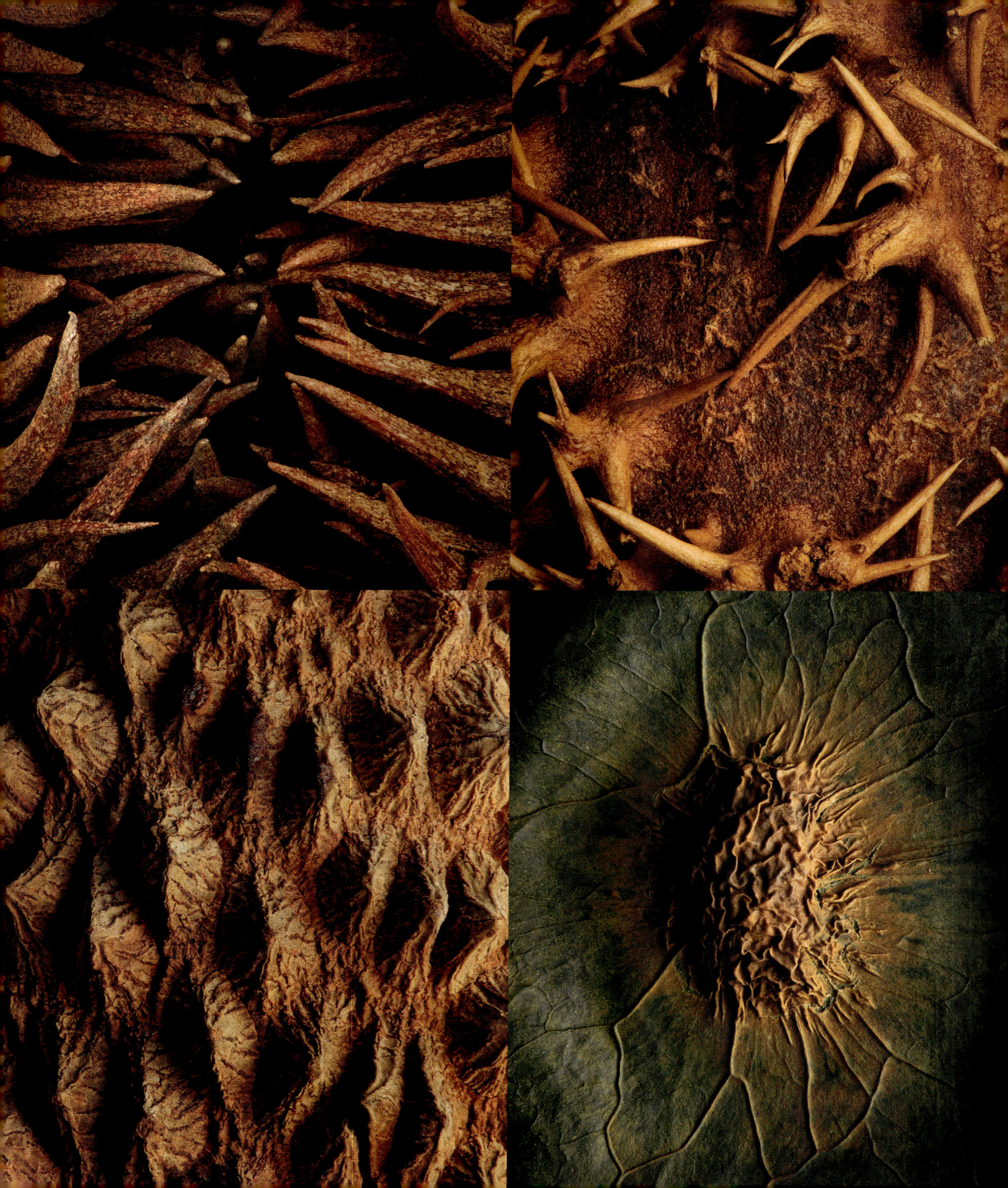

CEYLON DURIAN

Cullenia ceylanica (Malvaceae)

TOP LEFT: This large tree is endemic to Sri Lanka. Durian is known as the "king of fruits" in Southeast Asia, being revered for its unique taste and smell. However, this particular species has only a faint odor and is not eaten by humans. The fruit is covered with sharp, hard spines up to ⅜ inches (1 cm) long; people have been injured or killed by having the fruit fall on them from a tall tree. This specimen is one of the sections into which the fruit splits at maturity.

SRI LANKA

BARANGAN

Castanopsis megacarpa (Fagaceae)

TOP RIGHT: This large tree (to 148 feet/45 m tall) is found in Peninsular Thailand and Peninsular Malaysia, and on the islands of Borneo and Singapore. It belongs to the family Fagaceae, which also includes the beeches (*Fagus*) and oaks (*Quercus*). The specific epithet, *megacarpa*, refers to its large fruit. The hard spines of the fruit protect the nutritious nut within from predation by a wide range of rain-forest animals. The seeds are eaten by humans in times of food shortage.

INDONESIA

SILKWOOD

Flindersia sp. (Rutaceae)

BOTTOM LEFT: The genus *Flindersia* is distributed from the Moluccas to New Guinea, and from New Caledonia to East Australia. Common names in addition to "silkwood" include "hickory ash," "scented maple," and "silver ash." The large, hanging fruit are woody with warty projections on their outer surface; in some species, these develop into short spines. The fruit dries and splits into five parts, which often remain attached to the tree as they release their thin, winged seeds.

PAPUA NEW GUINEA

LANCEPOD

Lonchocarpus sp. (Fabaceae)

BOTTOM RIGHT: *Lonchocarpus* is a genus of trees typical of seasonal forests across the tropical Americas. These forests have a short dry season, to which most trees respond by shedding their leaves for two to four months. Visitors willing to tolerate the brutal heat of the dry season are rewarded by the opportunity to witness the synchronous flowering of many trees, including *Lonchocarpus*, whose bare branches seem to come to life with yellow, red, and purple blooms. In Trinidad and Tobago, the *Lonchocarpus* seedpod is called a "lancepod" because of its resemblance to a spear.

TRINIDAD AND TOBAGO

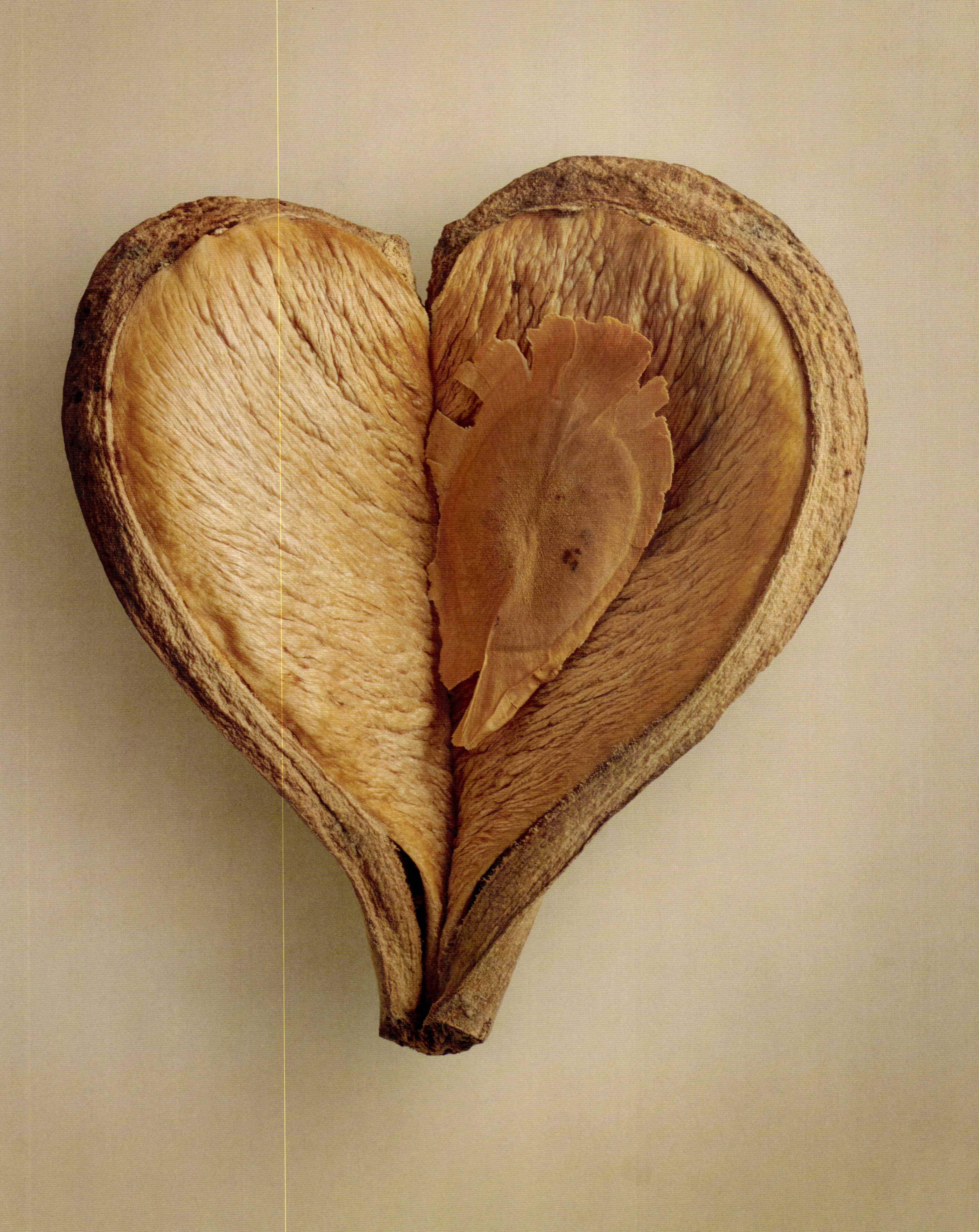

YELLOW PIQUIÁ

Aspidosperma tomentosum (Apocynaceae)

OPPOSITE: This specimen is a fruit that has opened to release its seeds and in so doing created a wonderful heart shape. It was collected from *Aspidosperma tomentosum*, a semideciduous shrub or tree ranging from 13 to 82 feet (4 to 25 m) in height. This species comes from South America, where it is found in Brazil, Bolivia, and Paraguay. It is widespread in seasonally dry savannah forests, especially those in Brazil's Cerrado biome, which have been the focus of research by RBGE botanists. These forests are threatened by conversion of the land for agricultural use. The thick, corky bark is an effective defense against damage from the periodic fires that are a natural and regular occurrence in its habitat.

BRAZIL

OPIUM POPPY

Papaver somniferum (Papaveraceae)

OVERLEAF LEFT: This species is cherished by gardeners for its long-lasting displays of pink, purple, or white flowers. However, it is also notorious for its association with drug misuse and drug-related crime. Across the world, the lives of millions of people are adversely affected by addiction to heroin and other opioids. Heroin is a highly addictive derivative of morphine, an alkaloid present in opium (the dried milky exudate of the unripe seed pods). Morphine itself has a legitimate place in medicine as a powerful analgesic agent; it is prescribed when other drugs have failed to relieve a patient's physical distress. The first medical uses of this species date back to perhaps as early as 4000 BCE, when it was used to treat asthma, stomach ailments, and poor eyesight. The natural range of the species is poorly understood due to its widespread cultivation over the course of millennia, but it is probably native to the eastern Mediterranean.

TURKEY

RHU BUKIT

Gymnostoma sumatranum (Casuarinaceae)

OVERLEAF RIGHT: Found across South East Asia, *Gymnostoma sumatranum* is often growing at high altitudes and in dry soil types such as that of *kerangas* (heath) forest. Its needle-like leaves and cone-like fruit give it a superficial resemblance to a conifer. However, the fruit is not a cone but a series of compressed, single-seeded samaras (winged fruits that do not split at maturity) surrounded by woody protective leaves. These leaves separate on drying, thus releasing the seeds. In Malaysia, this species is known as *rhu bukit* (from the Malay words *rhu*, a general term for this kind of tree, and *bukit*, meaning "hill").

MALAYSIA

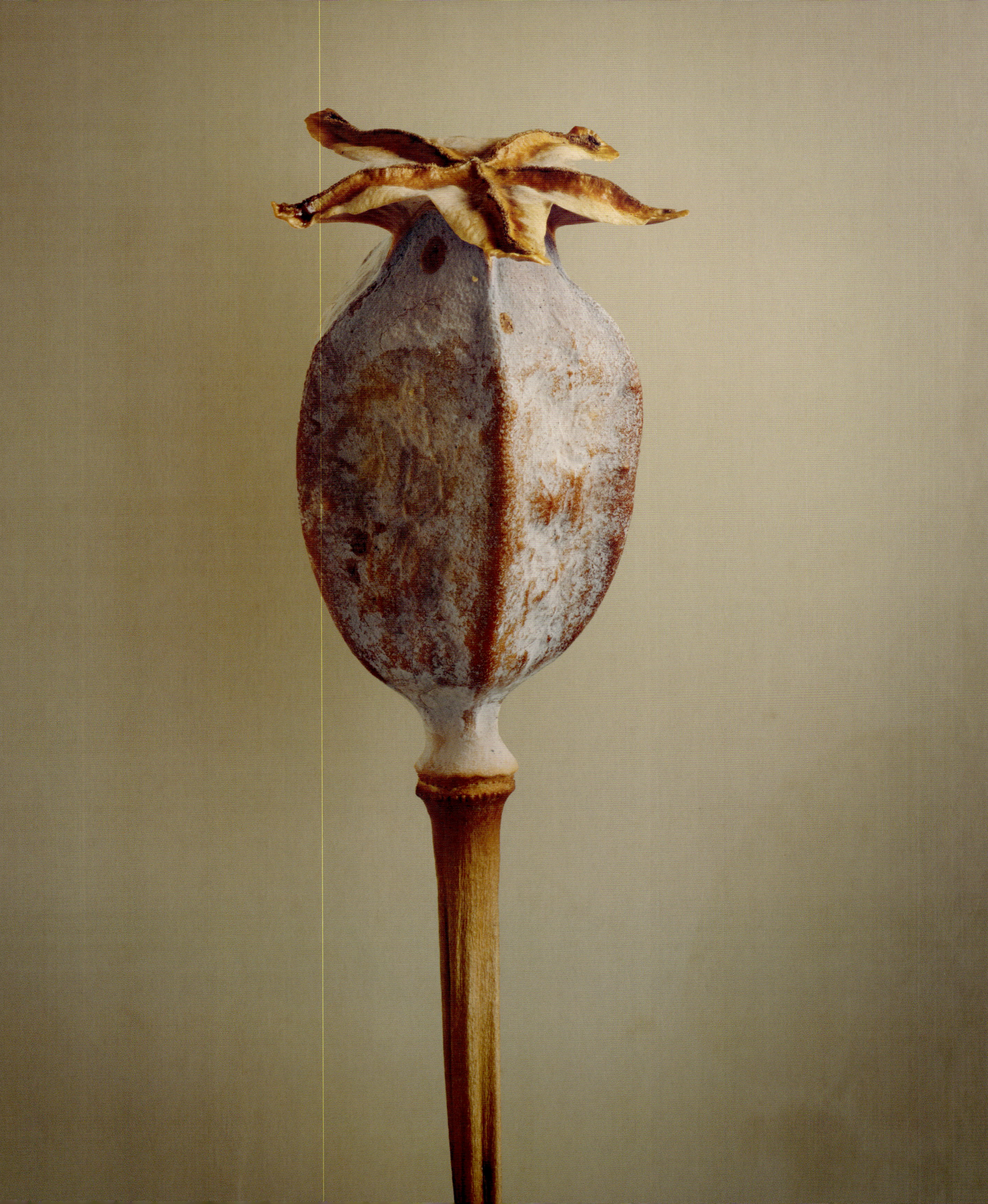

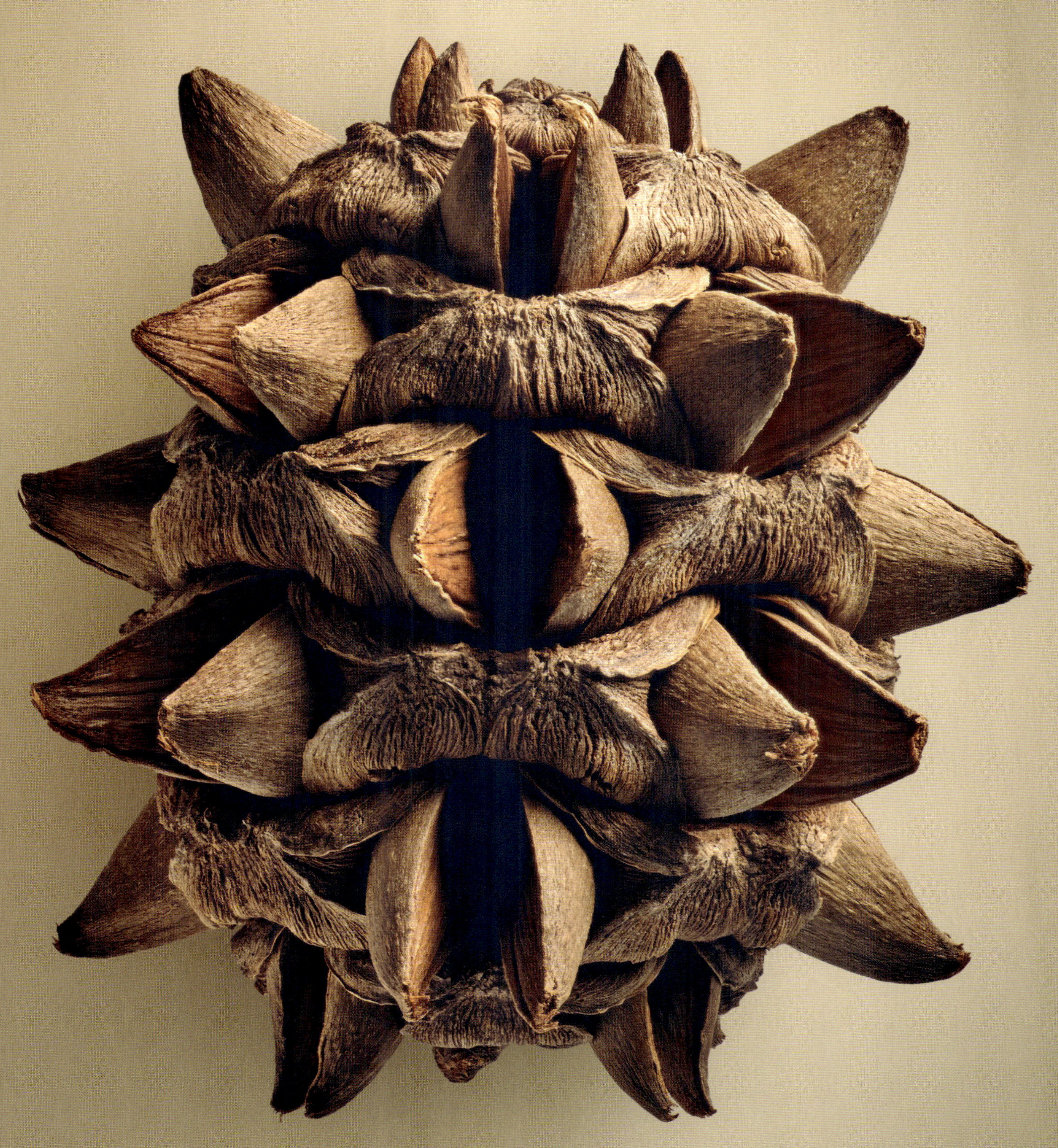

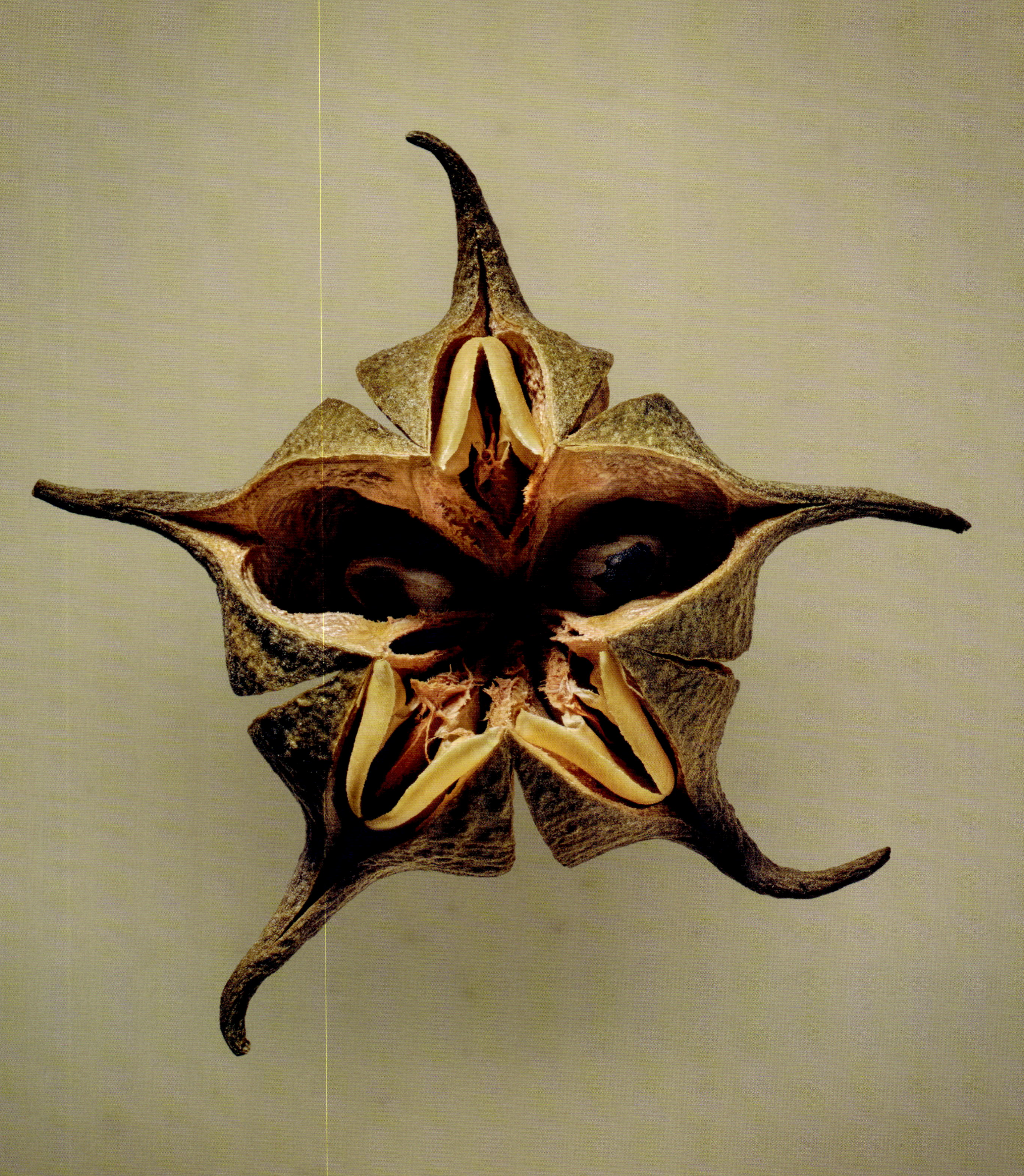

BOFIYU

Esenbeckia cornuta (Rutaceae)

OPPOSITE: This small tree in the citrus family is restricted to a small patch of dry forest in the remote Marañón valley in the north of Peru. The dry forests of the Americas are sometimes called "the forgotten forests"; little studied and inadequately protected, they are being destroyed by conversion to agricultural land and overgrazing. Research recently carried out by RBGE staff, working closely in partnership with botanists from universities and museums in Peru, has shown that a huge number of species are unique not only to dry forests generally but even to individual patches of dry forest. The dry forests of the Marañón valley, being separated by high mountains from the surrounding areas, owe their high degree of endemism (unique plants) to geographical isolation.

PERU

CANDLESTICK BANKSIA

Banksia attenuata (Proteaceae)

OVERLEAF LEFT: This shrub (or small tree) was given its scientific name in 1810 by Scottish botanist Robert Brown, whose extensive plant collections contributed greatly to our knowledge of the Australian flora. It is one of the many *Banksia* that have adapted to survive the bushfires that regularly sweep through their habitat. In terms of how these fire-resistant species regenerate in response to fire, they are either seeders or sprouters. *Banksia attenuata* is in the latter camp, regrowing from either the lignotuber, a tough storage organ at the base of the plant, or from buds hidden within its trunk. It is pollinated by the exclusively nectivorous marsupial known as the honey possum (*Tarsipes rostratus*).

AUSTRALIA

FIREWOOD BANKSIA

Banksia menziesii (Proteaceae)

OVERLEAF RIGHT: This tree is one of the many *Banksia* species that have adapted to survive the bushfires that occur naturally in their habitat and are necessary for their regeneration. The structures resembling beaks embedded in its cone-like fruit head are termed *follicles*. Each follicle has developed from a single pollinated flower and contains one or two winged seeds. These are released only when the fruit head is burned, causing the follicles to open. The amount of pigment in the seeds determines the color of the flowers in the plants they produce. The flowers of *Banksia menziesii* have more color variants than any other members of the genus; they can be pink, yellow, white, brown, or green.

AUSTRALIA

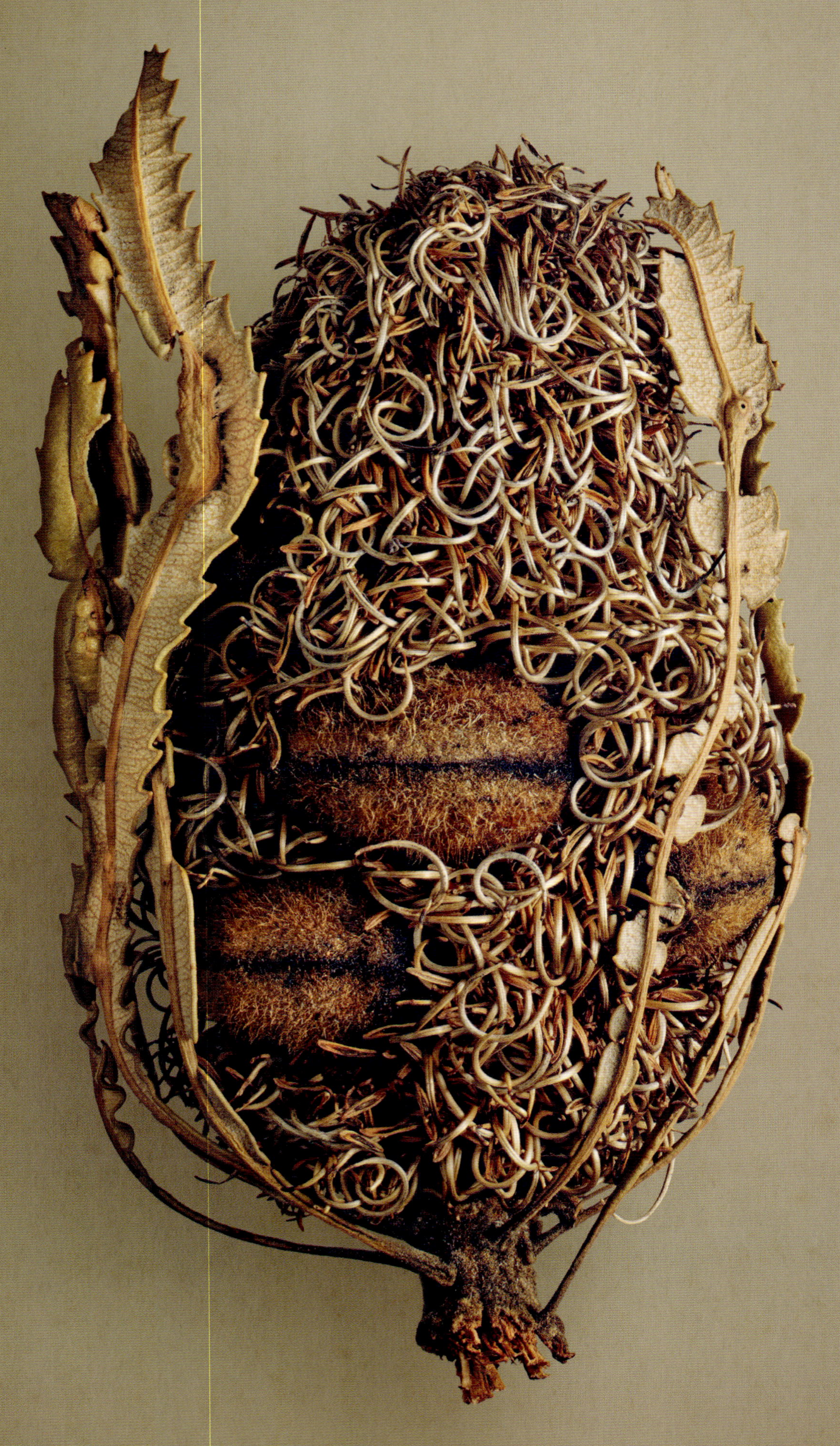

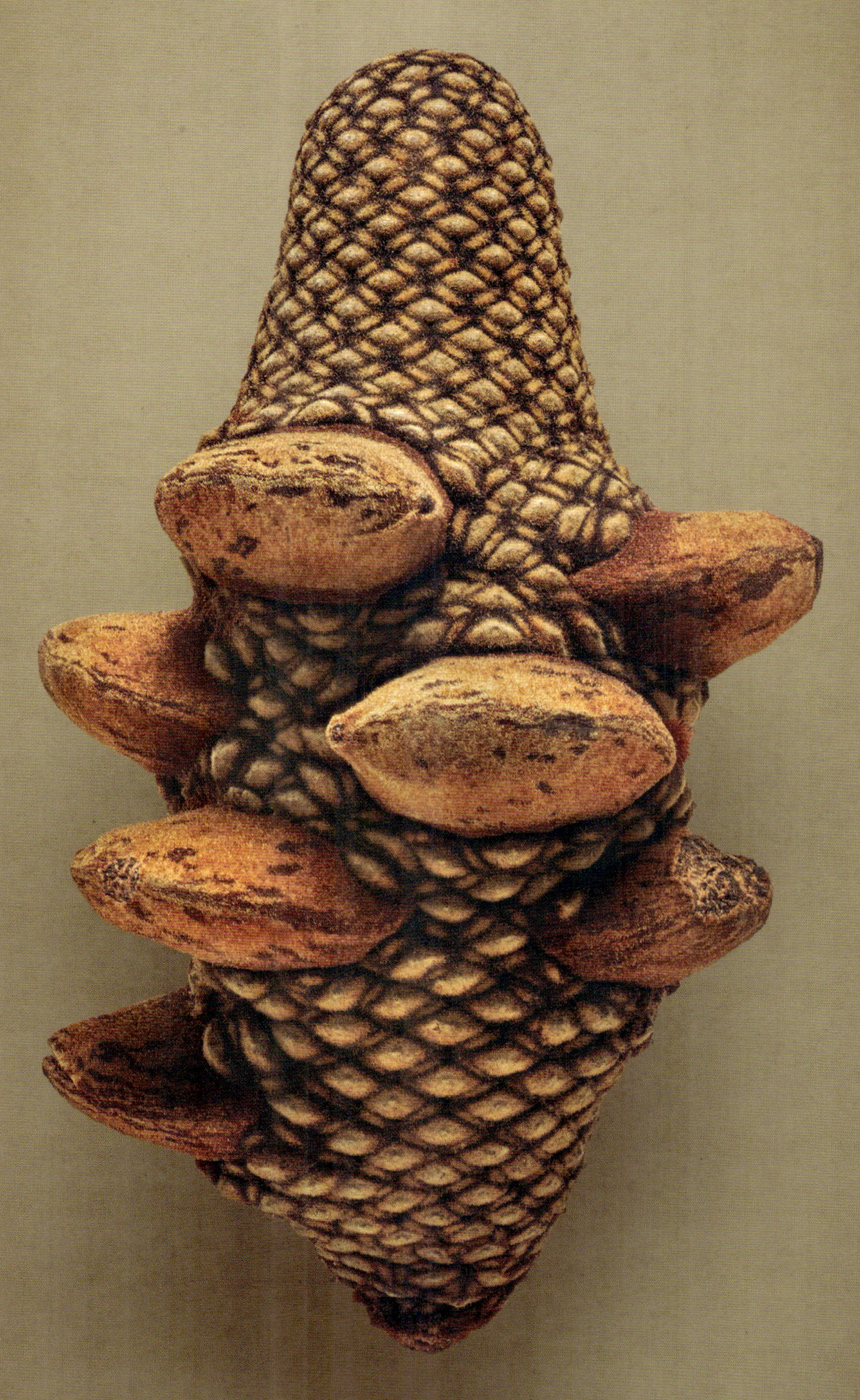

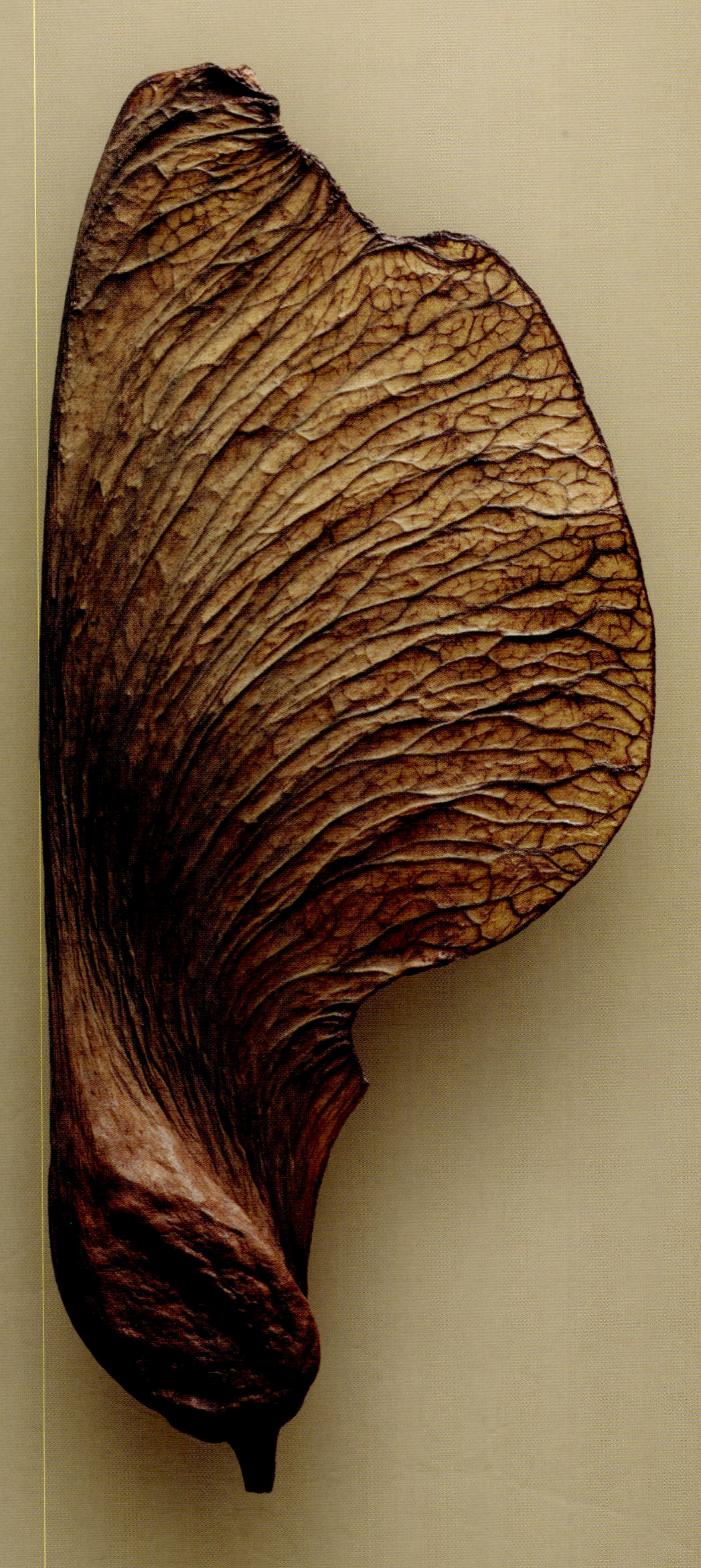

DUNGUN

Heritiera aurea (Malvaceae)

OPPOSITE: This species is endemic to the island of Borneo. It is a large tree (to 131 feet/40 m tall) found in the lowland rain forests. The timber is traded as a medium to heavy hardwood. The single-seeded fruits are wind-dispersed, aided by their thick wing. When fresh, the seed is mainly bright green (the wing has a red-brown tinge). When dry and ready for dispersal, the whole fruit is a pale brown-tan. In contact with water, the seed splits open and exudes a jelly-like substance; this may reduce insect predation or store moisture for germination. *Dungun* is the Malay word used on the island for this species, but it is also referred to by other names in the various languages spoken in the region.

MALAYSIA

PANDAN

Pandanus sp. (Pandanaceae)

OVERLEAF LEFT: This is a large genus of trees and shrubs with about six hundred recognized species. The label that accompanied this specimen does not specify where it was collected, only the collector name and collection number: *HS McKee* 3150. In cases such as this, the specimen records database at RBGE helps us to "fill in the blanks" in collection information. The database holds records for *McKee* collection numbers 3140 and 3164, from the year 1955, with New Caledonia stated as the location. Therefore, we were able to deduce that specimen *HS McKee* 3150 was collected on the same expedition. This allowed us to record the specimen and start trying to identify the species to which it belongs. The island of New Caledonia, which lies 750 miles (1200 km) east of Australia, is a biodiversity hot spot. Its remarkable flora is the consequence of evolution occurring over millions of years of isolation from the nearest landmass. Three-quarters of its plants are endemic (i.e. native to no other place on earth).

NEW CALEDONIA

DUTCHMAN'S PIPE

Aristolochia macrophylla (Aristolochiaceae)

OVERLEAF RIGHT: The common name of this species reflects its flowers' resemblance to Meerschaum pipes. It is a vigorous climber with large, heart-shaped leaves and small, brown-and-cream flowers, which are pollinated by insects. *Aristolochia* flowers attract insect pollinators by emitting a notoriously unpleasant smell of rotting meat, and that of *Aristolochia macrophylla* flowers is the worst of all! The fruits, which have the appearance of parachutes, split into six segments to release the flat, wind-dispersed seeds. This species is a host for the pipevine swallowtail butterfly (*Battus philenor*). The butterflies feed on the flower nectar, and their caterpillars on the leaves.

USA

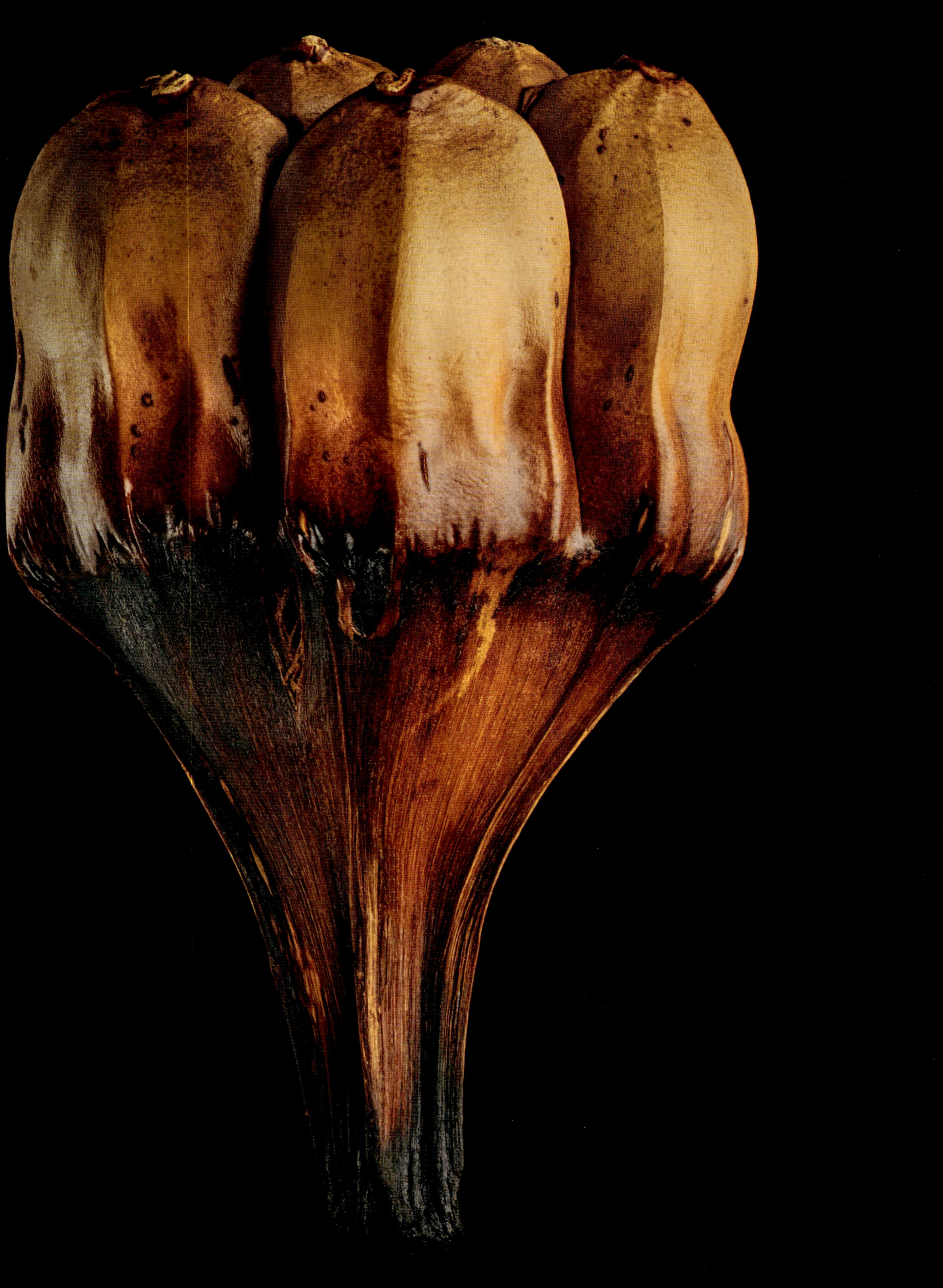

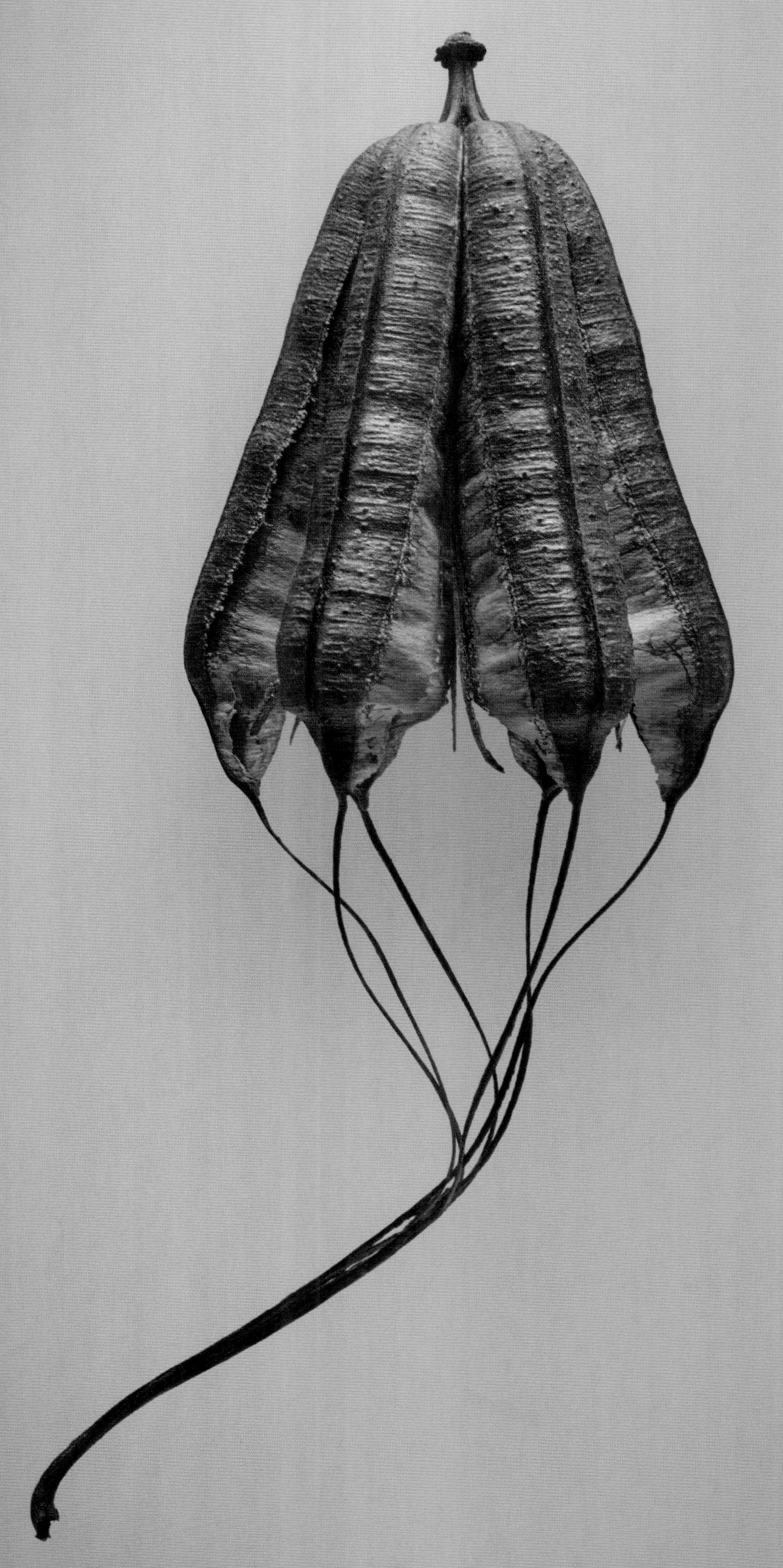

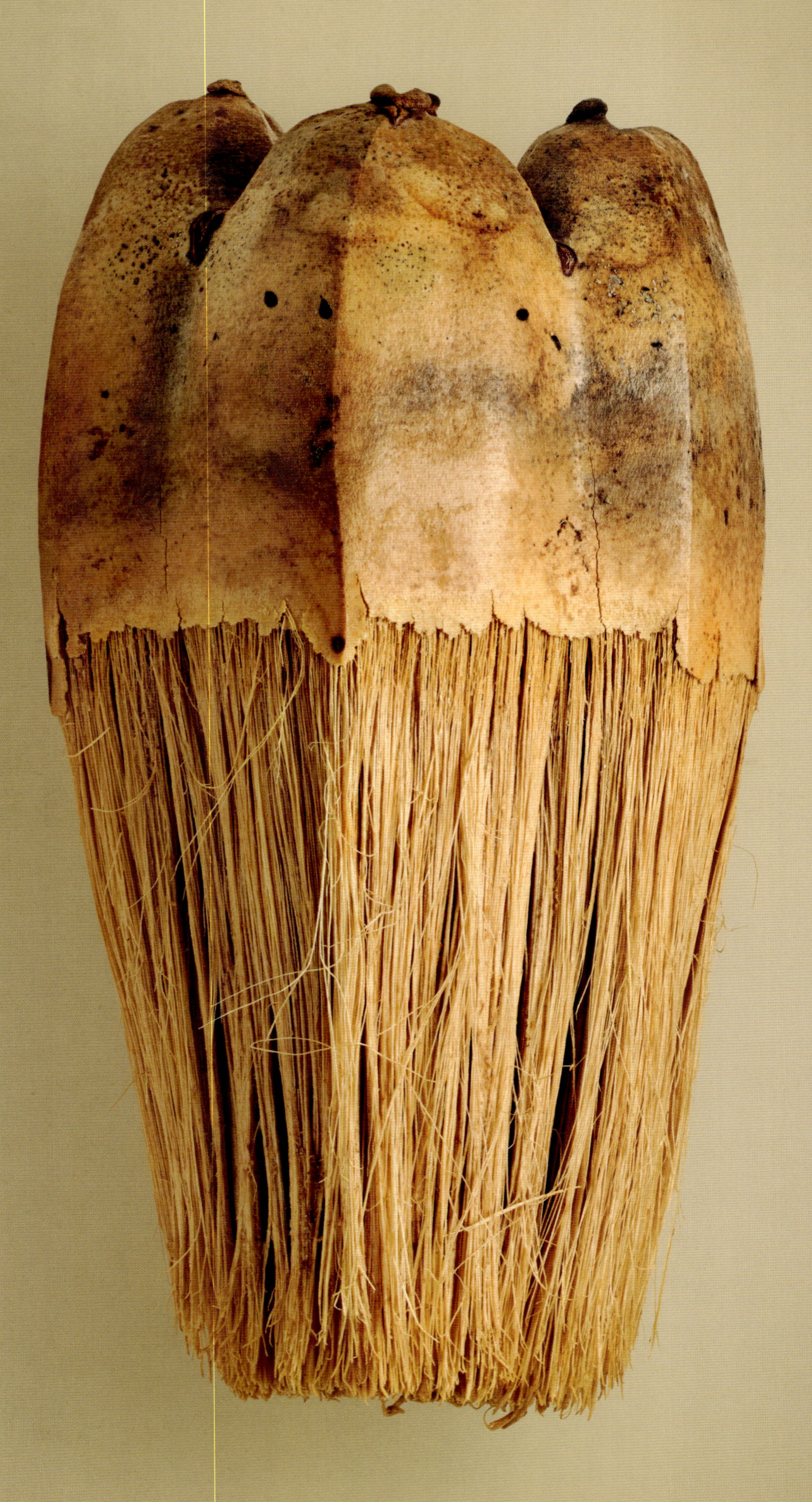

HATA

Pandanus hata (Pandanaceae)

OPPOSITE: Named by American botanist Harold St. John in 1975, this species is unique to the Rotuma island group, part of modern-day Fiji. St. John collected and described plants around the Pacific Islands and in later life worked at several institutions in Hawaii, including the Bishop Museum in Honolulu. The Museum now houses an extensive collection of his specimens in its Herbarium Pacificum. St. John is best known for his work on *Pandanus*, having discovered about five hundred species from around the globe. The specific epithet *hata* derives from the Rotuman name for this species. In traditional ceremonies, garlands known as *tefui* are made and worn. To create these garlands, the bright red skin is removed from the fruit and cut into diamond shapes that are then strung with white gardenia flowers.

FIJI

COCO DE MER

Lodoicea maldivica (Arecaceae)

OVERLEAF LEFT: This palm, the sole member of its genus, is found only on the Seychelles islands of Praslin and Curieuse. It produces the world's largest fruit from a wild plant and the seed is also the heaviest. Such huge seeds provide nutrients to allow the germinating seedling, as seen in this dissected specimen, to compete with other plants. Its name ("coconut of the sea") arose because the tree was originally thought to disperse its seeds by sea, as fishermen have sighted the shells of giant fruits floating offshore. The myth of sea-dispersal is disproven by the fact that seawater breaks down the outer coating of the fruit, making the seeds no longer viable. In fact, the seeds tend to germinate on land close to the parent tree where the soil is most nutritious. The fruits were traded for centuries as an ornamental item. Their export, however, is now illegal due to the species' Endangered *IUCN Red List* conservation status.

SEYCHELLES

MEDANG PAJAL

Ternstroemia sp. (Pentaphylacaceae)

OVERLEAF RIGHT: Named after eighteenth-century Swedish naturalist Christopher Ternstroem (a pupil of Linneaus), this genus of small trees is distributed across the tropics. It is composed of about 150 species: 3 in Africa, about 30 in Asia (including 17 on the island of Borneo), and the remainder in South America. Many species are found in mountainous areas. The fruit is orange-red when fresh, with a persistent thick calyx at its apex. This partial dissection of the fruit has exposed the seed which, although now dried out and a little bit degraded, would have been bright red when fresh and probably dispersed by birds. The wood is sold for use in light construction (trade name Tapmis) and sometimes for veneer. The bark is used to produce a fish poison, and in western New Guinea it is used to combat head lice.

MALAYSIA

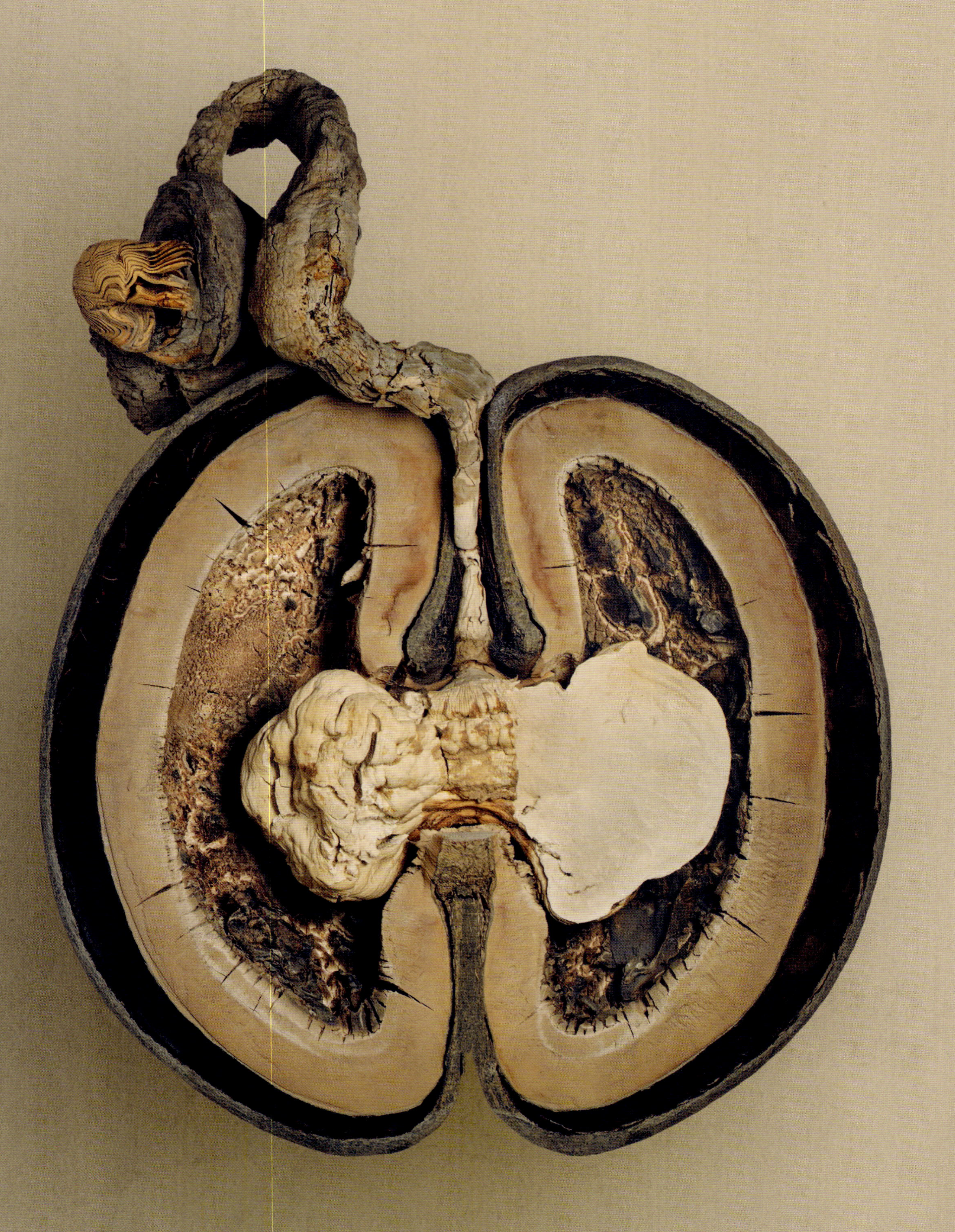

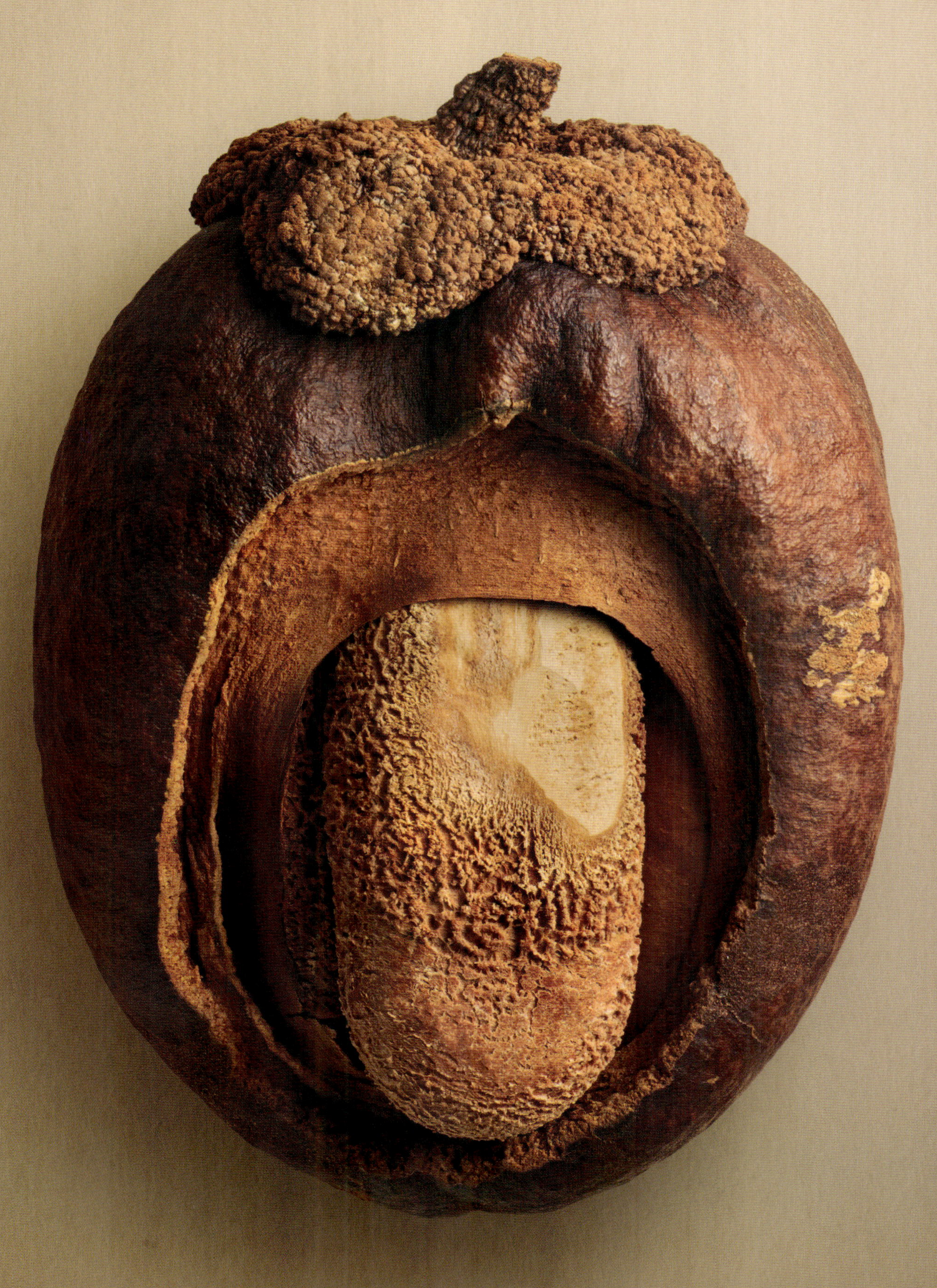

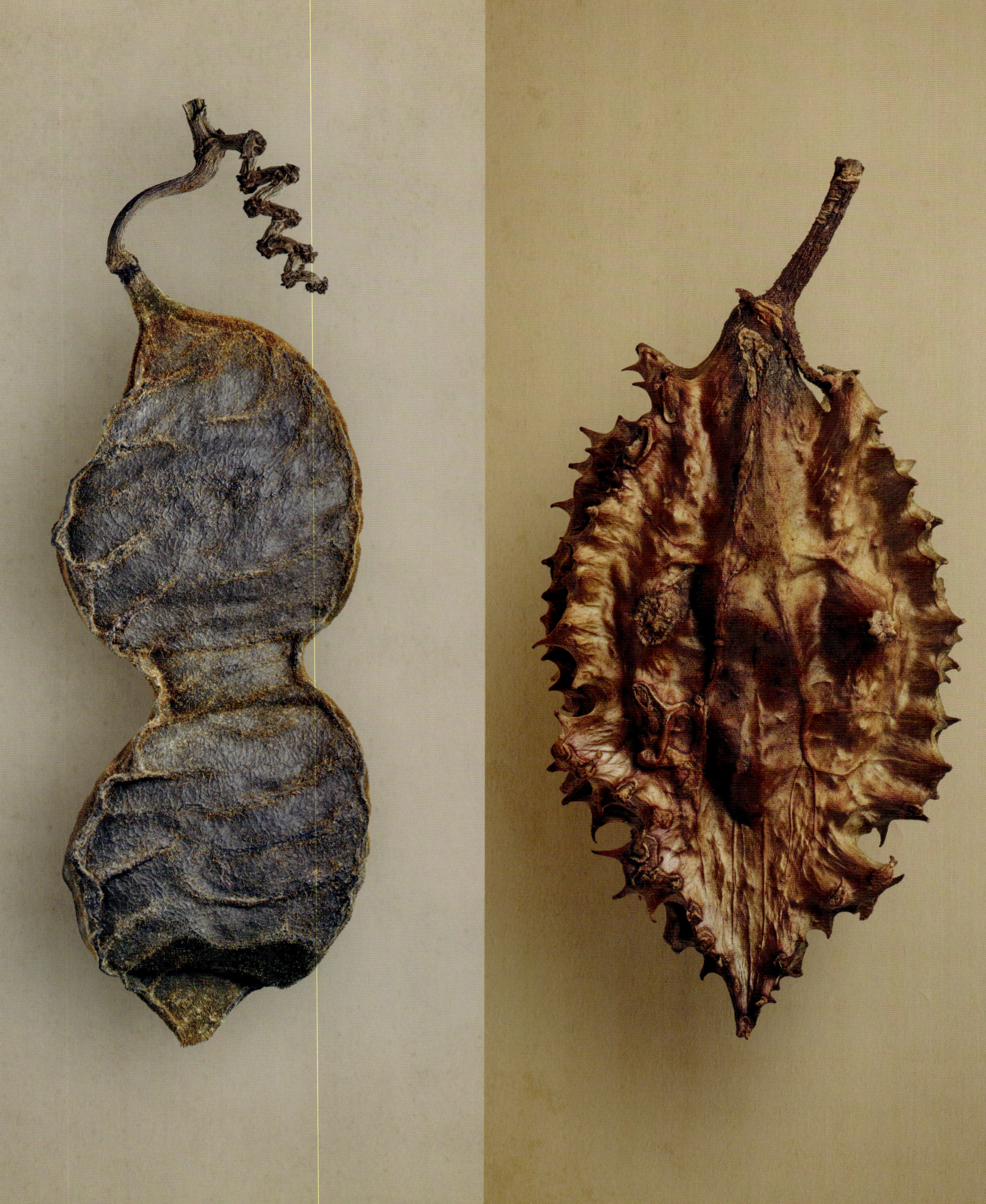

COW ITCH

Mucuna flagellipes (Fabaceae)

OPPOSITE LEFT: The fruits of some *Mucuna* are covered in hairs so nasty they will make a cow itch. It is a climber that grows on trees growing on riverbanks in West and Central Africa. The specific epithet comes from the Latin for 'whip' and refers to the 3- to 6-foot (1- to 2-m) long stalk from which the flowers and fruits hang. This is one of the several hundred tropical plants pollinated by nectarivorous bats. The flowers open at night, and their large size and white color make them easy to spot in the darkness. Their position, held clear of the branches and leaves, makes them easier for the bats to access. The pods each contain two or three rounded seeds. When ripe, they fall into the river below and are carried by the current to germinate at another site.

CENTRAL AFRICAN REPUBLIC

GRAPPLE PLANT

Harpagophytum zeyheri (Pedaliaceae)

OPPOSITE RIGHT: This herbaceous plant has attractive purple flowers that recall those of sesame (*Sesamum indicum*), to which it is related. Its scientific name, inspired by the fruit, derives from the word *harpago* in Latin. In domestic contexts, this referred to a spiked kitchen utensil used to hook and lift pieces of meat from a cooking pot. The same word was used by the Romans for the grappling iron used in warfare. If you ever accidentally step on one of these fruits barefoot, the resulting pain might well bring this association to mind! The species is sometimes called devil's claw, a name it shares with a closely related species used medicinally in Namibia, Botswana, and South Africa, as well as several other plants across the globe.

SOUTH AFRICA

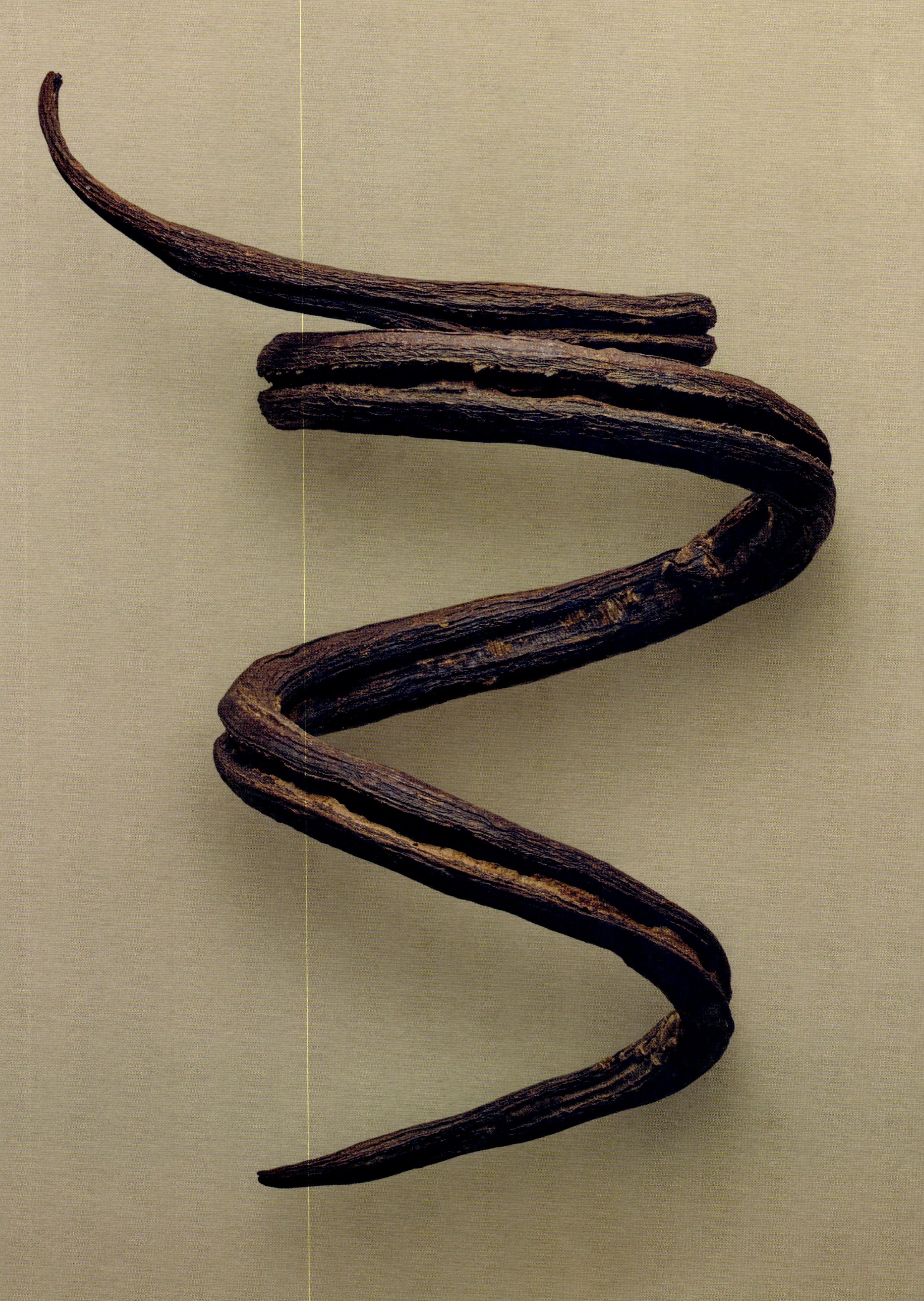

GOAT HORN

Skytanthus acutus (Apocynaceae)

OPPOSITE: This peculiar-looking specimen was collected from *Skytanthus acutus*, a member of the oleander family. The species is a yellow-flowered shrub found only in coastal parts of the driest and coolest desert on earth: Chile's Atacama Desert. Its low, sprawling habit and entangled stems trap drifting sand and seed, thus creating a refuge for wildlife, especially lizards. Its Chilean name, *cuerno de cabra* (Spanish for "goat horn"), refers to the long, curly, hard fruits in the shape of a coil. When mature, the fruits detach from the mother plant to be blown across the desert surface, dispersing their seeds as they go. They come to rest by hooking onto any patch of vegetation in their path, and it is here that their remaining seed germinate during the long-awaited spring rains.

CHILE

CÓGUIL

Lardizabala funaria (Lardizabalaceae)

OVERLEAF LEFT: This curious specimen belongs to *Lardizabala funaria*, a species of vigorous evergreen liana found only in the temperate rain forests of southern Chile. When mature, the liana develops thick, woody stems that twist around themselves and sometimes hang free from the canopy. Because of their great strength and flexibility, these stems have traditionally been used to make baskets. Male and female flowers are borne on separate plants. Once pollinated, the female flowers develop into distinctive, sausage-like fruits containing a thick white mucilage, within which the seeds are embedded. Being sweet, soft-textured, and edible, the fruits are considered a delicacy and offered for sale in local rural markets.

CHILE

SHELL GINGER

Alpinia sp. (Zingiberaceae)

OVERLEAF RIGHT: This specimen belongs to a species of *Alpinia*, a genus in the ginger family. *Alpinia* occur throughout the warmer parts of Asia, from Sri Lanka to some of the islands of the Western Pacific. They usually grow in forests but are also frequently found in disturbed areas at the edges of fields and forests. The round, hairy fruit shown here comes from a plant similar to galangal (*Alpinia galanga*), a species that is rare outside Southeast Asia. Like a cardamom pod (the fruit of *Elettaria cardamomum*, another ginger), it contains three rows of fragrant seeds. *Alpinia* currently holds more species than any other genus in the ginger family. However, over the coming years they will be divided among smaller genera to more accurately reflect the way in which they have evolved.

THAILAND

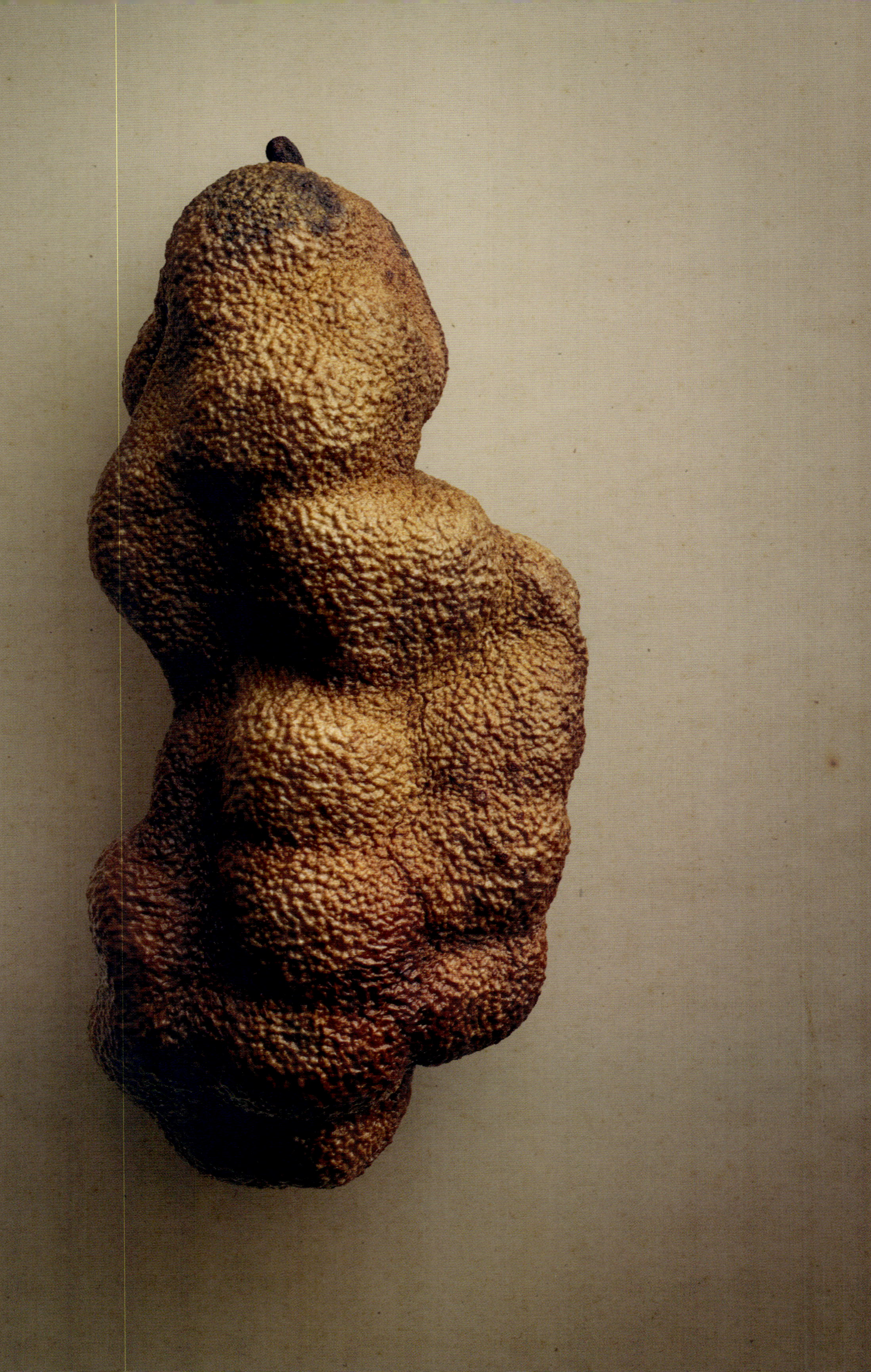

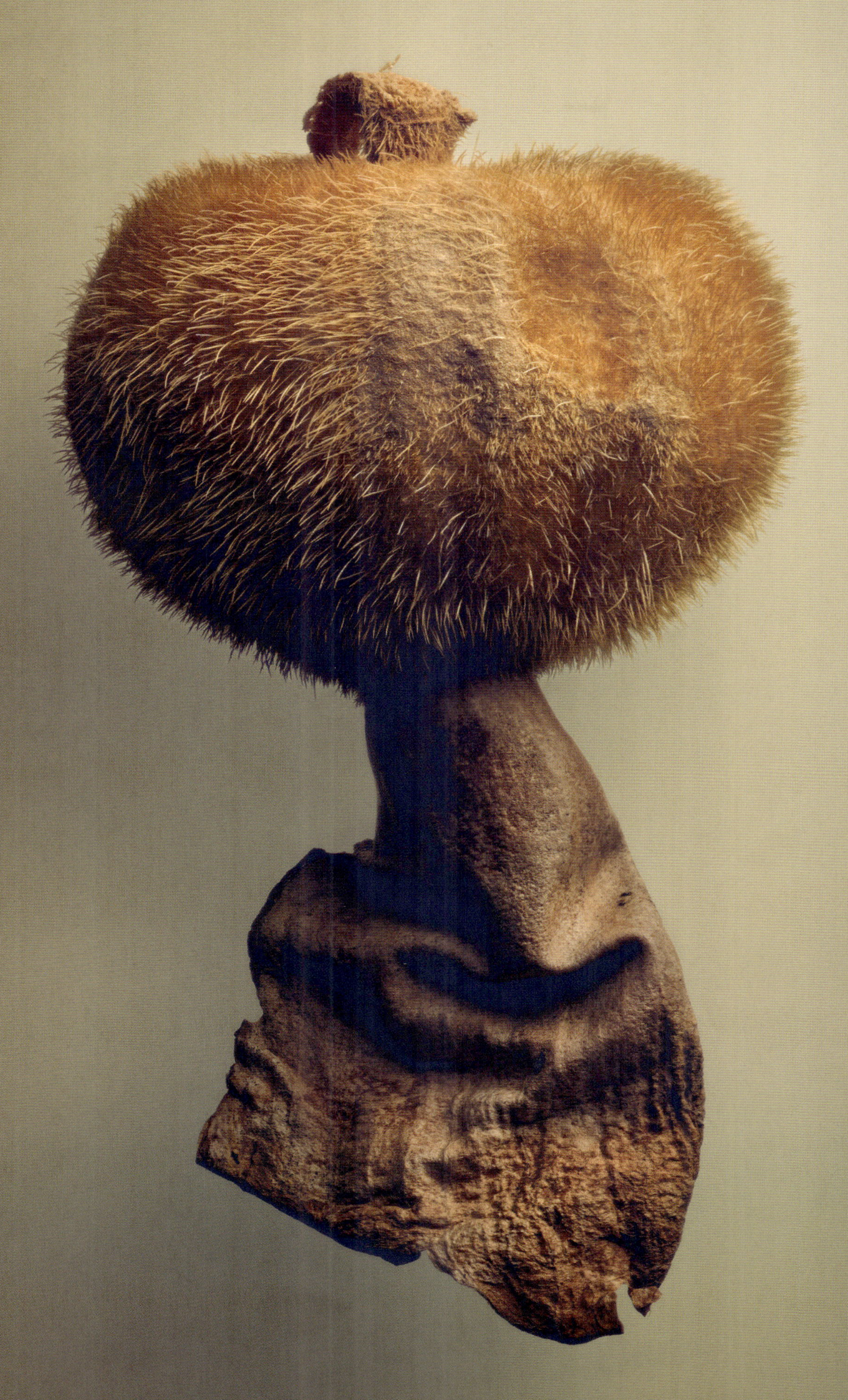

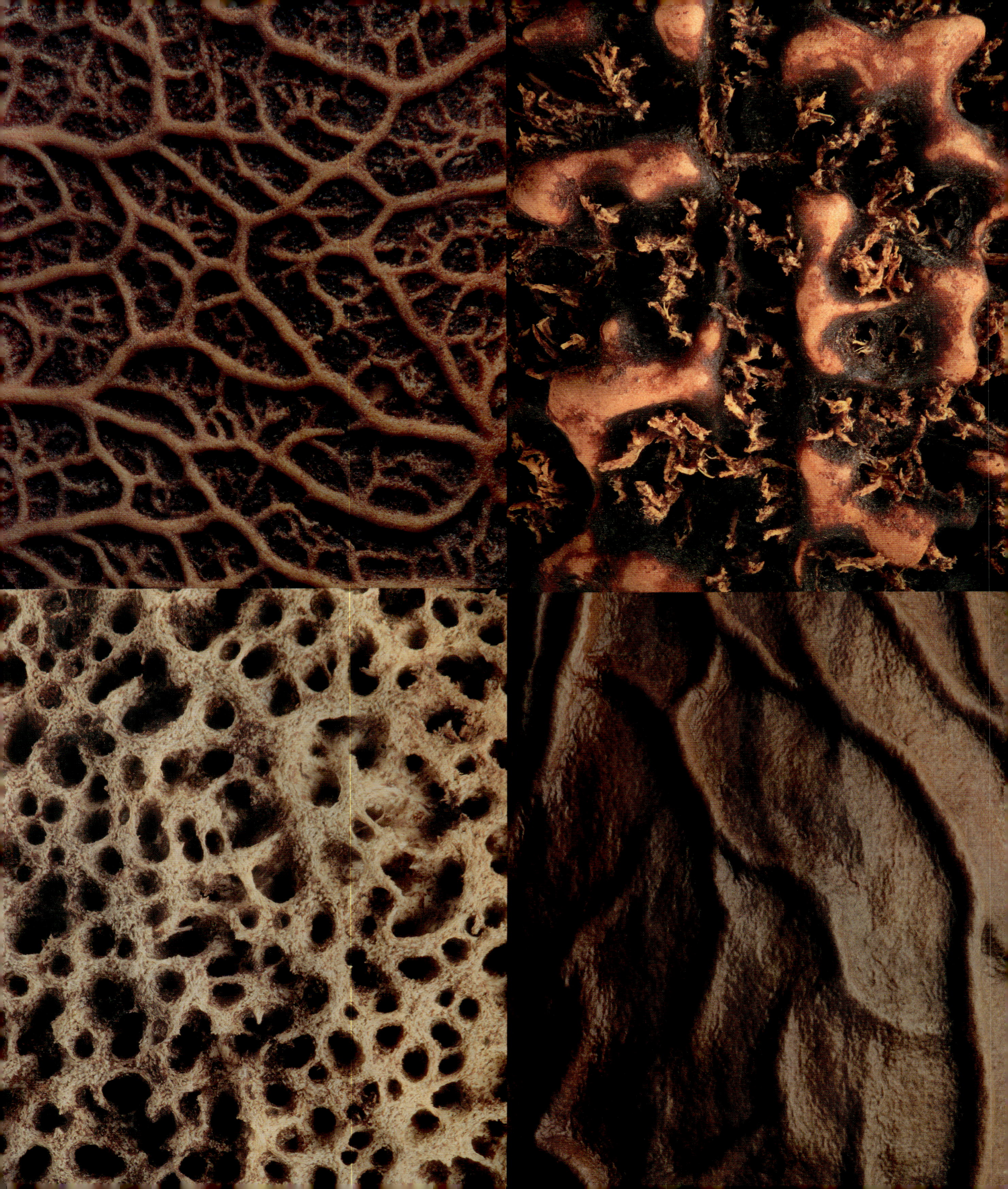

MYSORE THORN

Biancaea decapetala (Fabaceae)

TOP LEFT: This scrambling and climbing shrub is native to the Indian subcontinent and Southeast Asia. It has been introduced as an ornamental in many areas of the world because of its delightful, showy yellow flowers. It also works well as a barrier plant, forming a natural dense, thorny fence to mark boundaries in forests and farmland. However, it has become a nuisance in countries such as Australia and South Africa, where it is classed as an invasive weed. The seeds are released when the pods burst at maturity. This image highlights the intricate venation over the exterior surface of the fruit.

BHUTAN

OIL FRUIT

Elaeocarpus sp. (Elaeocarpaceae)

TOP RIGHT: This detailed image is of the wall of the stone, from the fruit of the genus *Elaeocarpus*. The family Eleaocarpaceae, which contains some six hundred species, is completely absent from continental Africa, although it occurs in Madagascar and other tropical continents. Plant families, which are widely dispersed, but are absent from whole continents, puzzle biologists. There is still much to understand about the evolutionary history of plants.

AUSTRALIA

MOKANA

Panda oleosa (Pandaceae)

BOTTOM LEFT: To forest elephants in the Central African Republic, the fruit of this tree is what a plum is to us: a tasty fruit with a hard stone. They use their trunks to pick up the fruits from the ground under the trees, then swallow them whole. This image is of the surface of a stone found in a pile of old elephant dung on the edge of Dzanga Bai. This clearing in the middle of the rain forest is one of the seven wonders of the natural world; it is where elephants congregate to eat the mineral-rich soil and to socialize. *Mokana* is the name given to this plant by the forest-dwelling Aka people. They extract the oily seeds from the stone by chipping at it with a machete.

CENTRAL AFRICAN REPUBLIC

MONKEY EGG

Dysoxylum gotadhora (Meliaceae)

BOTTOM RIGHT: This tree is native to India, from the central Himalayas down to Southeast Asia. When fresh, the fruit of this tree are bright orange when ripe. The fruit splits to reveal three to four dark brown shiny seeds and bright orange flesh. The common name in India is *bandor dima*, translating as "monkey egg." The tree is a member of the Meliaceae or mahogany family that contains many highly sought-after timbers.

BHUTAN

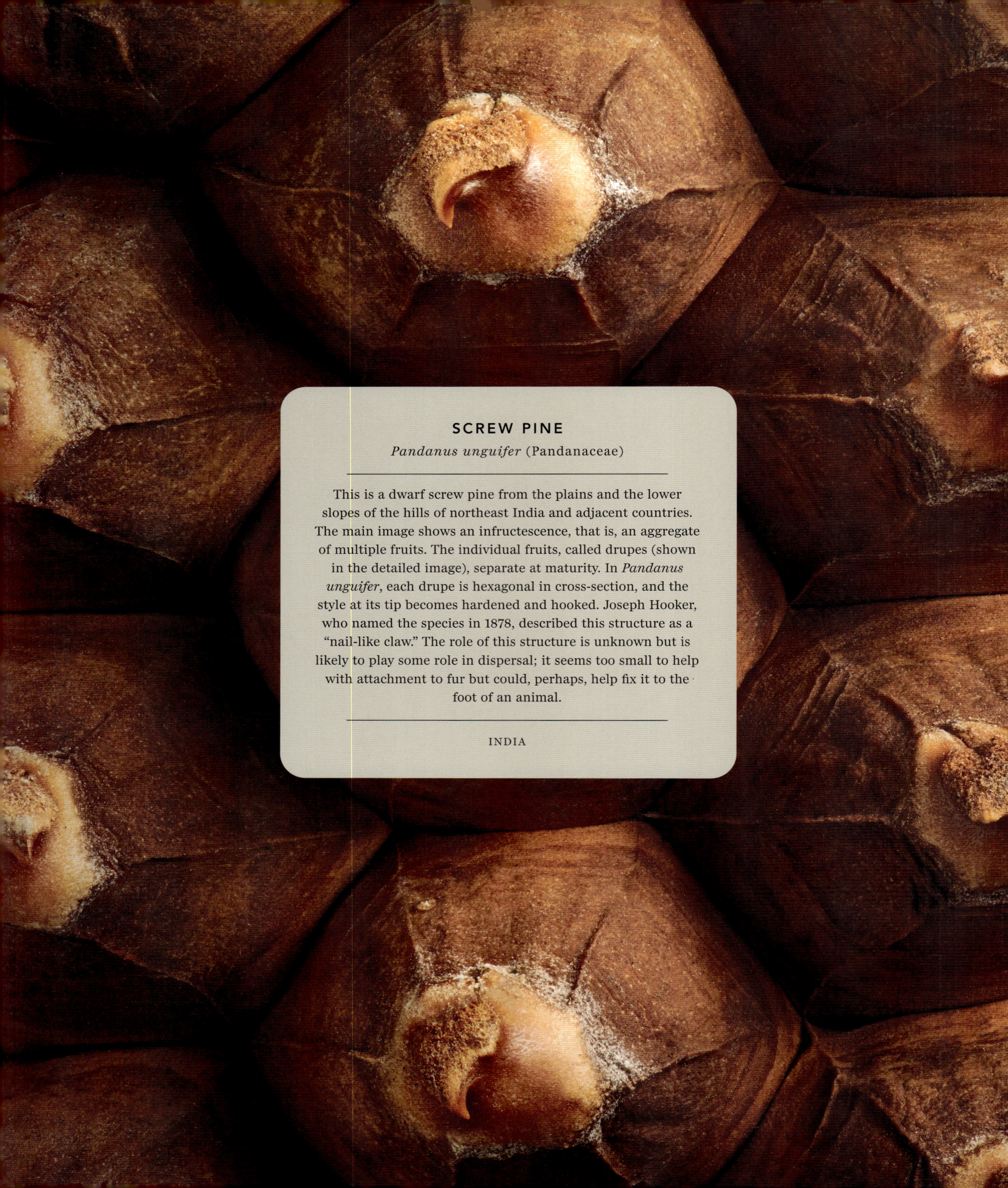

SCREW PINE

Pandanus unguifer (Pandanaceae)

This is a dwarf screw pine from the plains and the lower slopes of the hills of northeast India and adjacent countries. The main image shows an infructescence, that is, an aggregate of multiple fruits. The individual fruits, called drupes (shown in the detailed image), separate at maturity. In *Pandanus unguifer*, each drupe is hexagonal in cross-section, and the style at its tip becomes hardened and hooked. Joseph Hooker, who named the species in 1878, described this structure as a "nail-like claw." The role of this structure is unknown but is likely to play some role in dispersal; it seems too small to help with attachment to fur but could, perhaps, help fix it to the foot of an animal.

INDIA

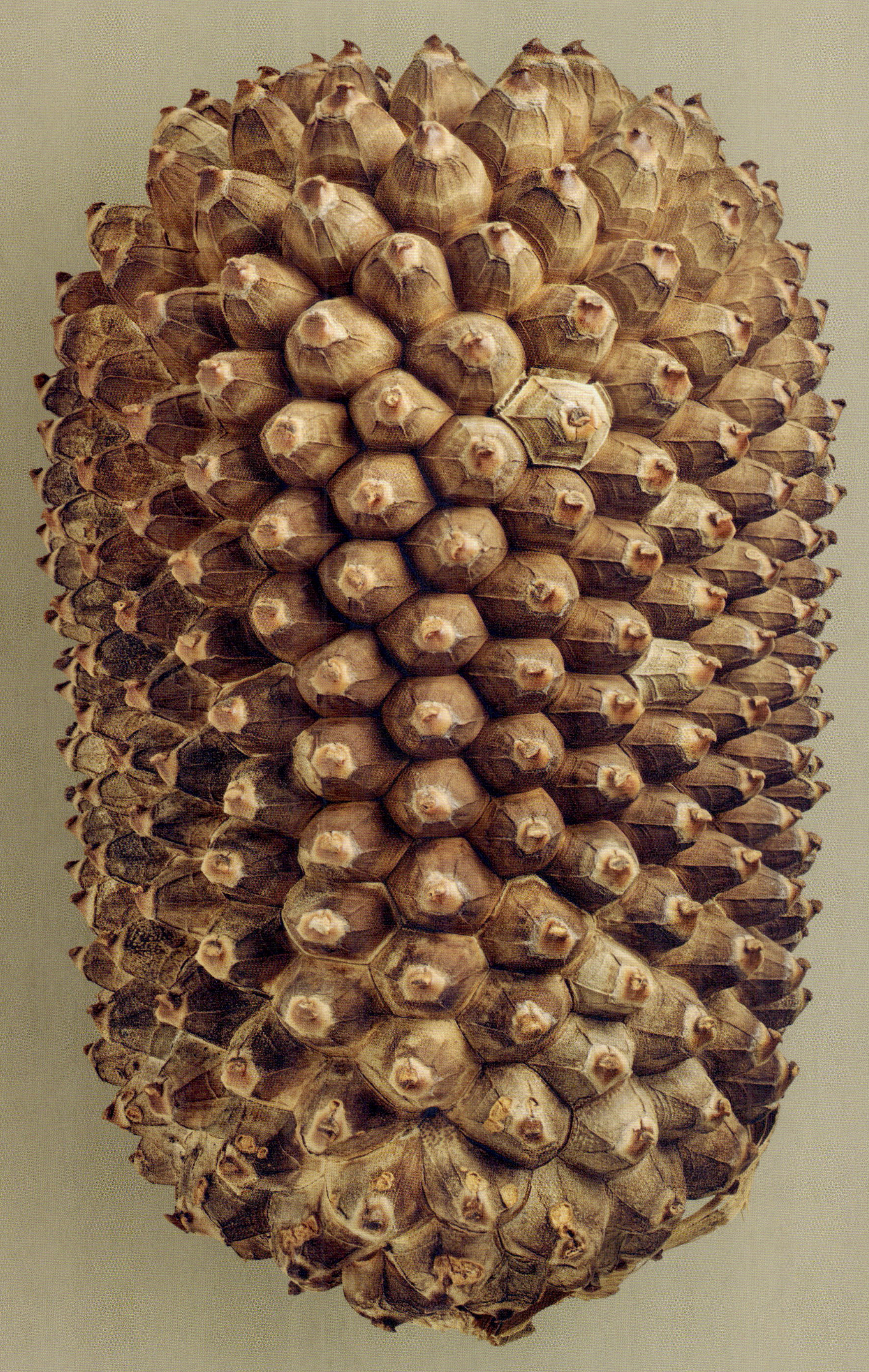

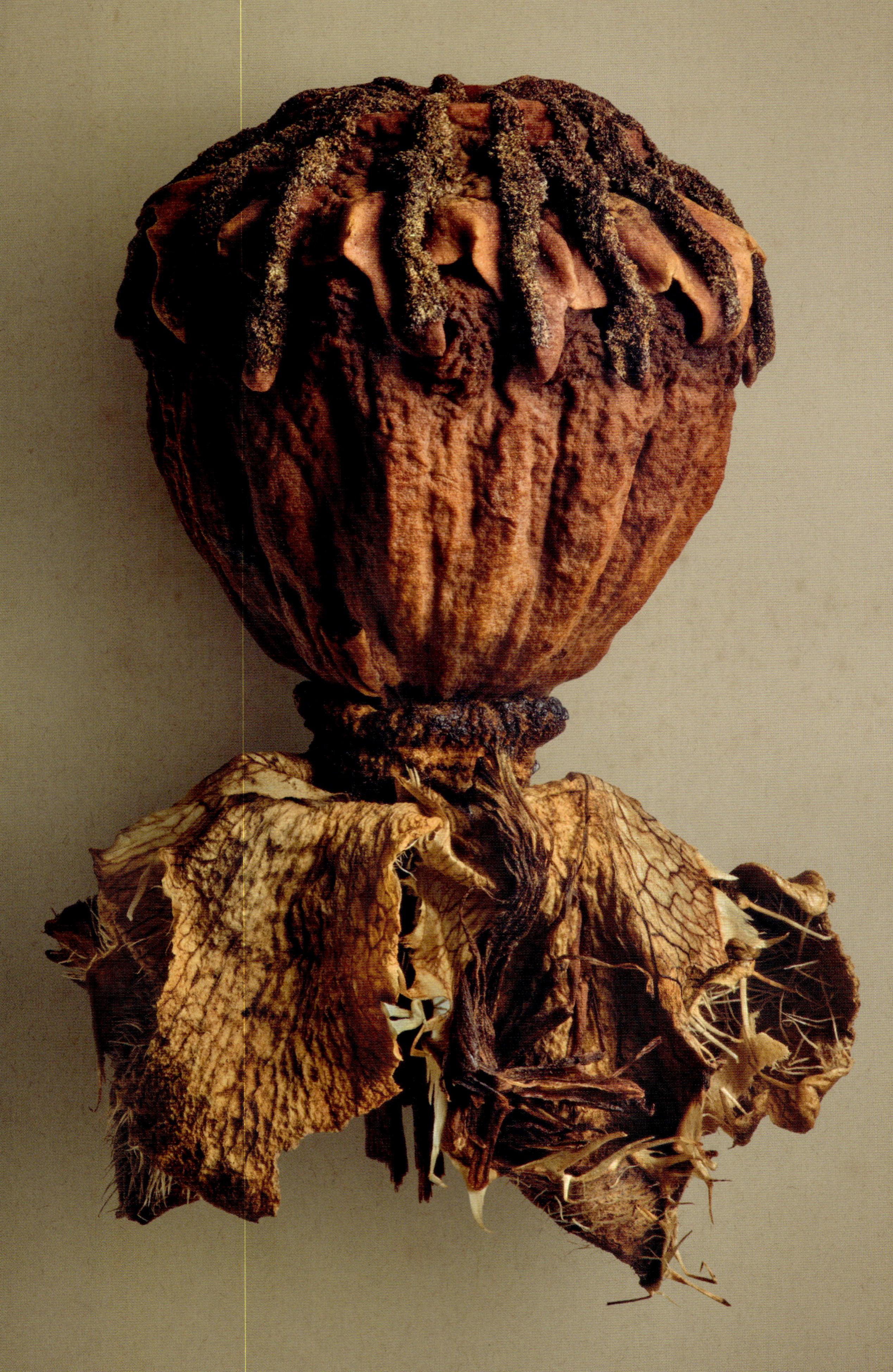

ORIENTAL POPPY

Papaver orientale (Papaveraceae)

OPPOSITE: This highly ornamental garden plant is native to Turkey, Georgia, Armenia, Azerbaijan, and Iran, where it inhabits meadows, stony places, and open forest glades in the subalpine zone just below the treeline. Like so many species, it was first described by the Swedish naturalist Carl Linnaeus (1707–1778). Linnaeus devised the formal system for naming organisms that we use today. The seeds of this and other poppies are dispersed when the wind is forceful enough to shake them free through small openings at the top of the fruiting capsule. This method of seed dispersal is called the censer mechanism, because seeds escaping from the capsule are reminiscent of smoke wafting from the incense burners swung on chains during religious ceremonies.

TURKEY

SANDILLÓN

Eriosyce aurata (Cactaceae)

OVERLEAF LEFT AND RIGHT: This species is a barrel cactus endemic to arid areas of central and northern Chile. The genus name *Eriosyce*, literally "woolly fig" in Greek, refers to the felt-like surface of the main body of the fruit. *Eriosyce aurata* can grow to almost 3 feet (1 m) in height and 18 inches (.5 m) across. Its longitudinal ribs are heavily armed with coarse, curved spines, a selection of which are shown here. Only mature plants produce the funnel-shaped red flowers; these can number up to fifty on a single plant. The white, globular fruits contain black seeds that are dispersed by the wind. At the highest end of the altitudinal range of this species (about 9,843 feet/3,000 m), it endures extraordinary climatic extremes, with night temperatures plunging well below freezing and intense heat and sunlight during the day.

CHILE

SANDPLAIN WOODY PEAR

Xylomelum angustifolium (Proteaceae)

FOLLOWING OVERLEAF LEFT AND RIGHT: Native to the sandplains of Western Australia, this small tree produces large fruits that look rather like pears. The woodiness of the fruit protects the two-winged seeds within it from granivores (seed-eating animals) and fire. It splits into halves longitudinally, either gradually over the course of several seasons of autumn rain followed by summer heat, or within hours in response to bushfire. This specimen, collected by Alexander Morrison in 1905, is what is left of the fruit once its seeds have been released; you can see the cavities in which they previously nestled. Scottish-born Morrison was appointed to the post of Western Australia's first official botanist in 1897. He bequeathed to the University of Edinburgh his large collection of specimens, about nine thousand of which are now held in the herbarium at RBGE.

AUSTRALIA

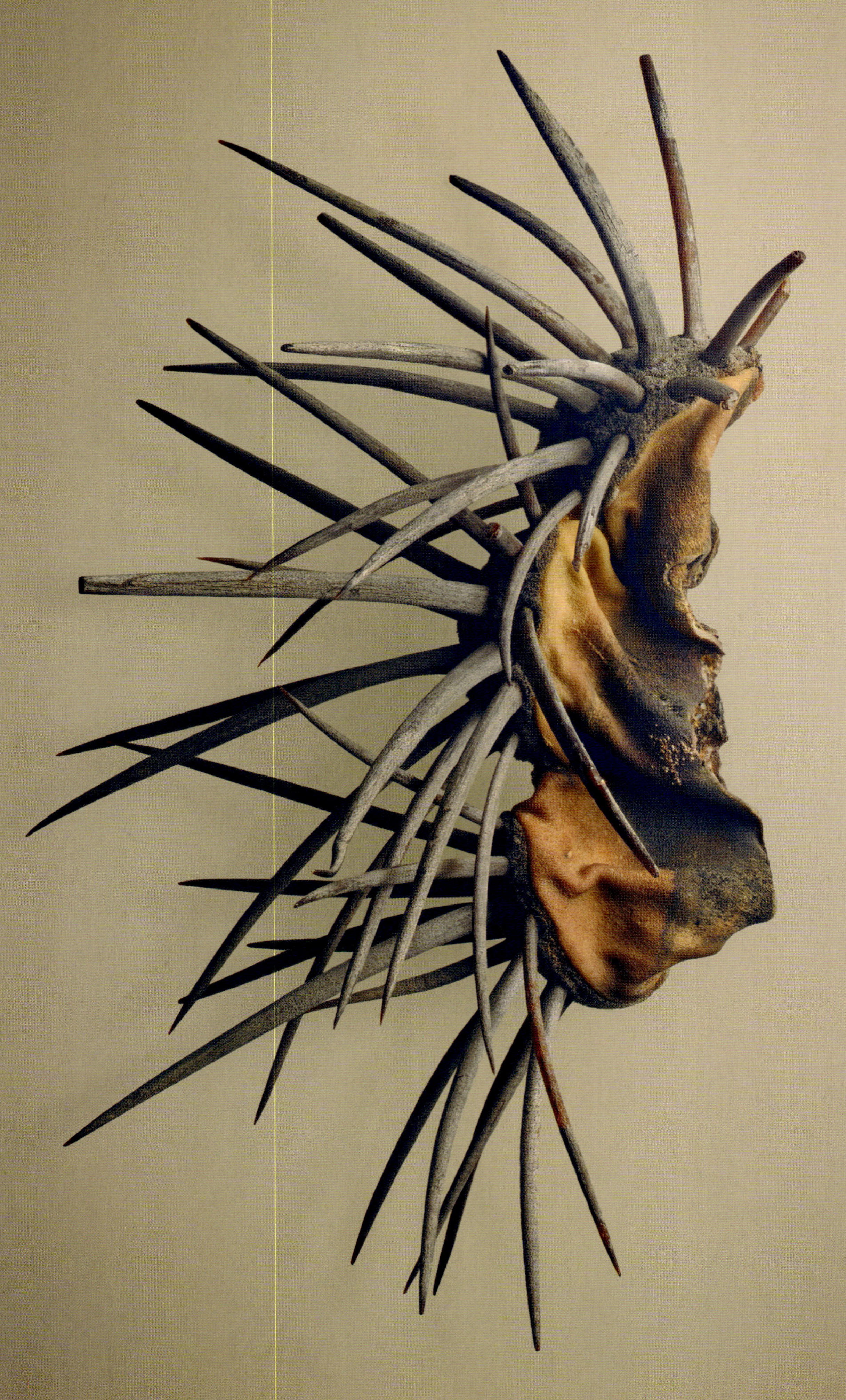

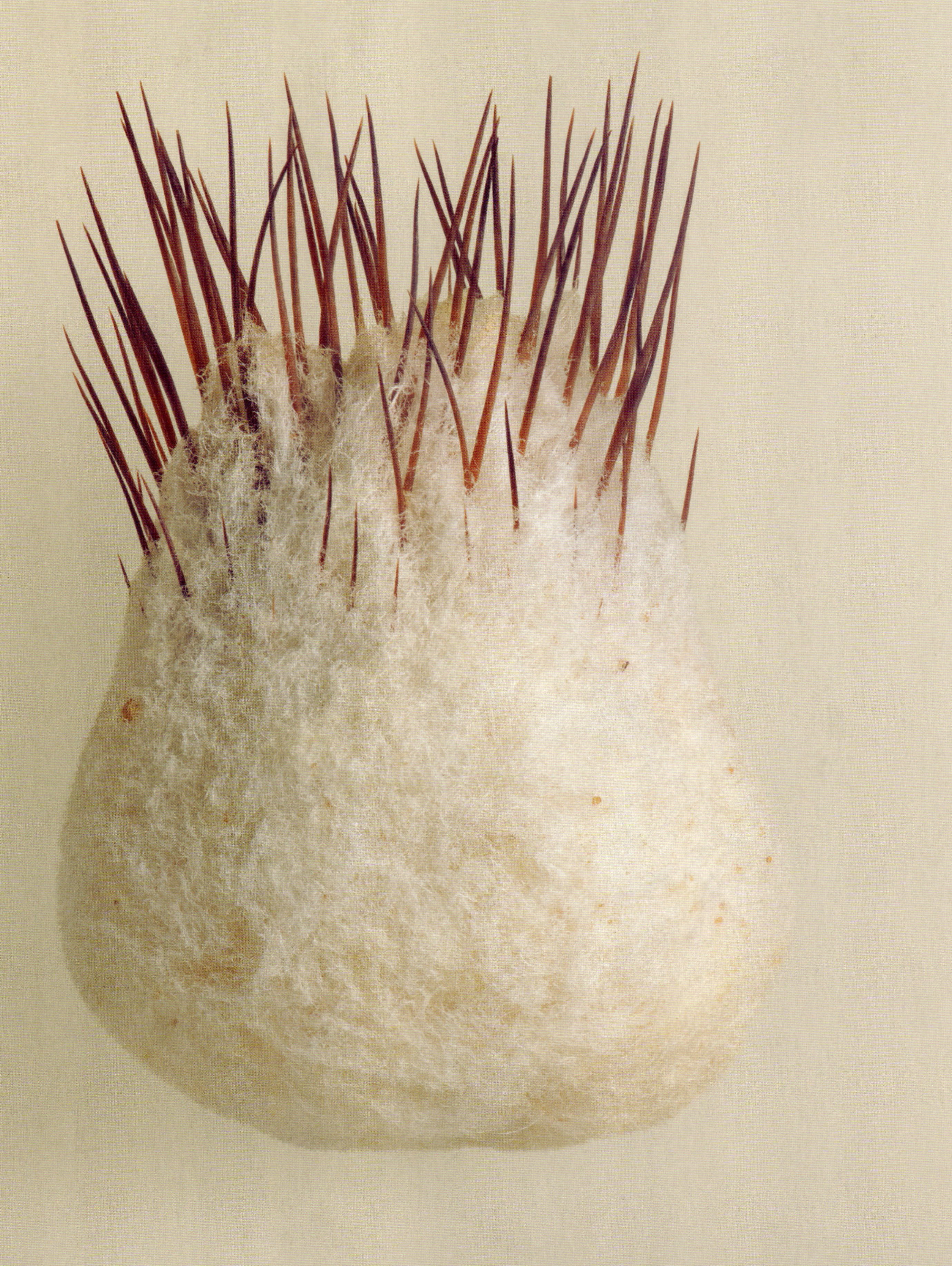

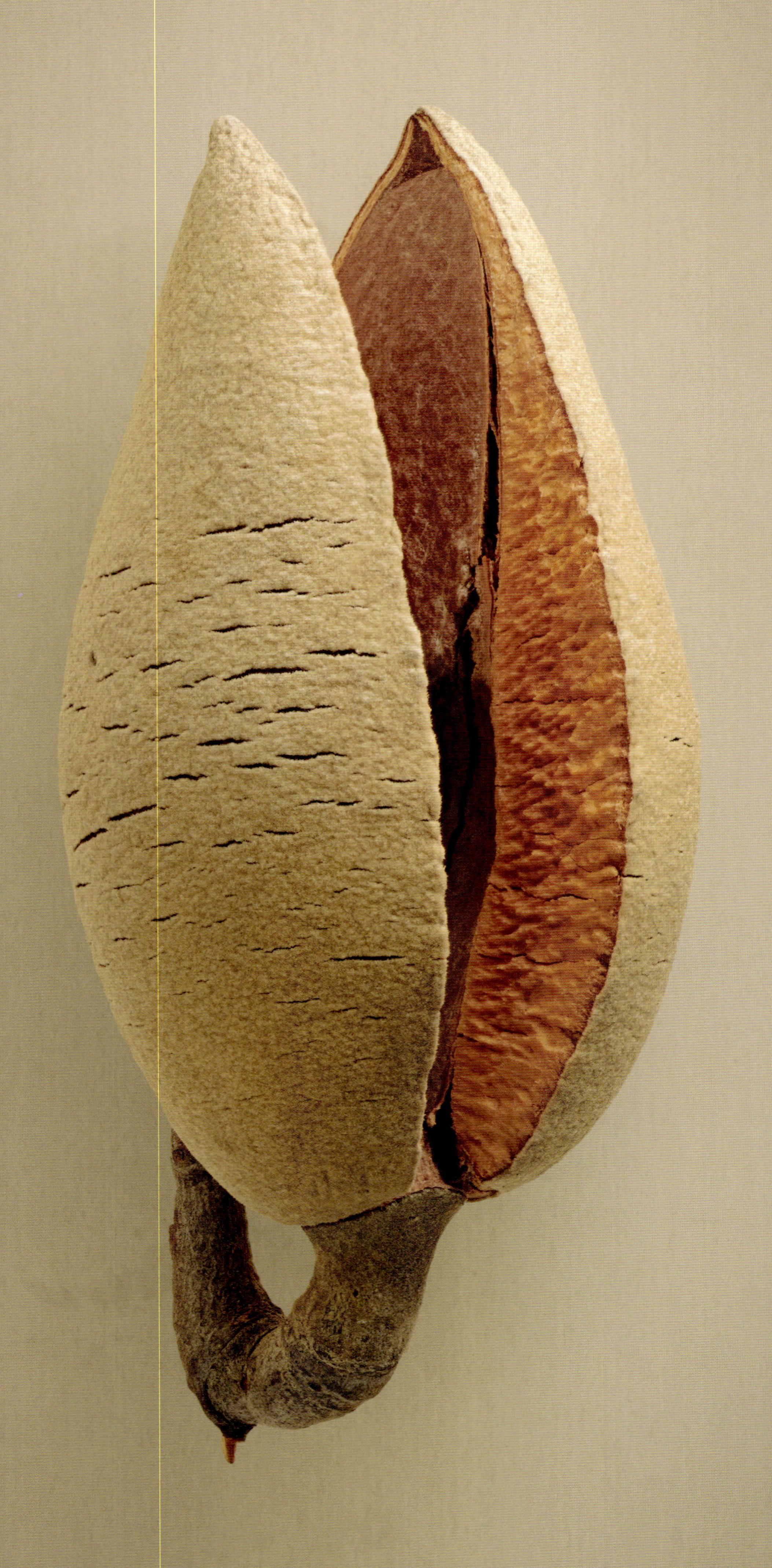

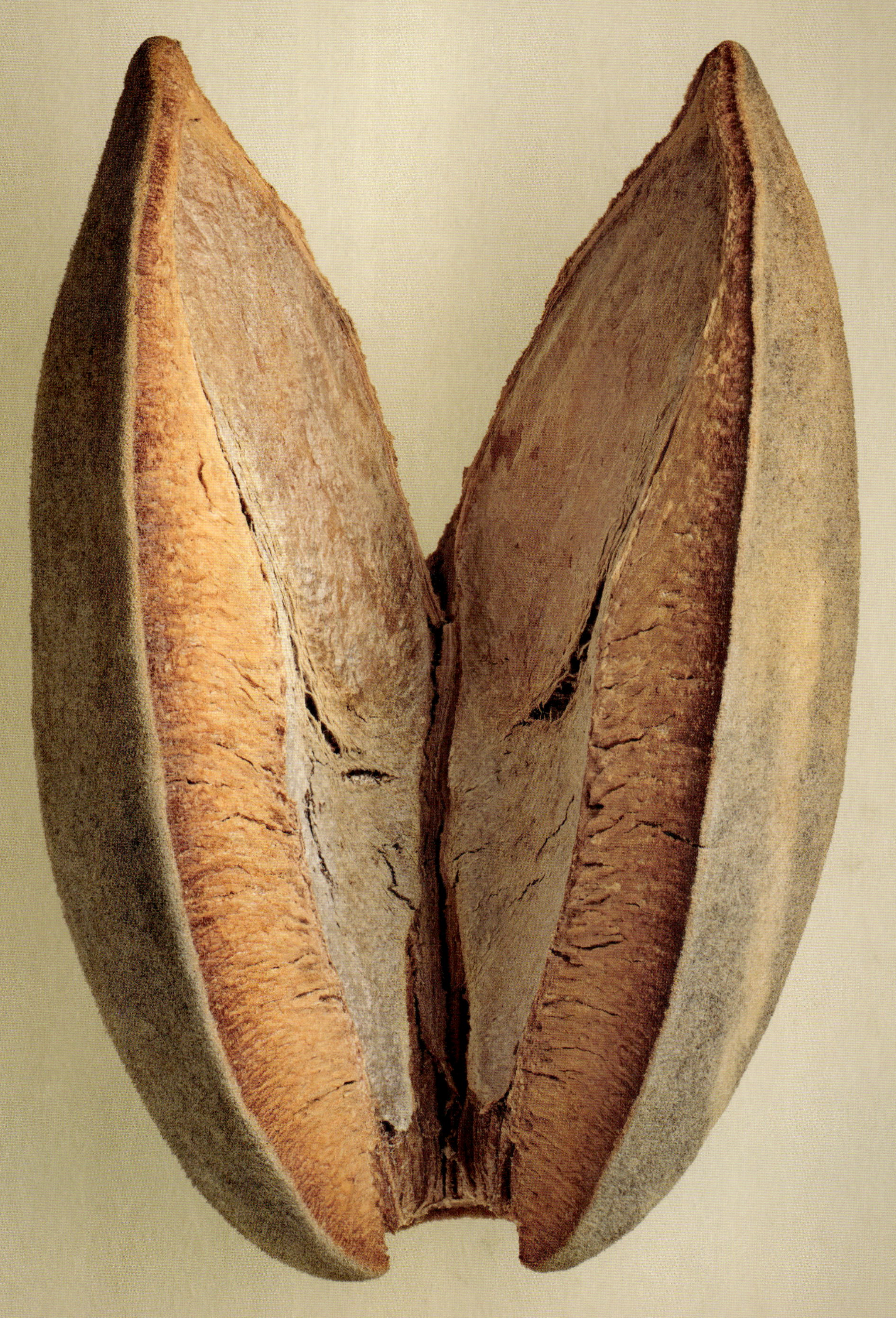

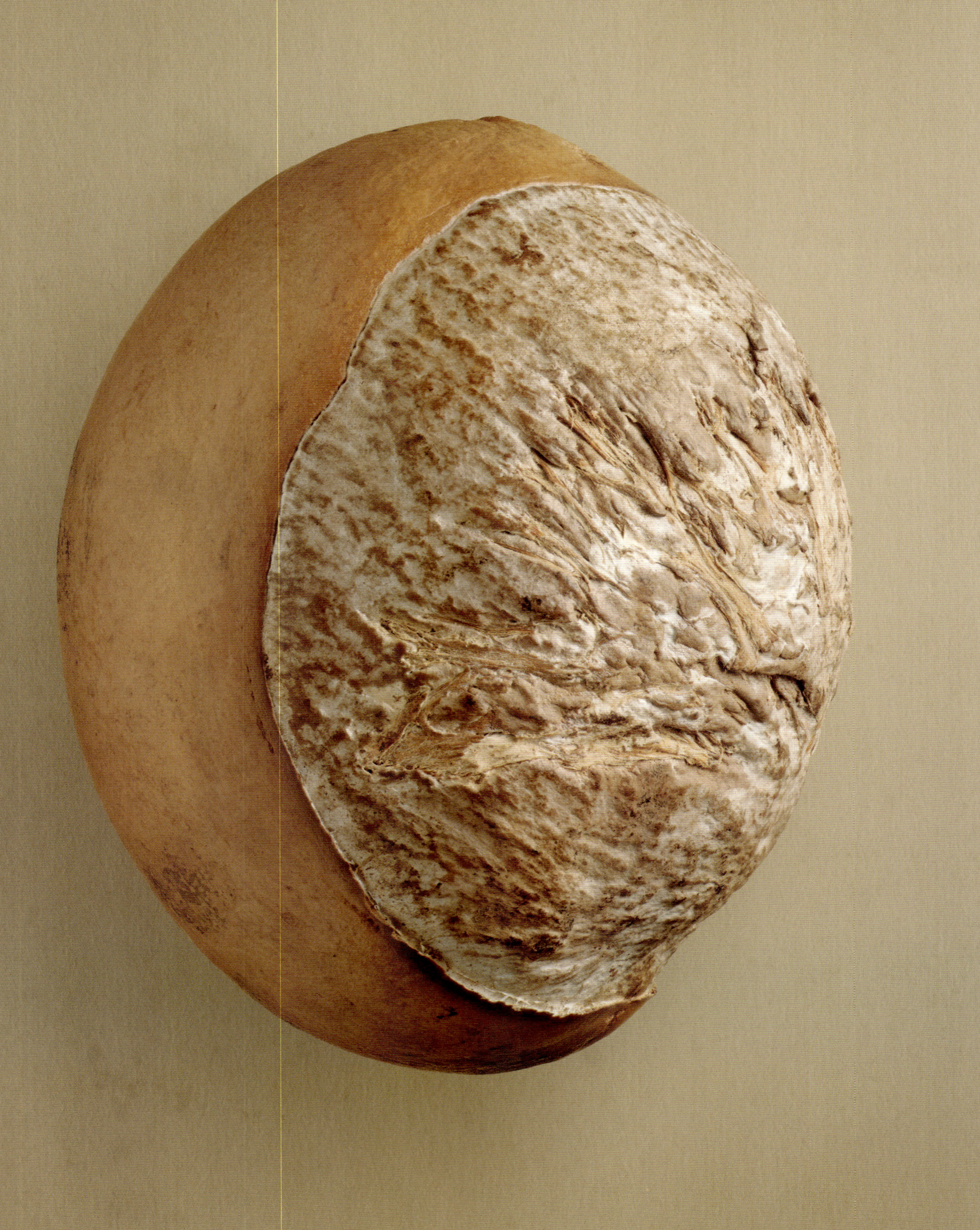

KAPISEN

Northia seychellana (Sapotaceae)

OPPOSITE: The genus is named after Victorian botanist and artist Marianne North. She spent her life traveling the world, producing vivid paintings of exotic plants in their natural habitats. Her work is permanently displayed at a dedicated gallery at the Royal Botanic Gardens, Kew. *Northia* is an isolated monotypic genus: It contains this single species, which is endemic to the Seychelles. It is often the dominant tree on high mountain ridges and is distinguished by its upward-pointing leaves with golden-copper undersurfaces. Its common name, Creole for "Capuchin," derives from the resemblance of the testa (the seed coat) to the hood of a monk belonging to this order, with the hilum (the scar marking the point of attachment to the fruit) suggesting his enigmatic face.

SEYCHELLES

FIELD MANIOC

Zeyheria montana (Bignoniaceae)

OVERLEAF LEFT: This shrub is endemic to the Cerrado of Brazil, a fire-dominated grassland ecosystem that rivals the Amazon in terms of species richness. The Portuguese name for this species, *mandioquinha do campo*, translates as "field manioc." This is confusing because it is not the true manioc; that would be *Manihot esculenta*, from a different plant family. However, the name shows a recognition that *Zeyheria montana* is a wild plant that looks like its cultivated near-namesake. Another name for it is *bolsa de pastor*, inspired by the resemblance of the pod to a bag once used by shepherds. The pod splits in half longitudinally to release its many wind-dispersed seeds.

BRAZIL

THORN APPLE

Datura stramonium (Solanaceae)

OVERLEAF RIGHT: This species is native to North and Central America and the Caribbean. As a member of the nightshade family, it contains tropane alkaloids, which are highly toxic and can induce hallucinations. Historically, small doses of this shrub were used by indigenous peoples of the Americas for medicinal and ceremonial purposes. It is also known as "jimson weed" (a corruption of "Jamestown-weed"). This name derives from Jamestown, Virginia, the first permanent English settlement in North America and site of a mass poisoning in 1676, when soldiers ate the leaves. It has spread worldwide as a common weed of cultivated fields and disturbed ground. Livestock are at risk of poisoning if the leaves or seeds are allowed to contaminate their feed. The large, trumpet-shaped flowers range from white through to purple, and the spiny seed pods split into four on ripening.

USA

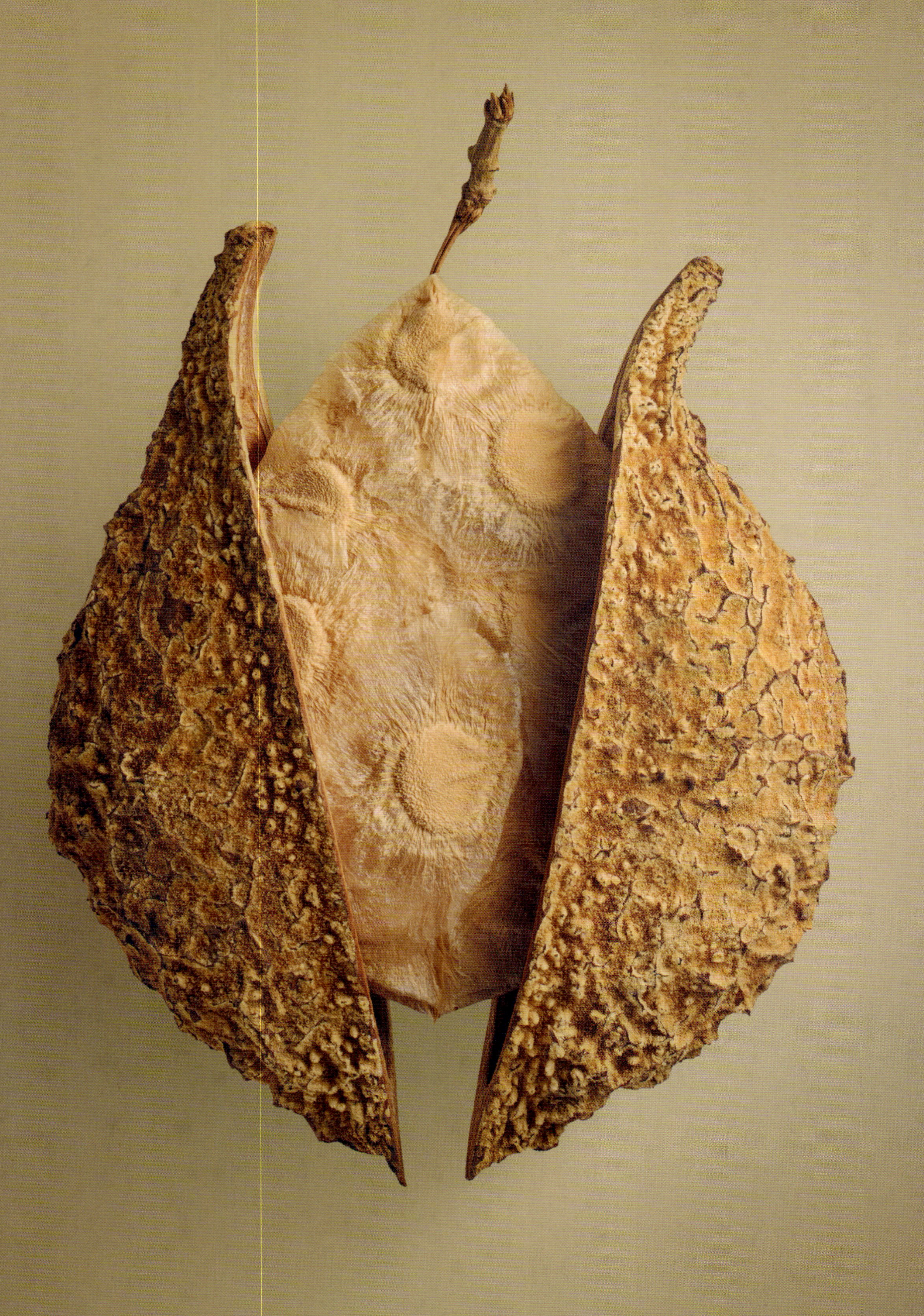

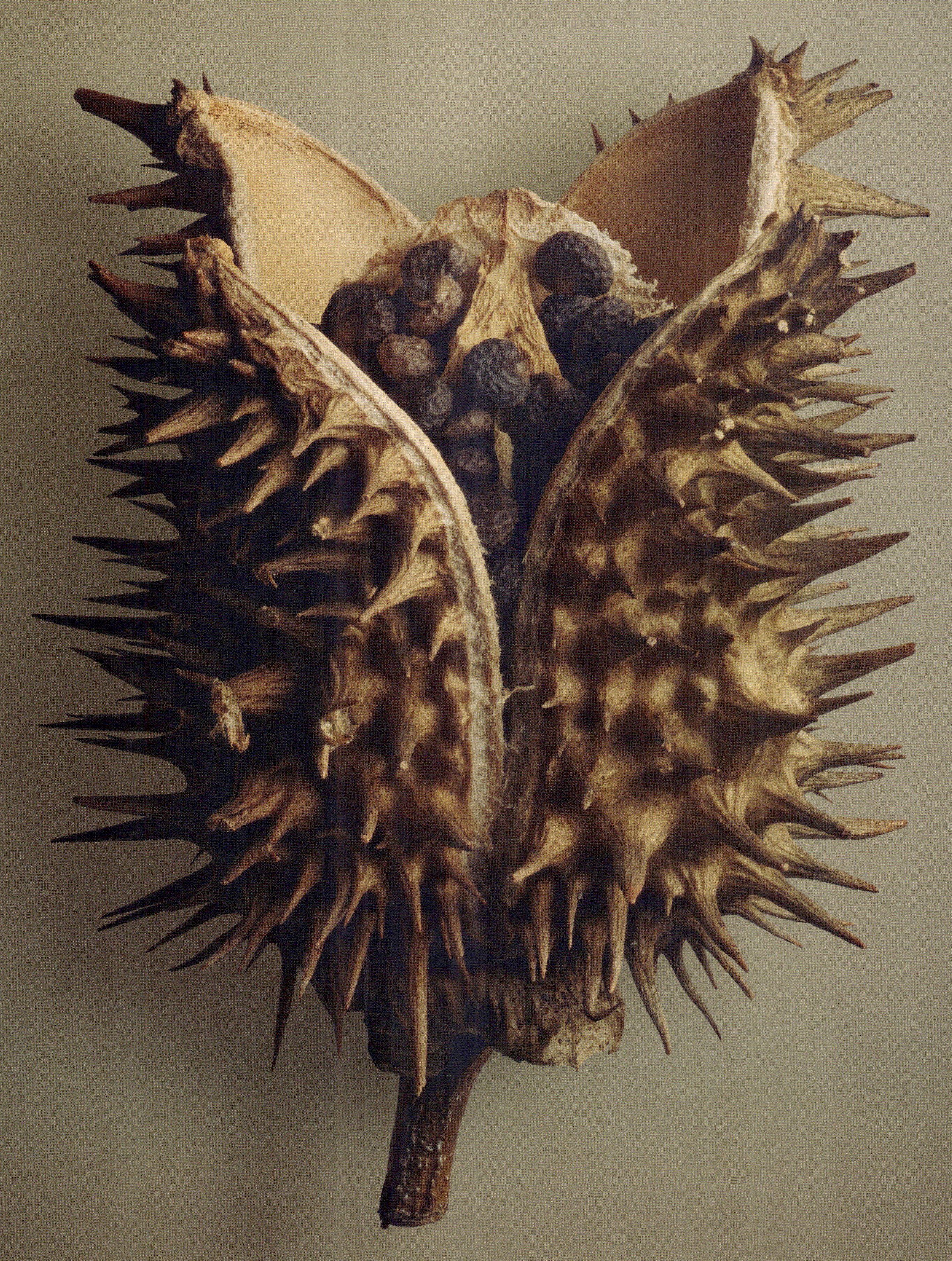

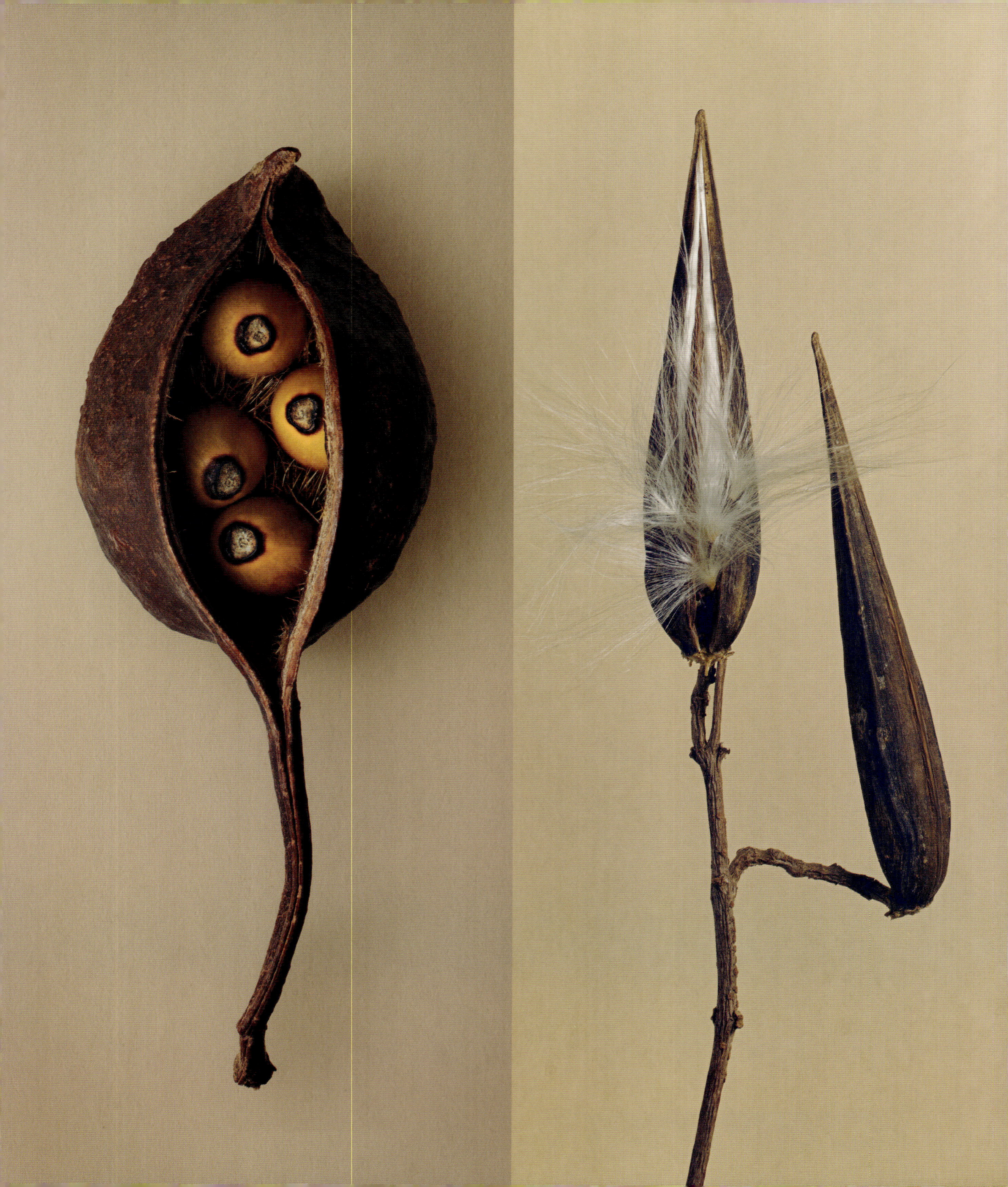

BOTTLE TREE

Brachychiton sp. (Malvaceae)

OPPOSITE LEFT: The genus *Brachychiton* comprises about thirty species of Australian trees and large shrubs. They typically have a trunk of seemingly excessive width relative to height, resulting in a flask-like shape. By storing water in the swollen trunk, the plants are able to tolerate drought. They provide welcome shade and ornament in gardens and parks. The genus name derives from the Greek words *brachys* ("short") and *chiton* (a kind of tunic worn in ancient Greece) and refers to the appearance of the seed coats. The seeds, roots, and shoots of some species were cooked and eaten by Australian Aboriginal peoples of Queensland.

AUSTRALIA

WAX-LEAVED CLIMBER

Cryptolepis buchananii (Apocynaceae)

OPPOSITE RIGHT: This species is also known by the names *krishna sariva* (Sanskrit) and *karanta* (Hindi). It is a leathery-leaved woody climber growing on trees and shrubs, using them both for support and for getting its seeds high up to maximize seed dispersal. It is found throughout the Himalayas, India, Southern China, and Southeast Asia. The fruits consist of two parts, which open longitudinally as they dry to release their plumed seeds. These are then carried away on the wind, each aided in its flight by a silky white coma (tuft of hairs). When cut, the plant exudes white latex, which is traditionally used to treat ulcers and coughs and to "purify" the blood. RBGE is working closely with Nepali partner organizations to build in-country capacity for plant biodiversity research, including a fieldwork program to remote regions to collect and record plants.

NEPAL

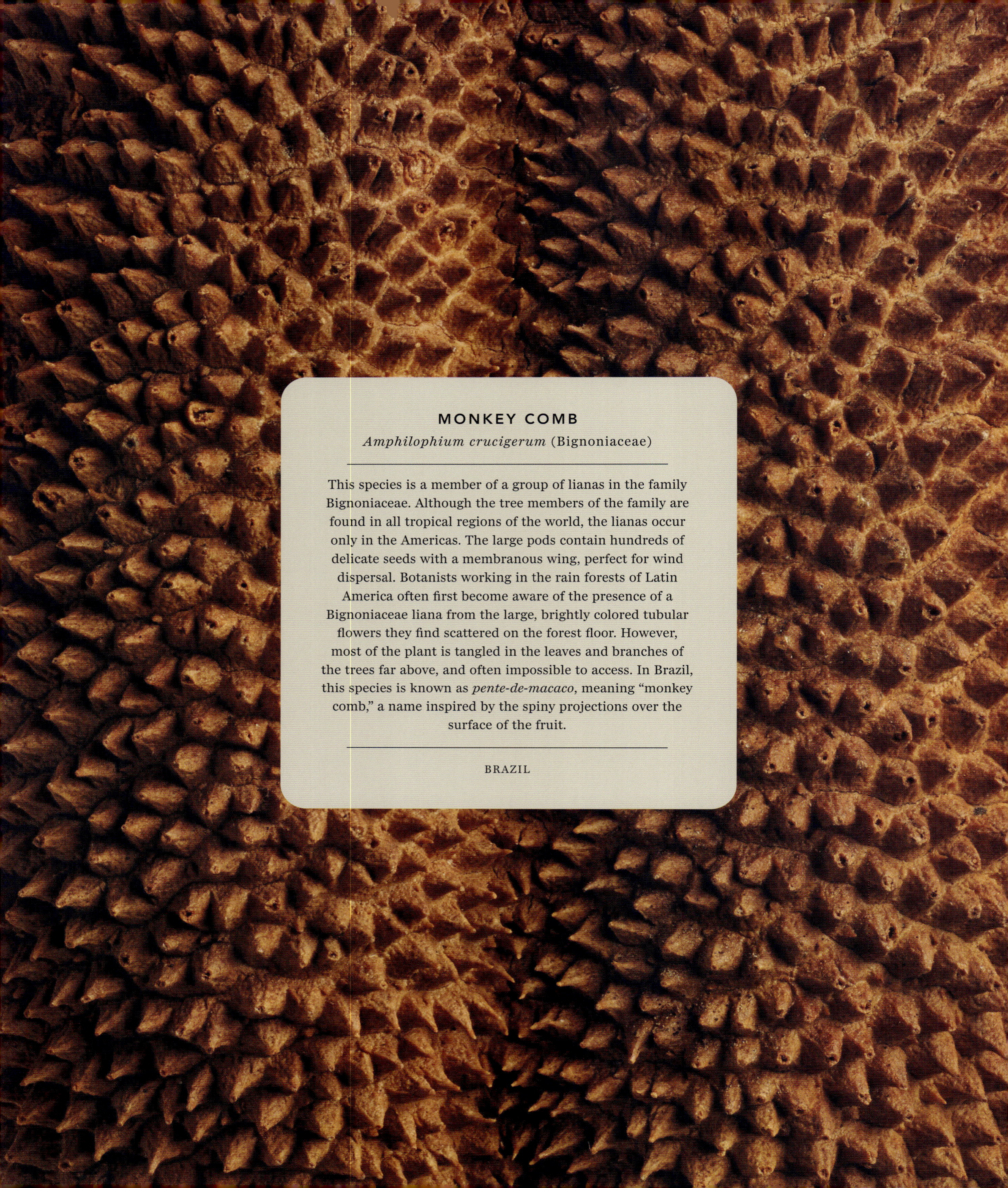

MONKEY COMB

Amphilophium crucigerum (Bignoniaceae)

This species is a member of a group of lianas in the family
Bignoniaceae. Although the tree members of the family are
found in all tropical regions of the world, the lianas occur
only in the Americas. The large pods contain hundreds of
delicate seeds with a membranous wing, perfect for wind
dispersal. Botanists working in the rain forests of Latin
America often first become aware of the presence of a
Bignoniaceae liana from the large, brightly colored tubular
flowers they find scattered on the forest floor. However,
most of the plant is tangled in the leaves and branches of
the trees far above, and often impossible to access. In Brazil,
this species is known as *pente-de-macaco*, meaning "monkey
comb," a name inspired by the spiny projections over the
surface of the fruit.

BRAZIL

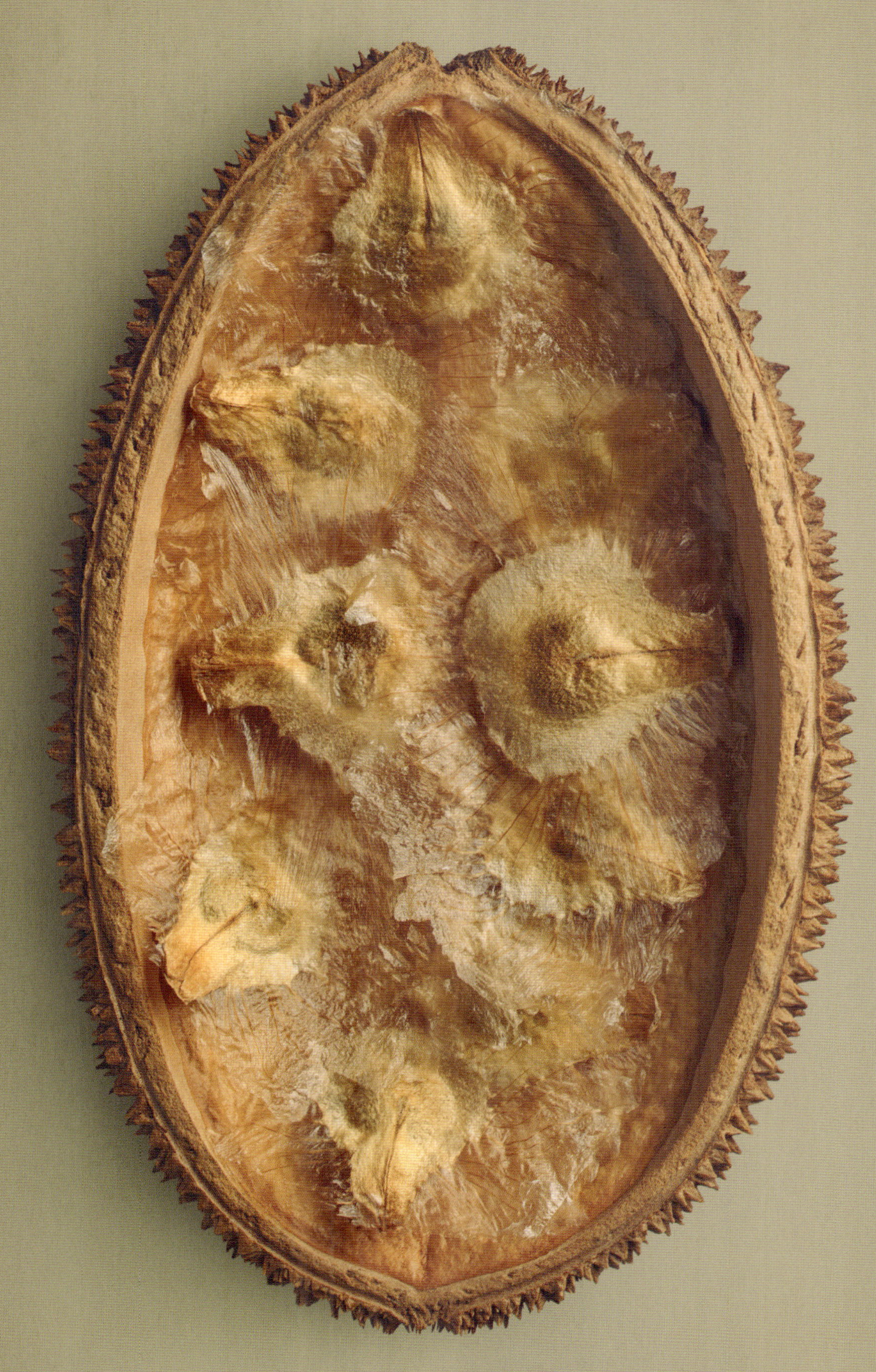

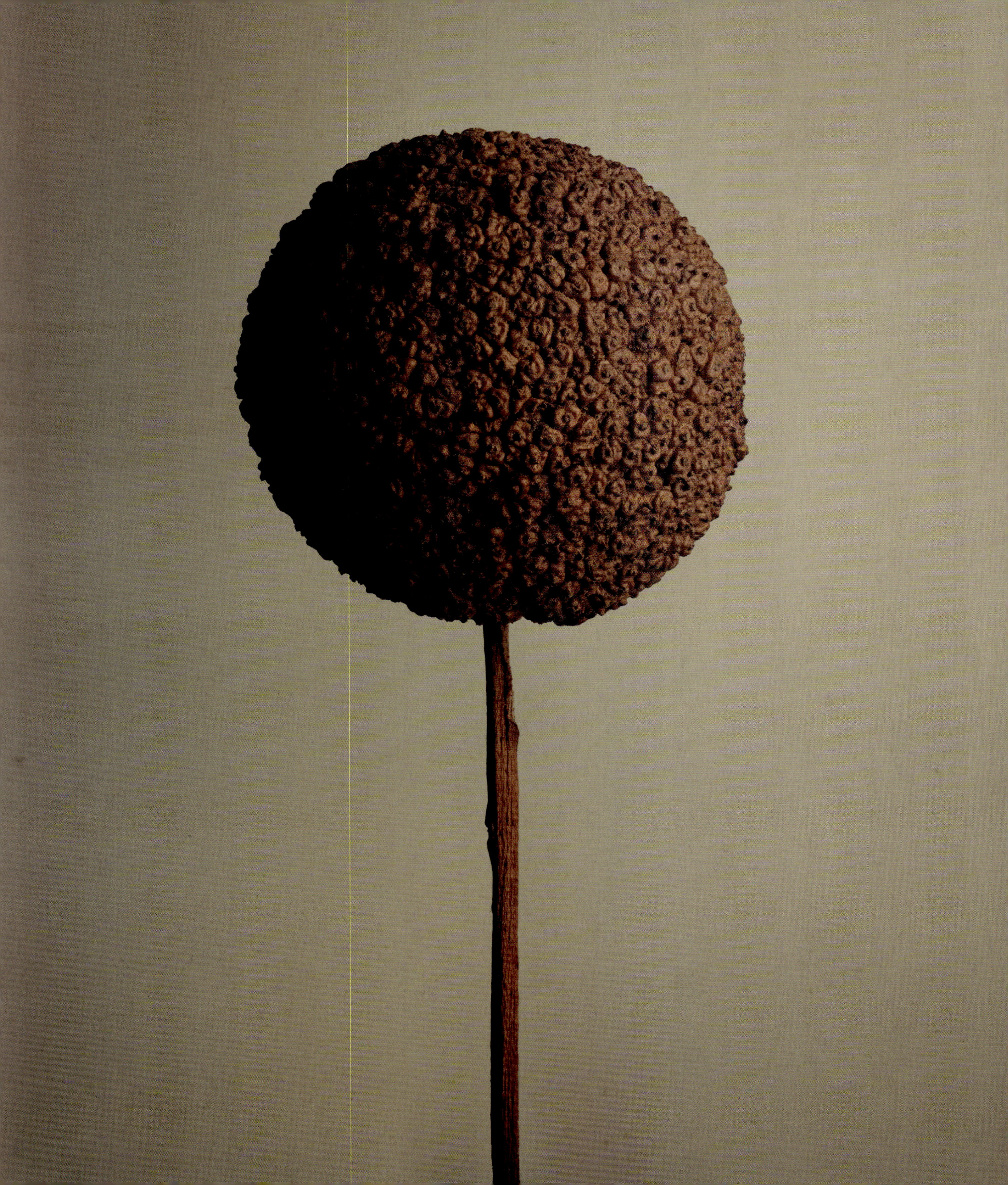

AMERICAN SYCAMORE

Platanus occidentalis (Platanaceae)

OPPOSITE: One of the largest trees in the deciduous forests of the eastern United States, the American sycamore is a commercially important timber resource. It is also increasingly being grown as a biomass crop because it has rapid early growth and coppices extremely well. The tiny fruits are tightly packed in spheres that hang down from the branches. The seeds within these fruits ripen in autumn and often overwinter on the tree before breaking free in spring. Each single-seeded fruit (achene) bears fine hairs at its base that catch the wind, thus ensuring a successful flight far from the shade of the parent tree. This species is completely unrelated to the European sycamore (*Acer pseudoplatanus*).

USA

CRUEL PLANT

Araujia sericifera (Apocynaceae)

OVERLEAF LEFT: This evergreen climber is native to Brazil and Argentina. It produces white or pale pink bell-shaped flowers, which are pollinated by moths, bees, and butterflies. The insects often die after becoming trapped in the flowers, hence one of the common names, "cruel plant." The fruit contains a multitude of black seeds, each of which has silky hairs to aid its dispersal by the wind. *Araujia sericifera* was introduced to cultivation in the nineteenth century and is a popular ornamental throughout the world. However, it can escape from gardens to become an invasive plant with damaging effects on natural habitats. In some countries, such as New Zealand, efforts are being made to remove it. Those doing this work are required to wear special clothing to protect their skin from the milky sap, which is an irritant.

RBGE CULTIVATED

CROWN FLOWER

Calotropis gigantea (Apocynaceae)

OVERLEAF RIGHT: This large shrub has beautiful purple flowers. Like most members of the family Apocynaceae, its fruit is composed of a pair of pod-like follicles, one of which can be seen here. The species is widespread in India and Southeast Asia; this specimen comes from Mumbai in western India. The field label charmingly describes the seeds as having been "packed [in the follicle] like fish scales" when it was picked, green and unripe. Each seed bears a terminal tuft of silky hairs (termed a *coma*), which can be used like kapok fiber for stuffing pillows and cushions. A fiber can also be extracted from the bark of the stems.

INDIA

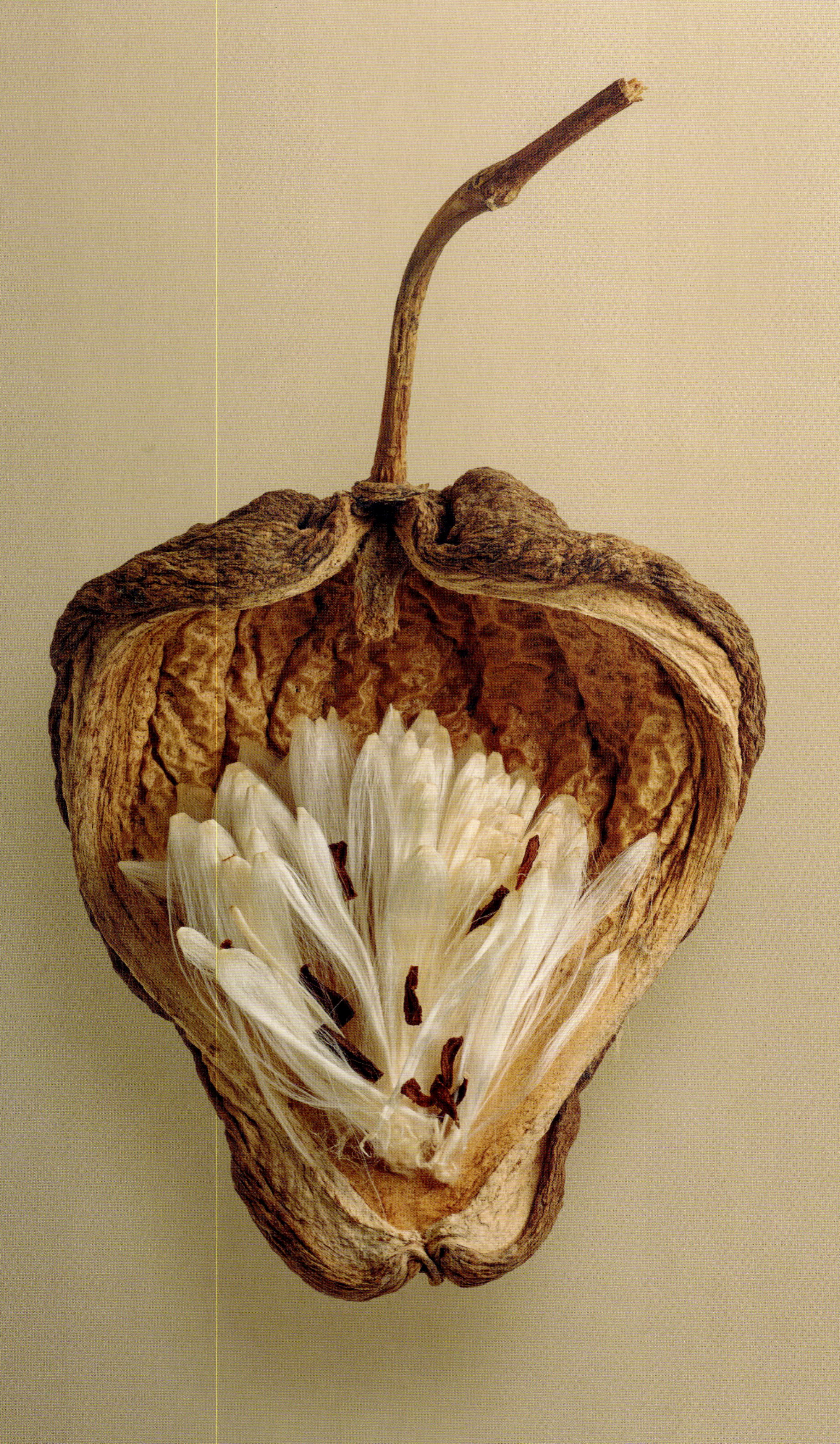

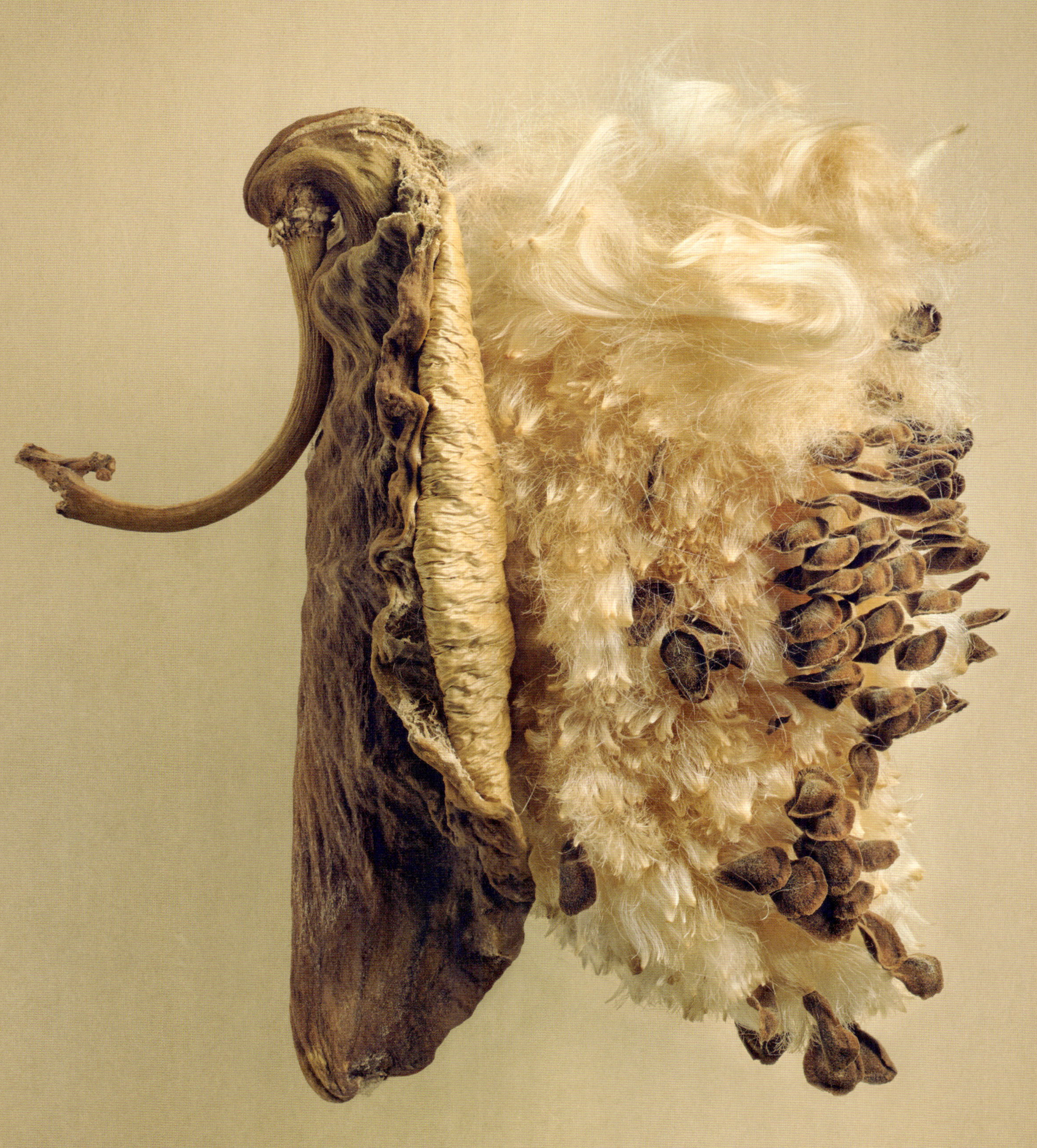

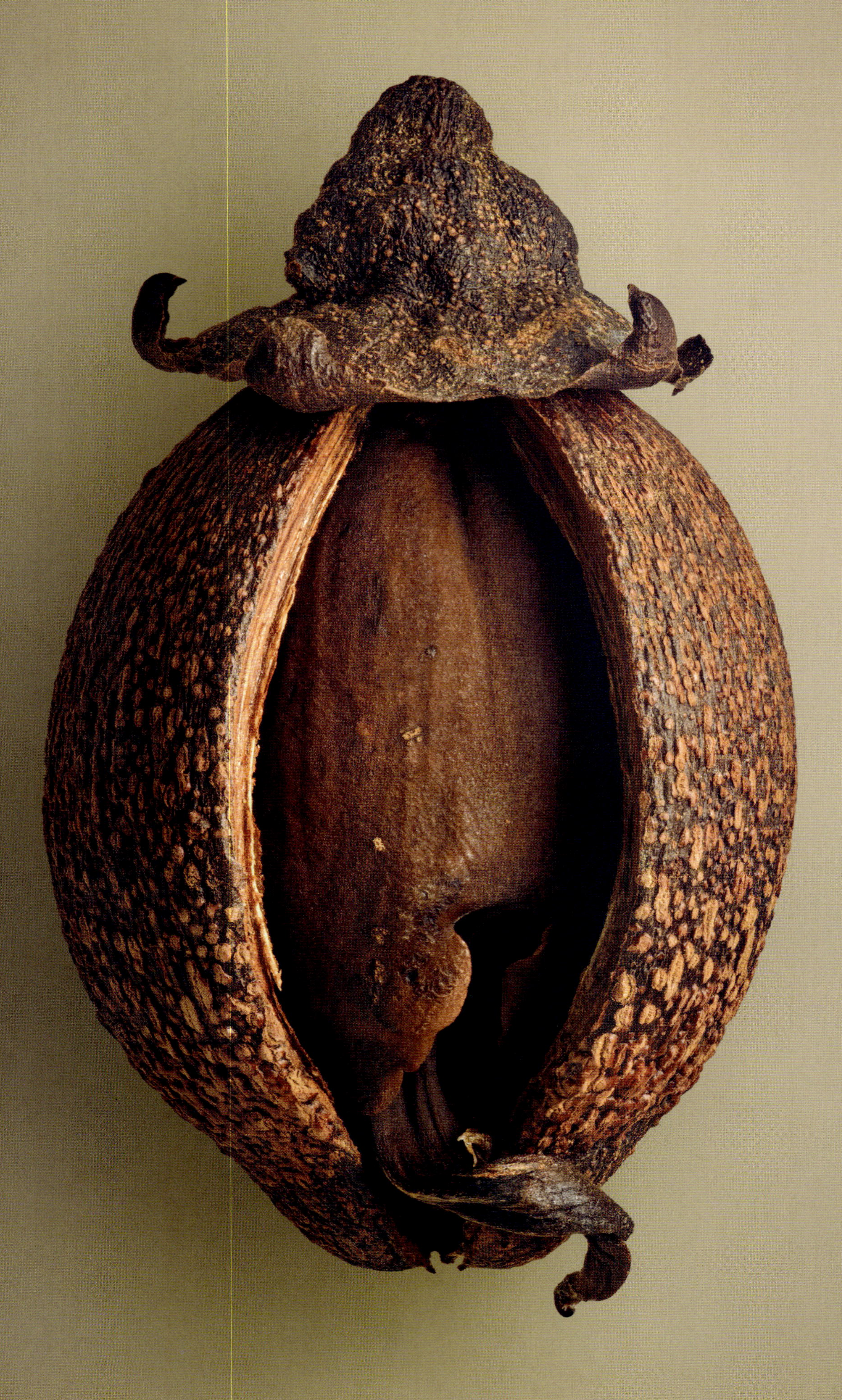

INDONESIAN KAPUR

Dryobalanops oblongifolia (Dipterocarpaceae)

OPPOSITE: This species belongs to Dipterocarpaceae, a family of hardwood tropical trees. It is extraordinarily diverse in Borneo: This island is home to well over three hundred dipterocarp species. Most form part of the forest canopy, whereas others emerge above it, growing to at least 164 feet (50 m) in height. They are under threat from commercial logging, being the source of the vast majority of timber felled in Indonesia and Malaysia. Forests that a century ago stretched from one side of the island to the other are now reduced to a few patches. *Dryobalanops oblongifolia* belongs to a genus of just seven species. Its timber is used in house construction to make window and door frames. The image shows a split in the fruit and a small tail emerging. This is the radicle, or first root of the seedling. One of the characteristics of this species is that the fruits germinate almost as soon as they hit the ground, quite a common characteristic of tropical rain forest trees.

INDONESIA

ELECTRIC SHOCK PLANT

Blumenbachia insignis (Loasaceae)

OVERLEAF LEFT: This white-flowered species, native to Brazil and Argentina, is one of a notorious group of plants found in the Americas: the rock nettles. Members of this family are typically covered with minute stinging hairs, each of which is heavily mineralized. If an animal tries to eat the plant, the tips break off, resulting in deposition of calcium phosphate and other noxious substances in and around its mouth. These substances elicit a sensation of being bitten—or receiving an electric shock. Thus, the hairs provide a defense against herbivores. The fruit is a five-chambered capsule. It is twisted in a counterclockwise direction, a character it shares with all other members of the genus.

RBGE CULTIVATED

COMMON PEONY

Paeonia officinalis (Paeoniaceae)

OVERLEAF RIGHT: This species is native to the low mountains and hills of southern Europe. Cultivated plants are abundant, especially the showier cultivars. However, wild populations have become threatened by habitat loss and the decline of traditional forest-clearing practices. Increasing forest cover has affected the ecology of open habitats, reducing the viability of populations of *Paeonia officinalis*; for this reason, the species has been listed for protection under French law. Fresh seeds germinate naturally in the autumn. In contrast, seeds that have been stored before sowing may take up to two years to germinate. This is because they must first undergo periods of heat alternating with cold and moisture to break down their hard seed coat.

RBGE CULTIVATED

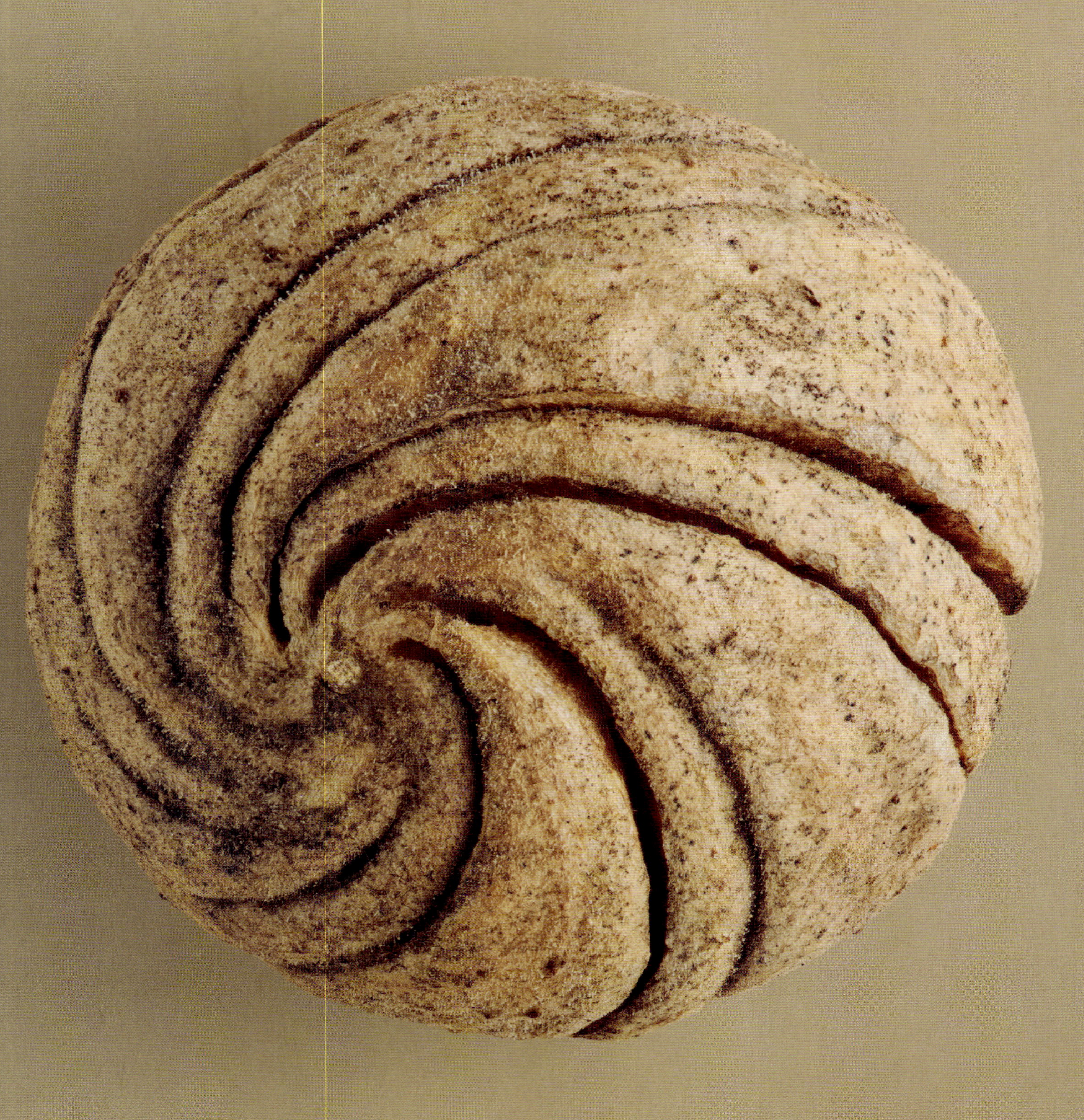

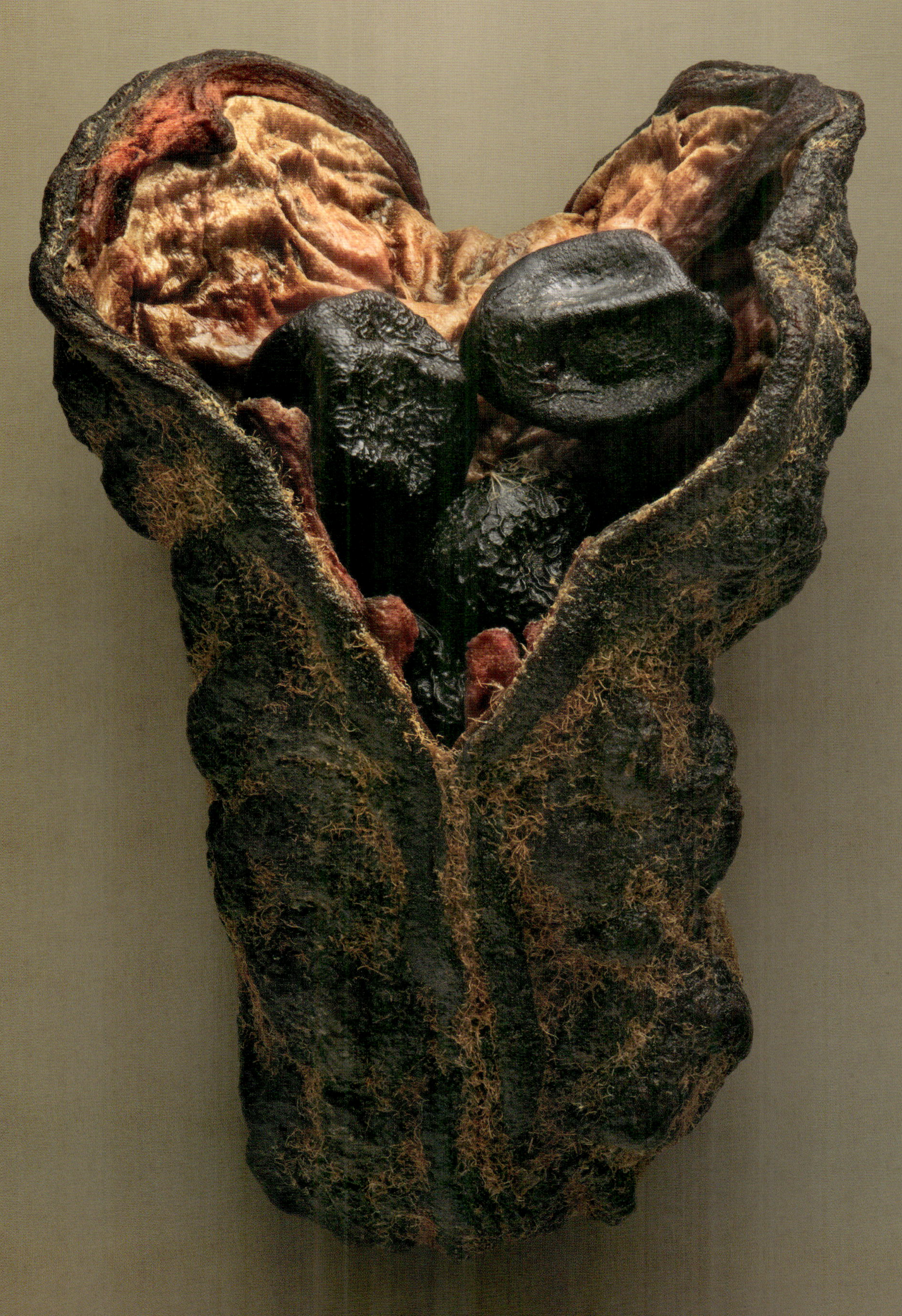

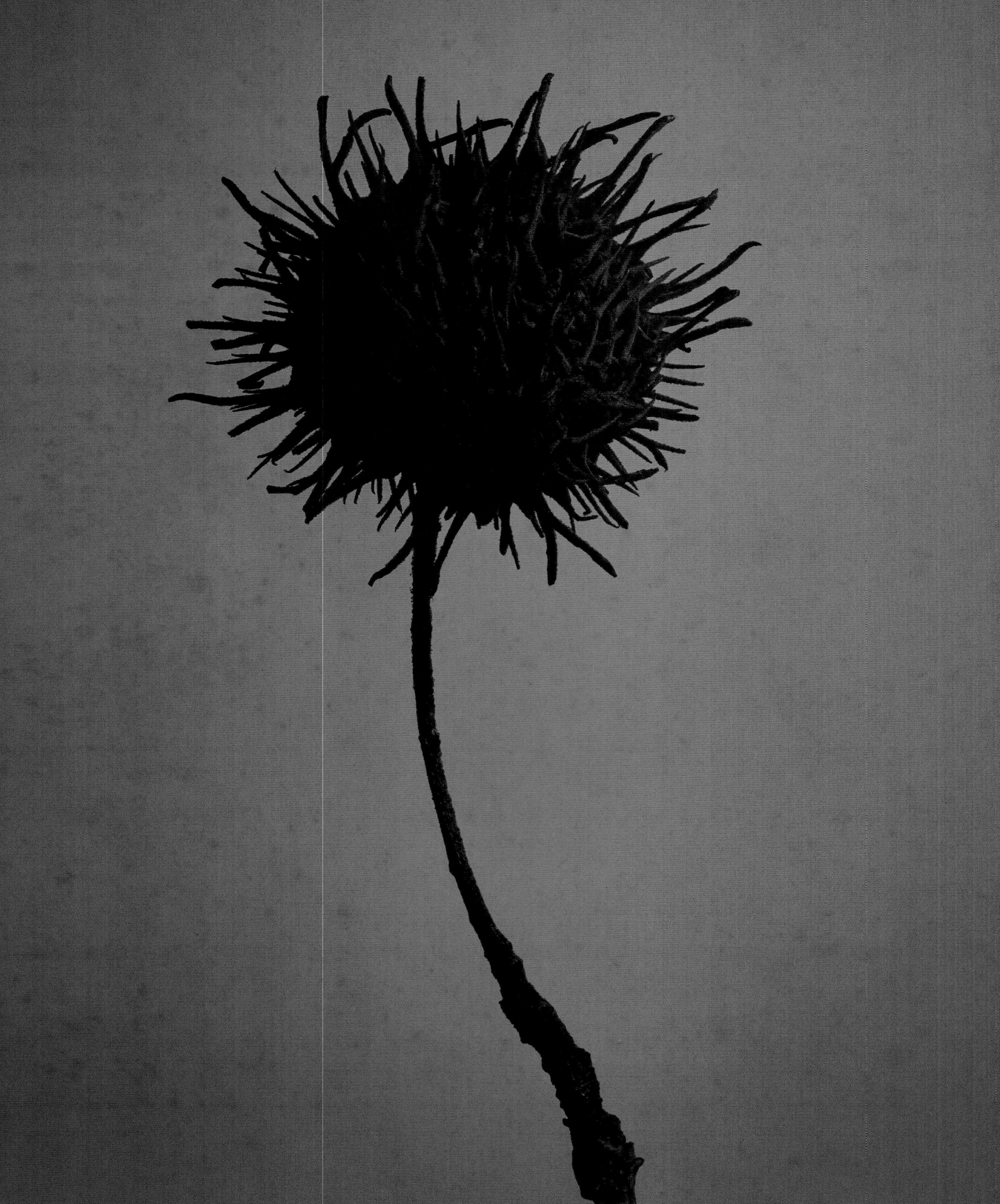

CHINESE SWEETGUM

Liquidambar formosana (Altingiaceae)

OPPOSITE: *Liquidambar* is the sole genus in the sweetgum family, Altingiaceae. Thirteen species are known today; more have been identified in the fossil record. This particular species is found in China, Laos, and Vietnam. These trees are often cultivated for their attractive lobed leaves, which turn a glorious red in autumn. The leaves are fed to silkworms to produce a particular kind of silk. Male and female flowers occur separately, but both on a single tree. The female flowers are arranged in groups to form ball-like inflorescences. These develop into fruit heads comprising many fruits fused to each other; they resemble prickly balls like the one in this image. Each individual fruit splits open when ripe to release the winged seeds.

LAOS

WEST AFRICAN WINE PALM

Raphia hookeri (Arecaceae)

OVERLEAF LEFT: These palms grow to a height of about 33 feet (10 m). They are cultivated in villages across West and Central Africa and also occur in vast stands in swamps. When an individual tree has reached the right stage of development, men climb to the top of the trunk and cut away at its tip. They then use a calabash or plastic container to collect the sap, which is left to ferment at the top of the tree. After the first day, the resulting wine tastes sweet and has a low alcohol content. Further fermentation time allows the naturally occurring yeasts to convert the sugars to alcohol, thus producing a much stronger beverage. The wine has great cultural significance.

REPUBLIC OF THE CONGO

SERAYA DUAN KASAR

Shorea fallax (Dipterocarpaceae)

OVERLEAF RIGHT: This is an emergent tree: growing up to 197 feet (60 m) in height, it is able to rise above the rain-forest canopy. The species is endemic to the island of Borneo. The name of the family to which it belongs, Dipterocarpaceae, derives from the Greek words *di* ("two"), *pteron* ("wing"), and *karpos* ("fruit"), although many species have a different number of wings. The wings—relatively small in *Shorea fallax*—facilitate wind dispersal of the seeds, enabling them to fall in a helicopter motion away from the parent tree. The Malay name, *seraya duan kasar*, translates as "the leaves are coarse." The wood is traded as a commercial timber under the name *meranti*.

MALAYSIA

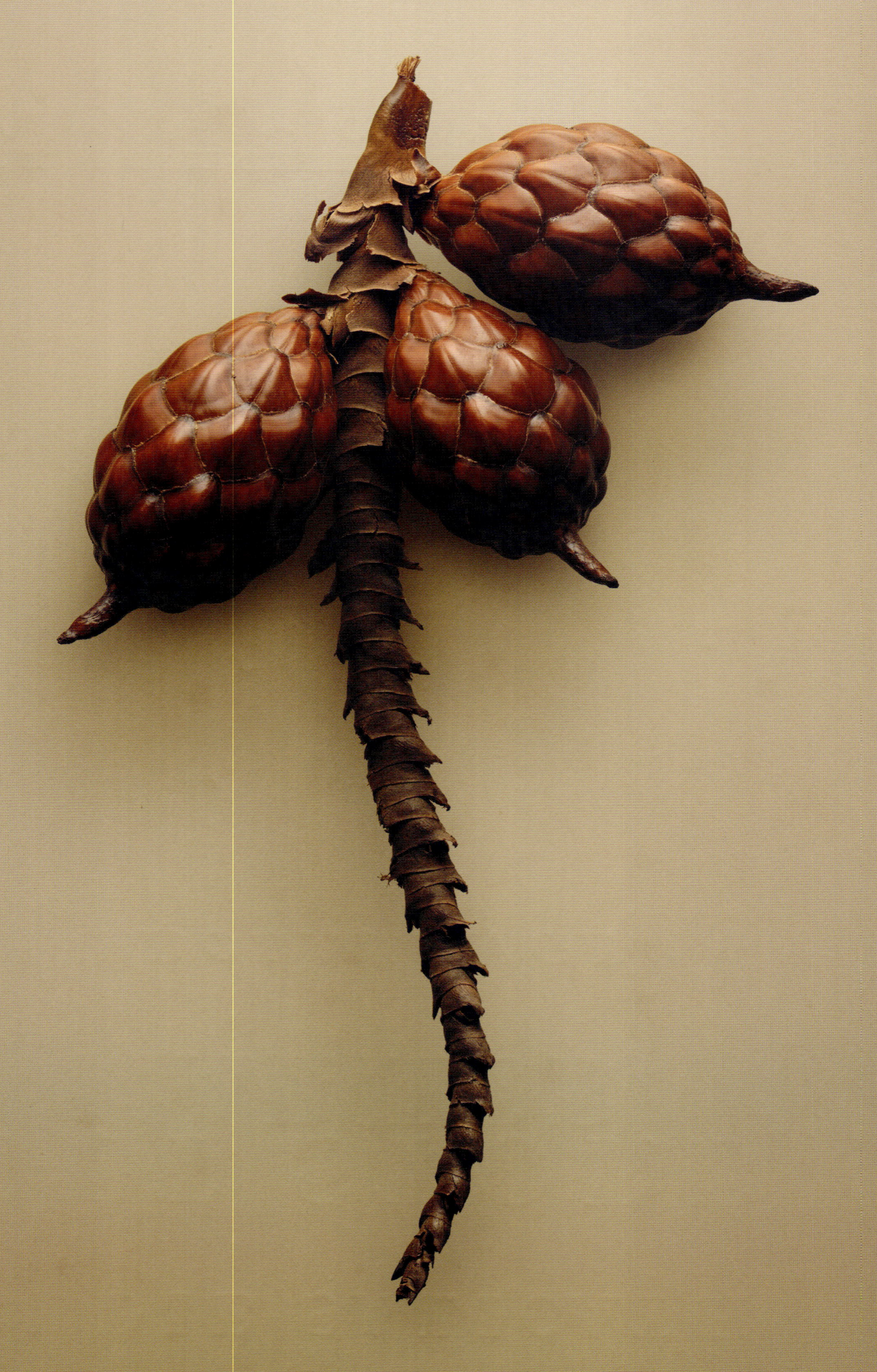

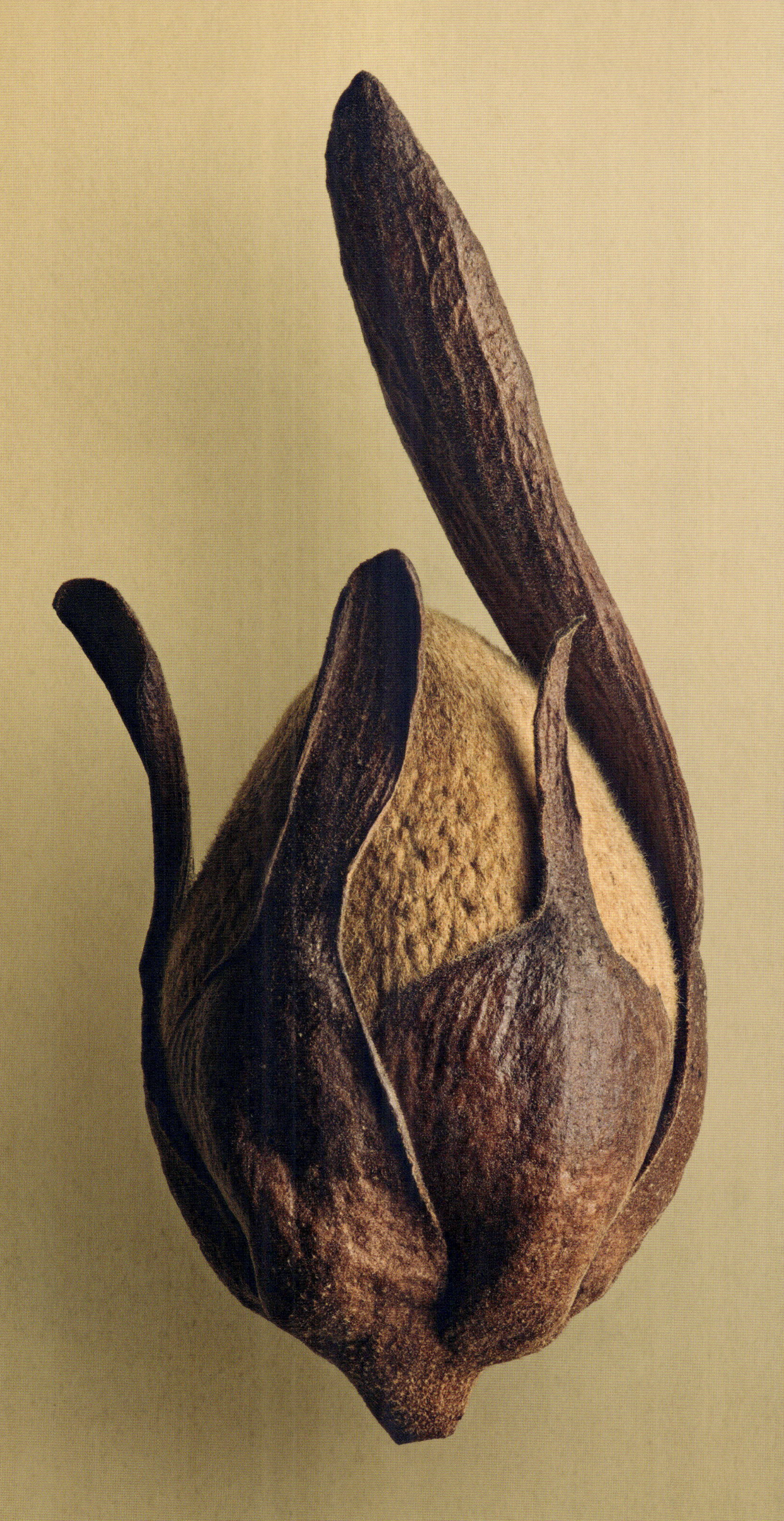

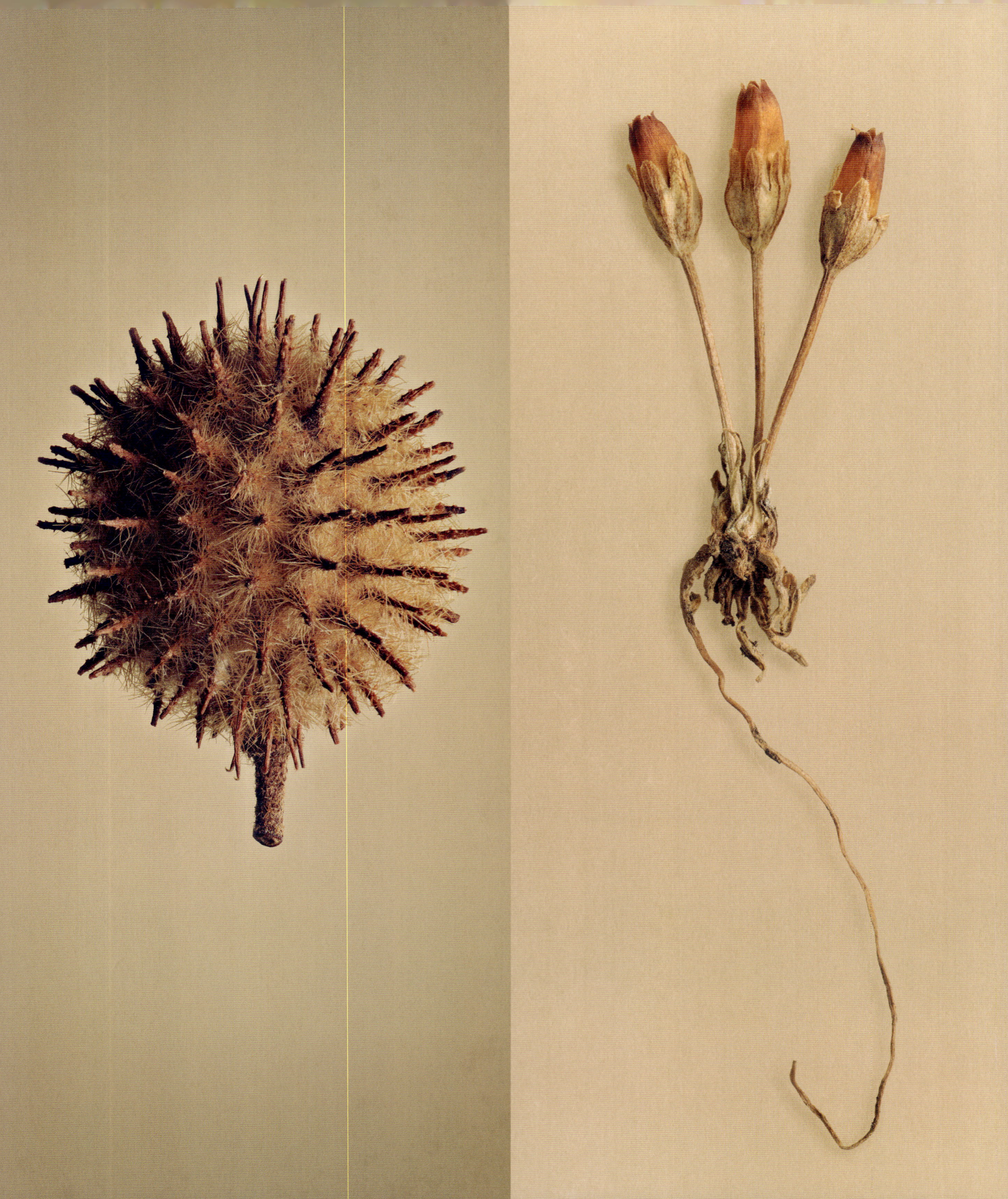

BURBARK

Triumfetta appendiculata (Malvaceae)

OPPOSITE LEFT: The first Australian collections of herbarium specimens of *Triumfetta* were made by Robert Brown, naturalist aboard the HMS *Investigator* on its 1801–1803 voyage. The ship's commander, Matthew Flinders, had been tasked with charting the parts of the coastline of Australia unknown to the British government in London. The voyage culminated in a circumnavigation of Australia. This species was described in 1862 by German-Australian botanist Ferdinand von Mueller, then director of the botanical gardens at Melbourne. The bristles that cover the surface of its mature fruit catch onto the fur or wool of passing animals, so that the seeds can be transported to germinate far away from the parent plant.

AUSTRALIA

SCOTTISH PRIMROSE

Primula scotica (Primulaceae)

OPPOSITE RIGHT: This tiny specimen was collected on the island of Orkney by Orcadian botanist Henry Halcro Johnston in 1919. The average height of the species is only 1.5 inches (4 cm), and this specimen is even smaller, at just 1 inch (2.5 cm). The bright purple flowers are self-fertile and so do not require pollination to set viable seed. This species is unique to Scotland, growing only in the grasslands of the north coast and Orkney, where it is under threat from habitat loss and overgrazing. This is a target species in the first phase of the groundbreaking Darwin Tree of Life Project, a collaboration between scientists at RBGE and elsewhere with the aim of sequencing the genome of two thousand species from the British Isles; it will provide invaluable insights into their biology, ecology, conservation, and potential uses.

SCOTLAND

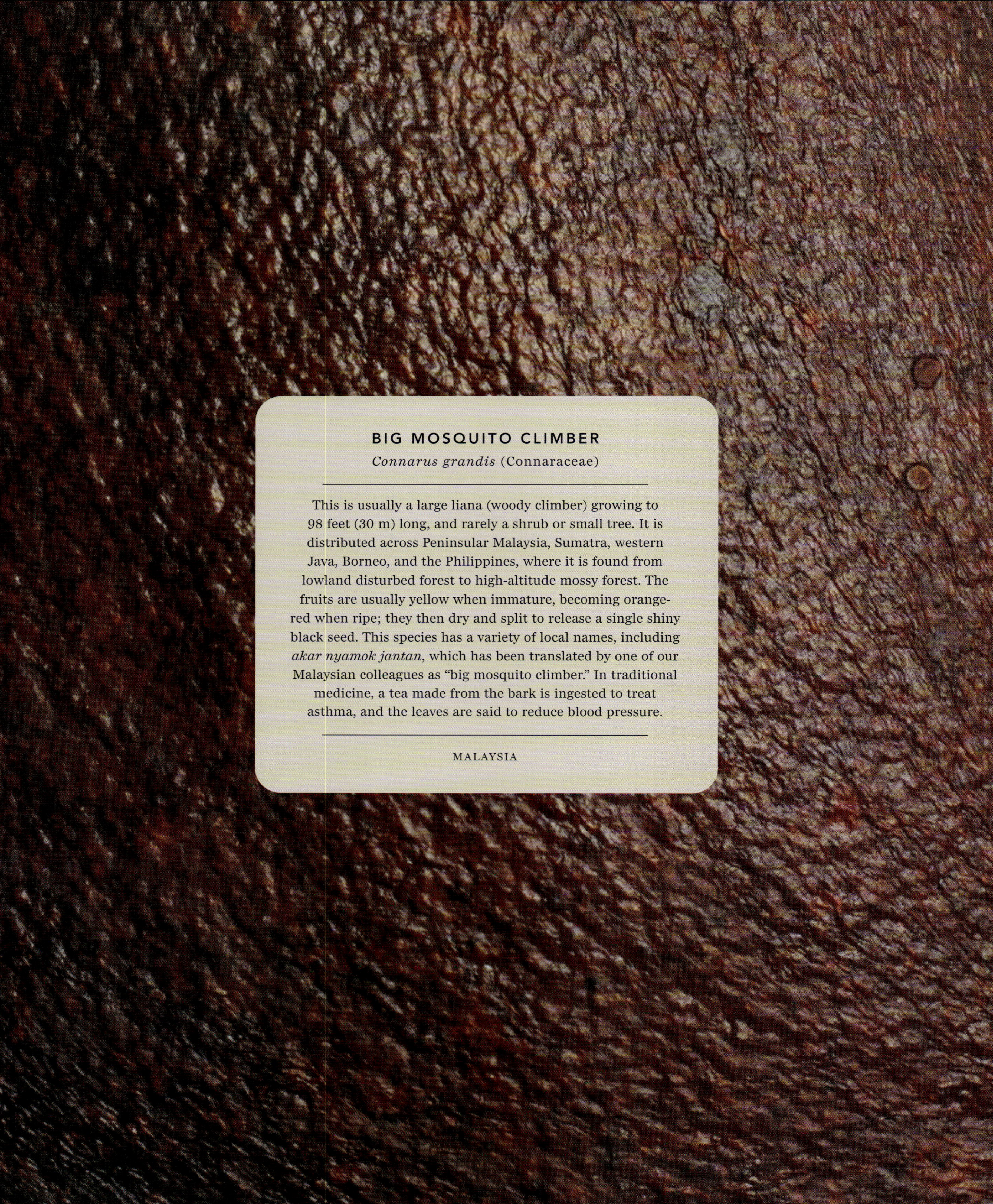

BIG MOSQUITO CLIMBER

Connarus grandis (Connaraceae)

This is usually a large liana (woody climber) growing to 98 feet (30 m) long, and rarely a shrub or small tree. It is distributed across Peninsular Malaysia, Sumatra, western Java, Borneo, and the Philippines, where it is found from lowland disturbed forest to high-altitude mossy forest. The fruits are usually yellow when immature, becoming orange-red when ripe; they then dry and split to release a single shiny black seed. This species has a variety of local names, including *akar nyamok jantan*, which has been translated by one of our Malaysian colleagues as "big mosquito climber." In traditional medicine, a tea made from the bark is ingested to treat asthma, and the leaves are said to reduce blood pressure.

MALAYSIA

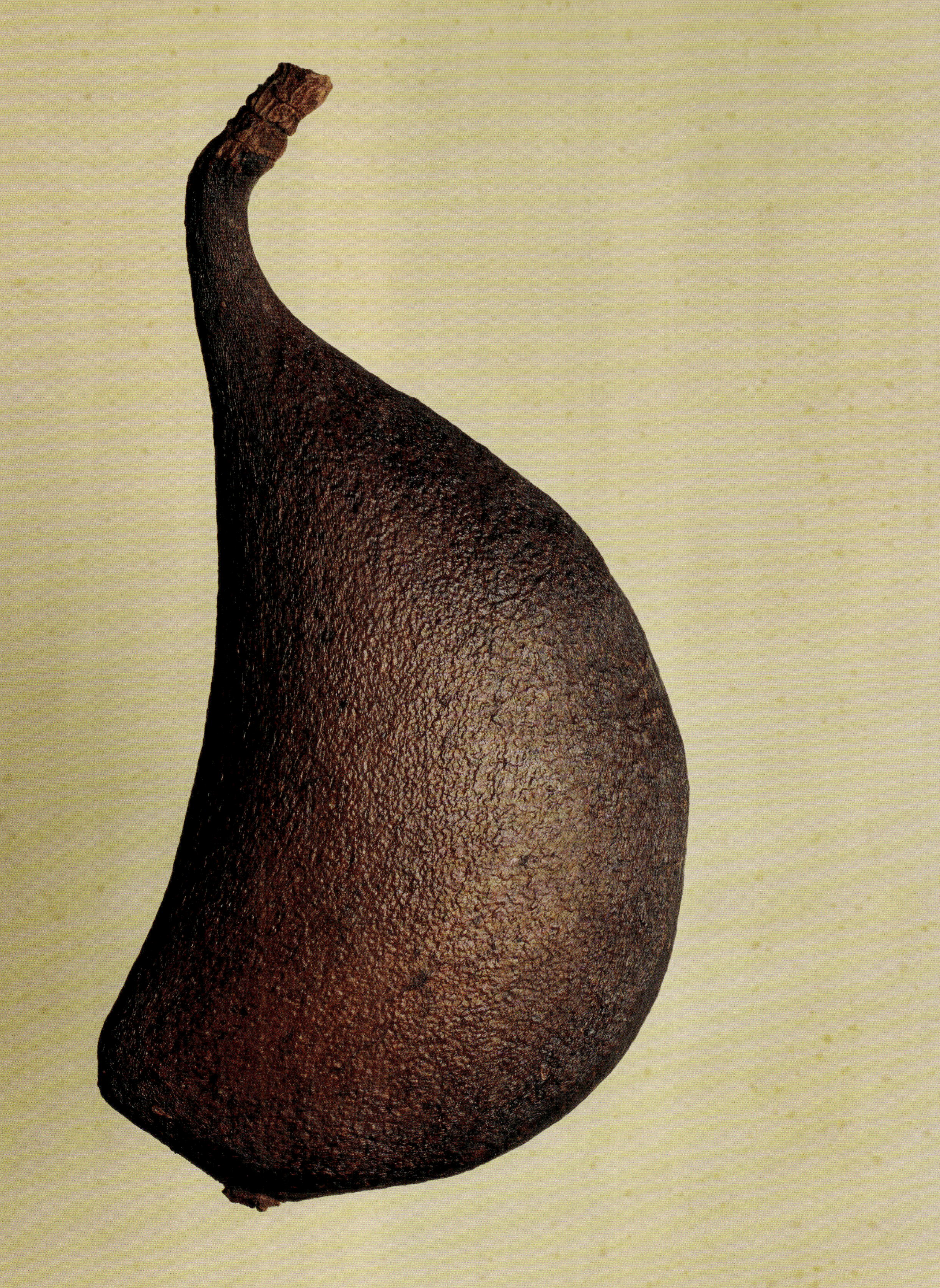

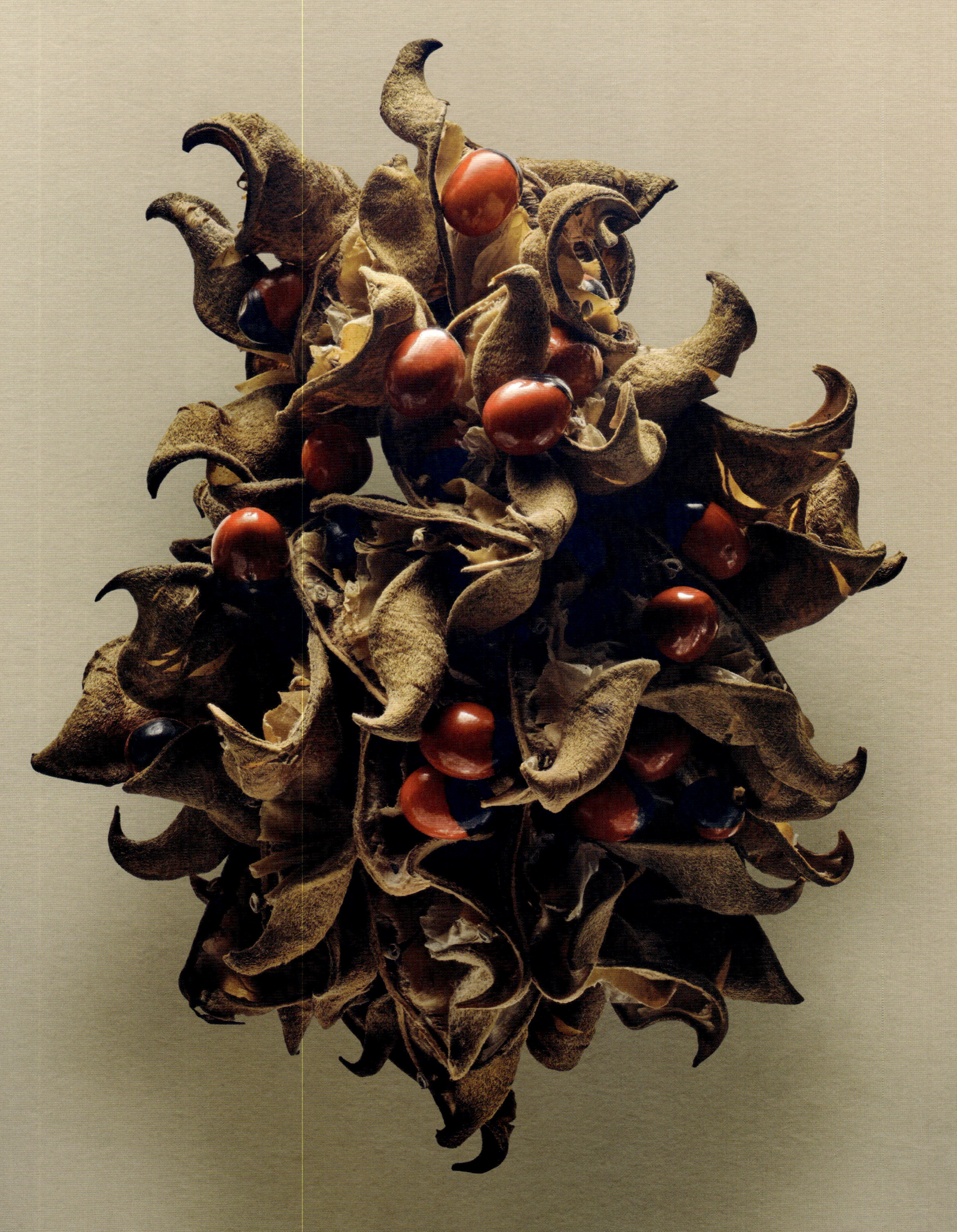

ROSARY PEA

Abrus precatorius (Fabaceae)

OPPOSITE: The eye-catching, primarily bright red seeds of this climber look very much like spotless ladybirds (known as ladybugs in North America). Their attractive appearance makes them widely valued as ornamental beads, and they are also used to decorate musical instruments. They are highly toxic and potentially fatal if chewed or eaten raw. However, in common with many other plants containing powerful phytochemicals, various health benefits have been ascribed to this species provided that the plant material is prepared correctly. In Ayurvedic medicine, the leaves, roots, and seeds—having first been crushed or boiled to reduce their toxicity—are used to treat a wide range of ailments from fevers to arthritis, and also as an aphrodisiac. A native of India south to Malaysia and parts of Australia, it is now found across the tropics and subtropics.

RBGE CULTIVATED

EBONY

Diospyros sp. (Ebenaceae)

OVERLEAF LEFT: *Diospyros* is a genus of more than seven hundred species of tree distributed from the tropics to warm temperate zones of the world. They produce a number of delicious fruits, chiefly persimmons and date plums. The wood of some species, much admired for its dark color and durability, is used in musical instruments. Trade in ebony is restricted, because the species that produce it are all under threat, not only due to felling of forests generally but also because the trees are actively sought out. Unusually for plants, the sexes are often separate, so male and female trees must grow together for pollination to occur. The species from which this specimen was collected has yet to be identified and may even be new to science.

LAOS

KURRAJONG

Brachychiton populneus (Malvaceae)

OVERLEAF RIGHT: This drought-tolerant tree is native to Eastern Australia. Its fruits take the form of canoe-shaped pods hanging in clusters of three to five. They are particularly attractive when they split open at maturity to reveal the yellow seeds within. These are coated with hairs that can irritate the skin and eyes. The species owes its common name to Dharuk, a language once widely spoken by Australian Aborginal peoples who lived in the area around Sydney. *Kurrajong* derives from the Dharuk word for "fishing line," reflecting one of their uses for the bark.

AUSTRALIA

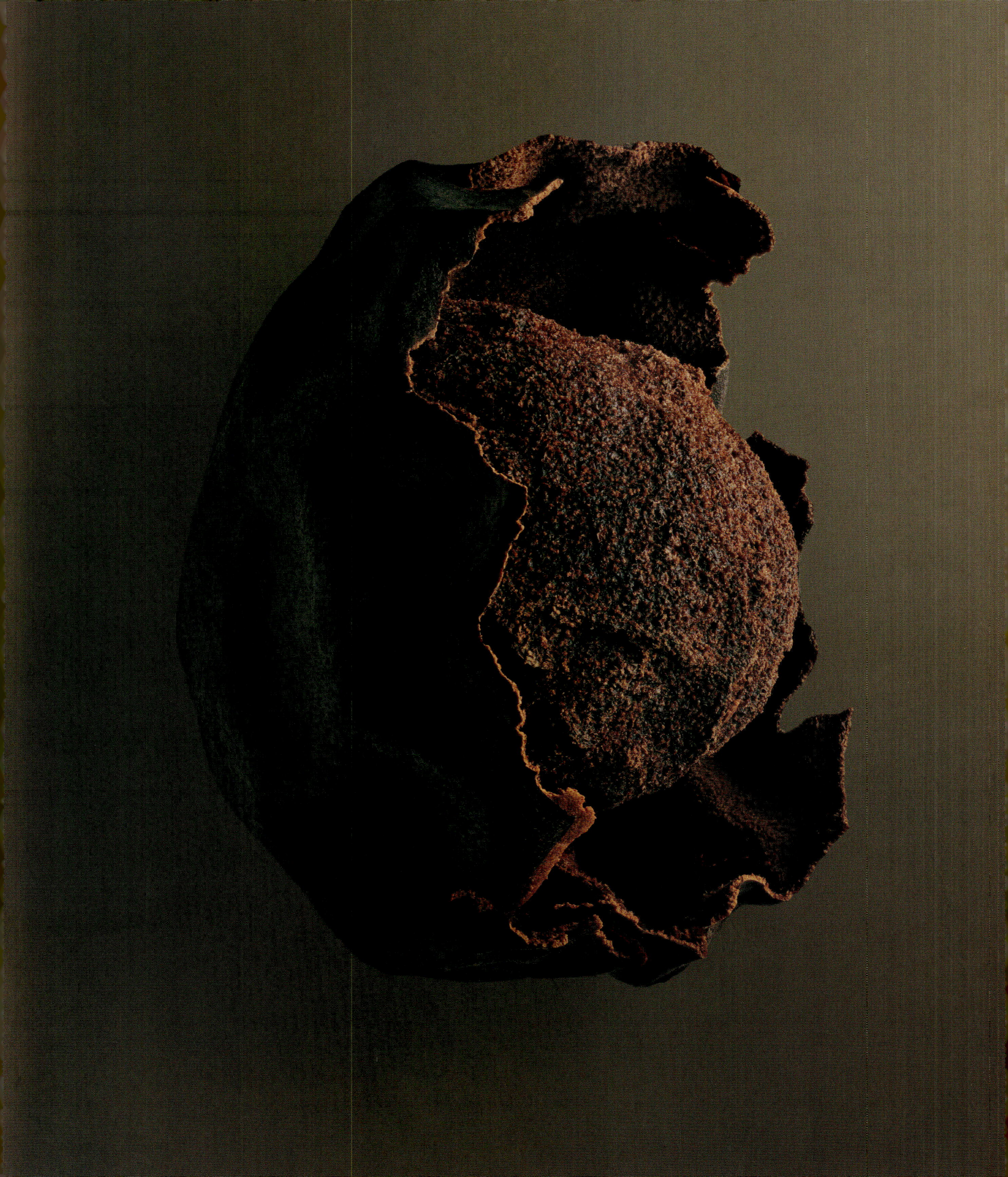

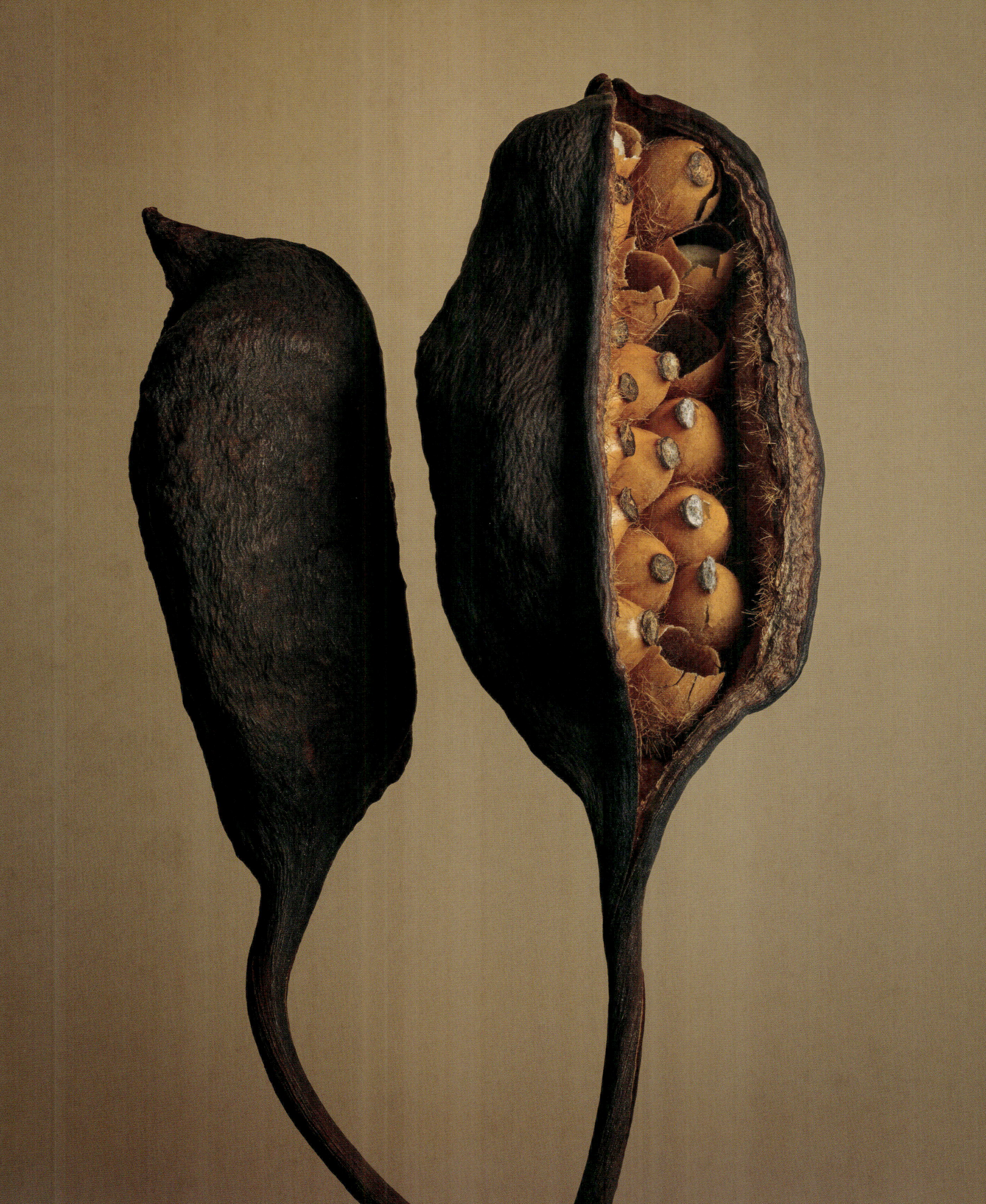

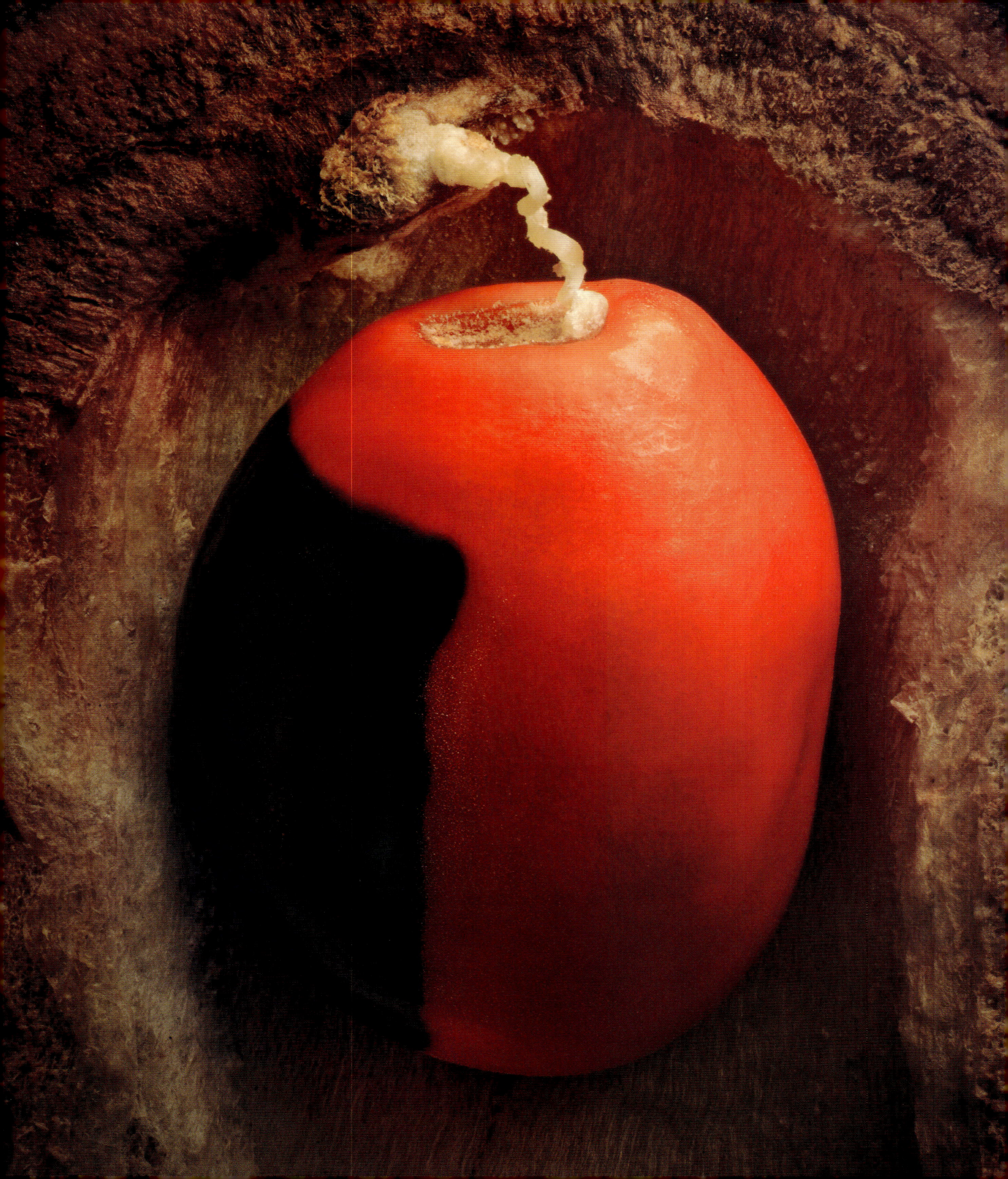

LUCKY SEEDS

Ormosia coccinea (Fabaceae)

OPPOSITE: This Latin American legume is an evergreen rain-forest tree that can attain a height of 115 feet (35 m). Its timber, like that of many other tropical forest trees, is highly prized. The wood is described as beautifully figured, meaning that it has unusual and interesting markings on its side-grain surfaces. It is also resistant to fungal infection and termites. The pretty red-and-black seeds are used to make necklaces and bracelets. These are a popular item for sale in local artisan markets but make unsuitable gifts because the seeds are poisonous. The common name refers to the supposed powers of the seeds to attract good fortune and ward off negative energy. Other names include "crab's eye" and "ladybug seeds."

PERU

PIQUIÁ

Caryocar villosum (Caryocaraceae)

OVERLEAF LEFT: A majestic tropical emergent tree of Amazonia that can reach the astonishing heights of 131–164 feet (40–50 m). Rich in carbohydrates and proteins, its large golden-yellow flowers are a prized food for forest animals. When the tree is in bloom, hunters take advantage of the game that are attracted to the thousands of flowers scattered on the ground. The fruits, which are the size of a grapefruit but more irregular in shape, contain a bright yellow pulp from which oil can be obtained. The oil is used in cooking and is especially good for frying fish. The wood is high quality, being compact, heavy, and slow to decompose; it is commonly used to build boats. This specimen is an old discarded fruit, probably collected from the forest floor, with the single seed exposed and with the remains of the outer pulp at the base in a decayed state due to desiccation.

BRAZIL

BLISTER POD

Sacoglottis amazonica (Humiriaceae)

OVERLEAF RIGHT: This tree is native throughout the north of South America, but as the species name suggests, occurs most commonly in the lower reaches of the Amazon River. It is one of the tiny number of plant species that produce drift fruit—fruit adapted for long-distance seed dispersal by salt water. Drift fruit can even cross the Atlantic on the Gulf Stream. The soft outer layer of each *Sacoglottis amazonica* fruit decomposes to leave a hard stone. The bumps all over the stone are the outer surfaces of the air-filled cavities ("blisters") that provide it with buoyancy. The interiors of these cavities become exposed as the pod is eroded by seawater over months, and sometimes years, of drifting.

BRAZIL

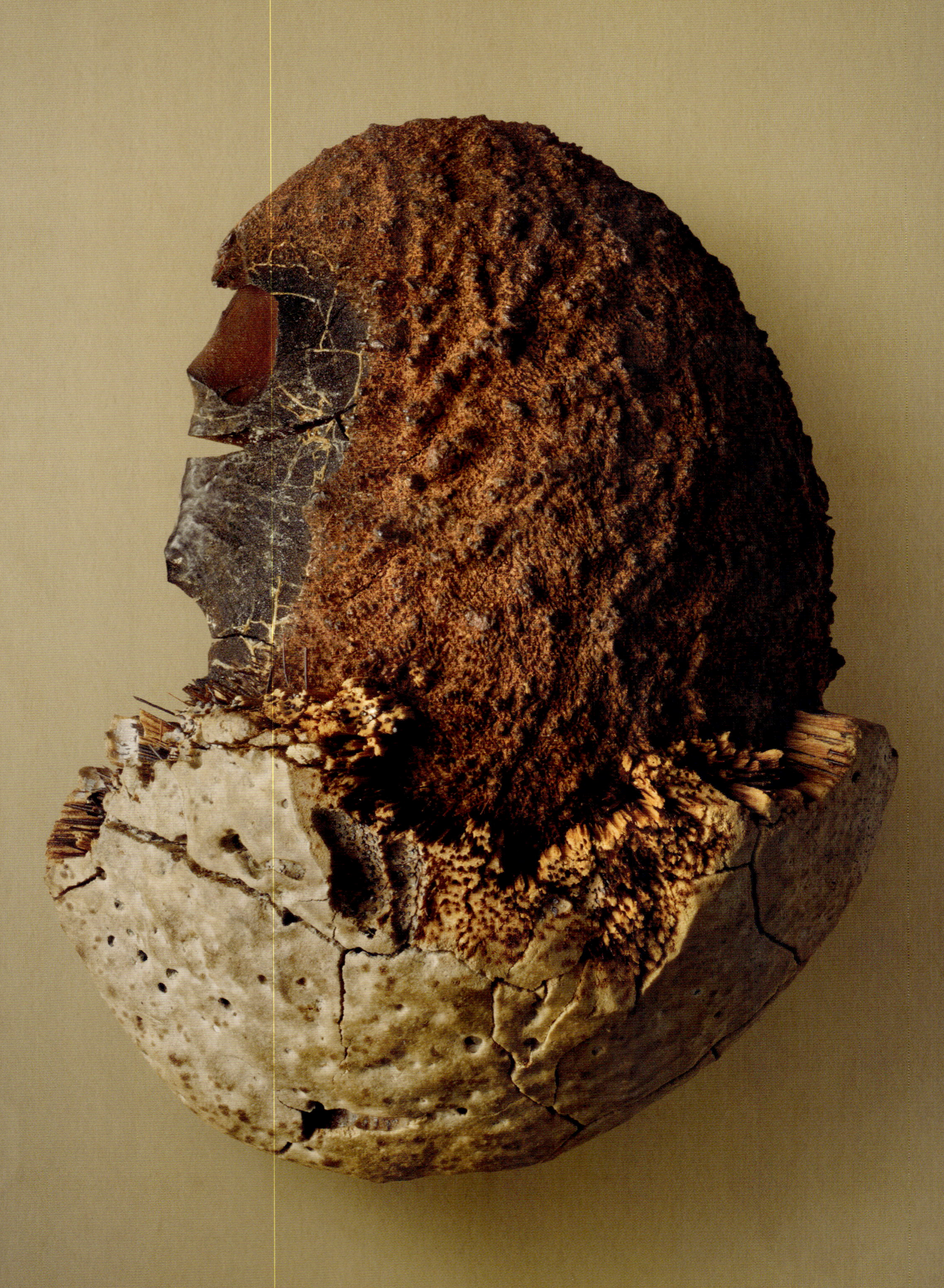

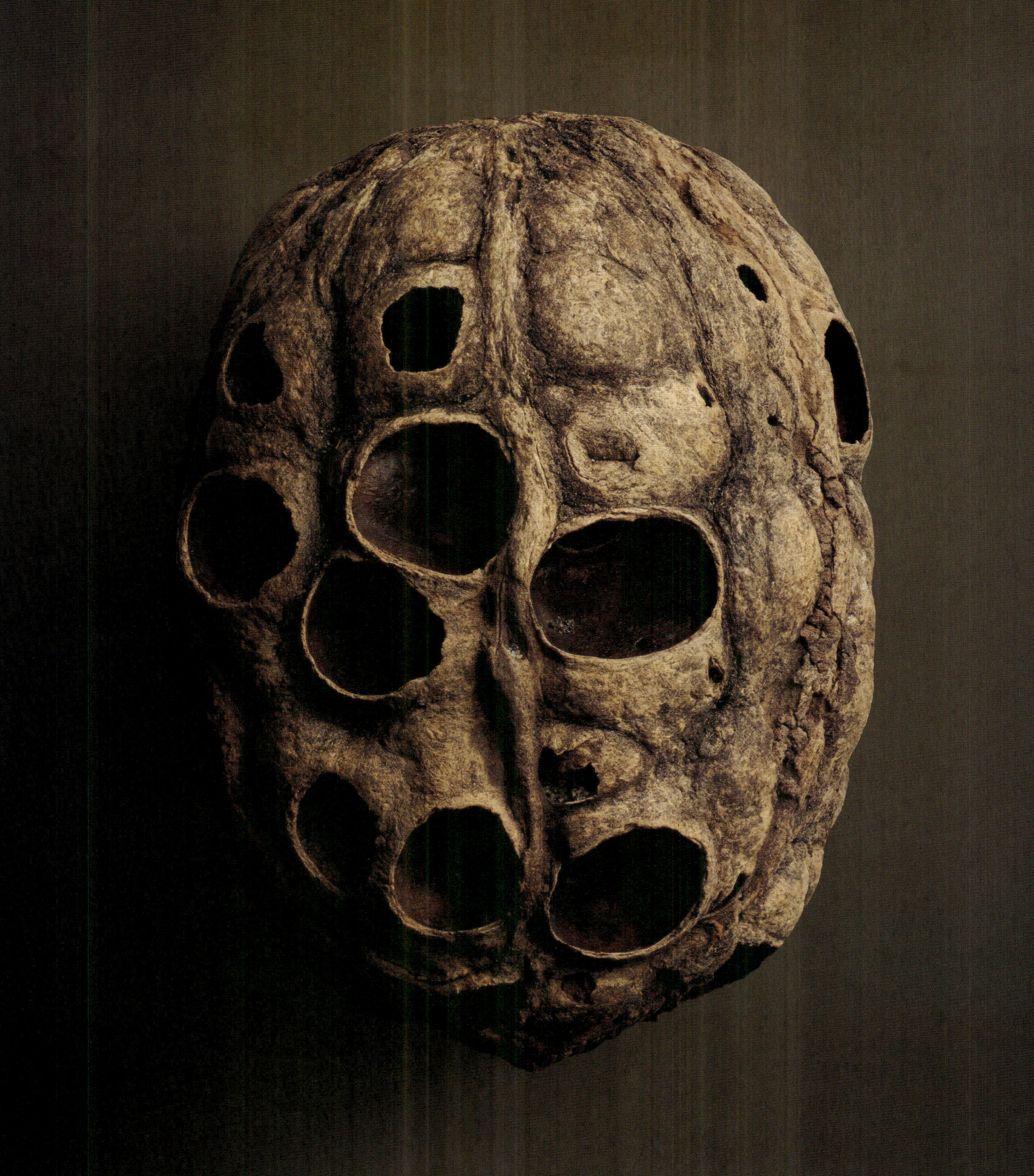

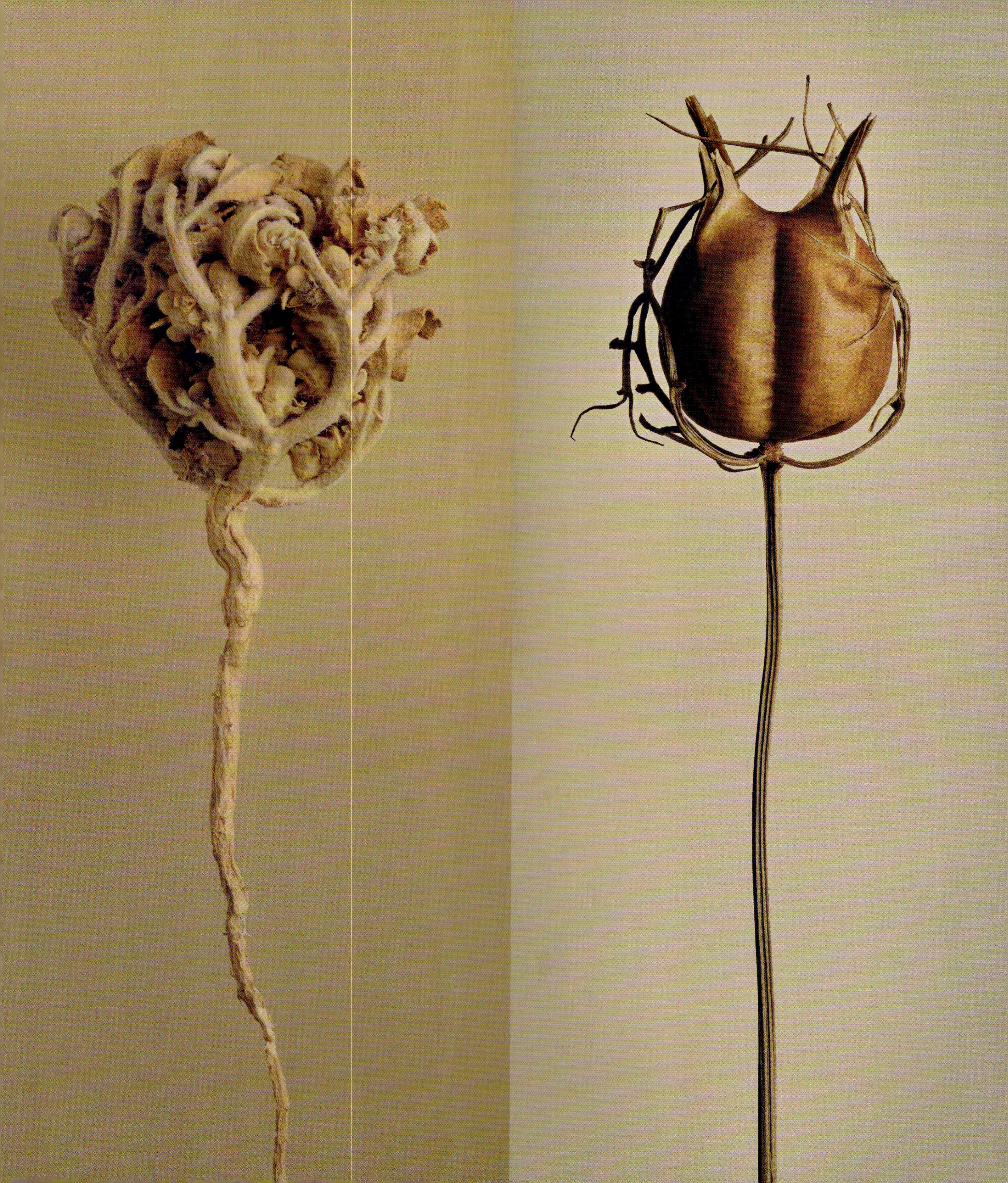

RESURRECTION PLANT

Anastatica hierochuntica (Brassicaceae)

OPPOSITE LEFT: This annual herbaceous plant, also known as "rose of Jericho" or *kaf Mariam* ("Mary's hand"), is native to deserts and drylands from the Canary Islands, across North Africa and Arabia, to Iran. It is particularly common in small depressions or sandy deposits. It is remarkable for its ability to survive long periods—sometimes years—curled in on itself in a state of desiccation, only to revive and expand when exposed to moisture in the air. This process causes the fruits to open and release their seeds. In some countries, an herbal tea prepared from the dried plant is traditionally drunk by expectant mothers in the belief that it will ease childbirth. However, consumption of *Anastatica hierochuntica* has not been proven to be safe during pregnancy.

BAHRAIN

LOVE-IN-A-MIST

Nigella damascena (Ranunculaceae)

OPPOSITE RIGHT: Although this species is widely cultivated as a garden plant in northern Europe and North America, its natural distribution is considerably farther south. It is found in all countries surrounding the Mediterranean, east to Iran, where it flowers in early spring in cultivated areas such as olive groves and in open habitats on unimproved ground. It has two other highly evocative common names: "ragged lady" and "devil in the bush." The first of these is inspired by the plant's untidy arrangement of leaves and bracts. The second derives from the resemblance of the fruit to the head of a horned fiend hidden behind branches. Like the closely related *Nigella sativa* (black cumin), *Nigella damascena* is traditionally used as a condiment and healing herb in southern Europe and Southwest Asia. In India, the seeds are also placed among clothes and bed linen to repel moths, and some physicians consider the seeds to be a stimulant.

RBGE CULTIVATED

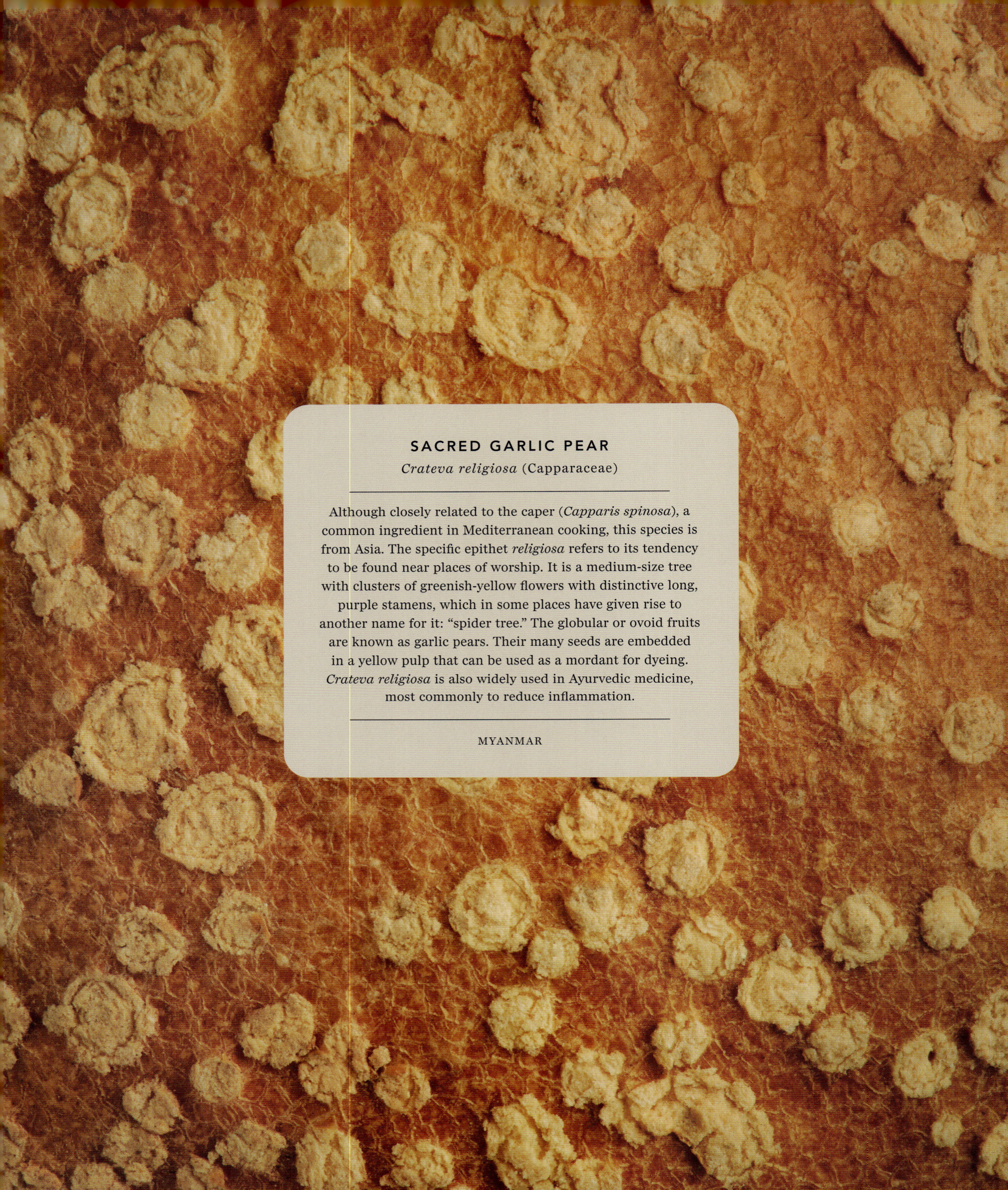

SACRED GARLIC PEAR

Crateva religiosa (Capparaceae)

Although closely related to the caper (*Capparis spinosa*), a common ingredient in Mediterranean cooking, this species is from Asia. The specific epithet *religiosa* refers to its tendency to be found near places of worship. It is a medium-size tree with clusters of greenish-yellow flowers with distinctive long, purple stamens, which in some places have given rise to another name for it: "spider tree." The globular or ovoid fruits are known as garlic pears. Their many seeds are embedded in a yellow pulp that can be used as a mordant for dyeing. *Crateva religiosa* is also widely used in Ayurvedic medicine, most commonly to reduce inflammation.

MYANMAR

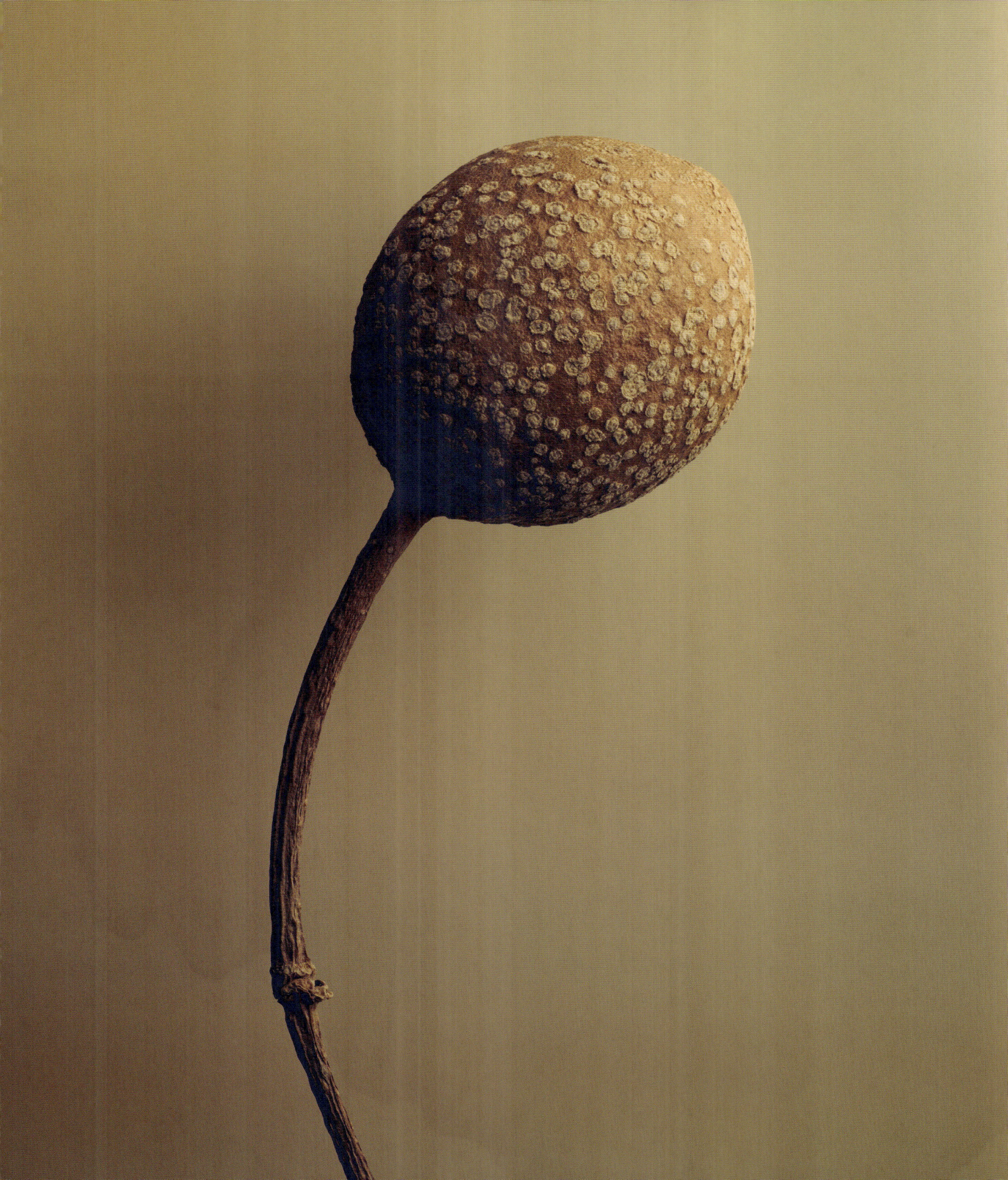

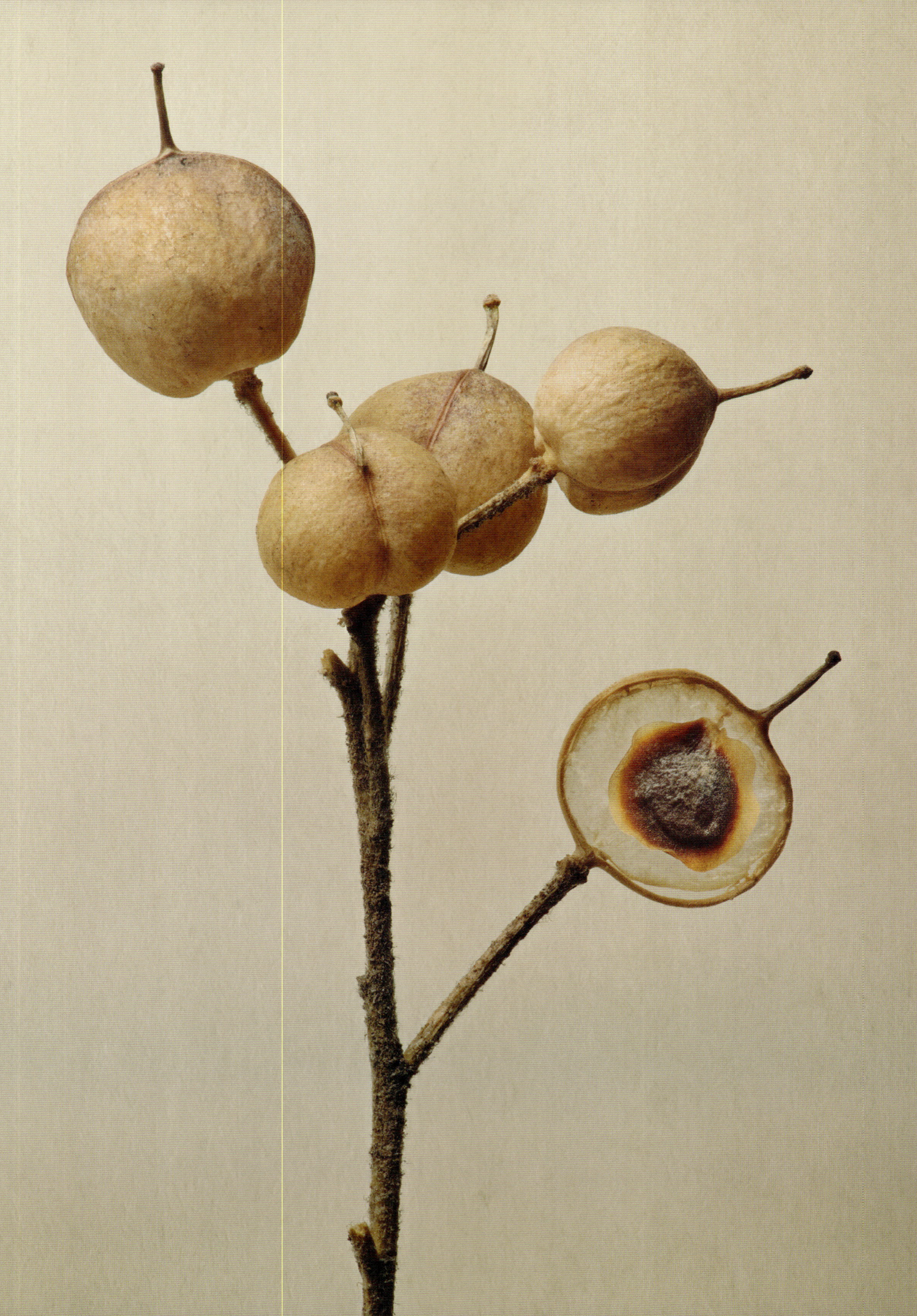

CRETAN ALYSSUM

Lutzia cretica (Brassicaceae)

OPPOSITE: This shrub, formerly known as *Alyssum creticum*, is endemic to Greece. It was first described in 1753 by the renowned Swedish botanist Carl Linnaeus, from a plant growing on the island of Crete. It is usually confined to cliffs, gorges, or rocky outcrops. Its attractive gray leaves are covered in soft gray or white hairs. Bright yellow flowers appear from February to April and are followed by distinctive inflated fruits in May and June. In this specimen, the fruits form an elegant grouping. Although *Lutzia cretica* has no significant history of use as a medicinal plant, extracts have been evaluated for their antimalarial activity and their activity against the parasites responsible for the disease leishmaniasis.

GREECE

CODESO

Adenocarpus complicatus (Fabaceae)

OVERLEAF LEFT: This specimen comes from an attractive broom-like shrub native to the Mediterranean region, with many occurrences in the Iberian Peninsula as well as records from north Africa and Turkey. It typically occurs in open forest and scrubland. A profusion of bright yellow pea-like flowers are followed by fruits that are densely covered in short, sticky glands. On drying, the fruits twist open to catapult the seeds to a new location. The plant is a source of essential fatty acids and antioxidants.

MADEIRA

COW'S EYES

Firmiana malayana (Malvaceae)

OVERLEAF RIGHT: This species is recorded from Sumatra, Java, Peninsular Malaysia, and Borneo. "Cow's eyes" is the translation of its Malay name, *mata lembu*. When in flower, and later in fruit, the tree loses its leaves. This results in a spectacular display of bright orange flowers on bare branches. The flowers are superseded by the fruits, each consisting of a papery wing bearing one or two green seeds on its edges. The wing changes from green to crimson as it matures, before drying to a silvery tan color. It is then carried on the wind to disperse the seeds at a distance from the parent plant. This specimen was collected at the Forest Research Institute Malaysia, with which RBGE has enjoyed a long-standing collaboration.

MALAYSIA

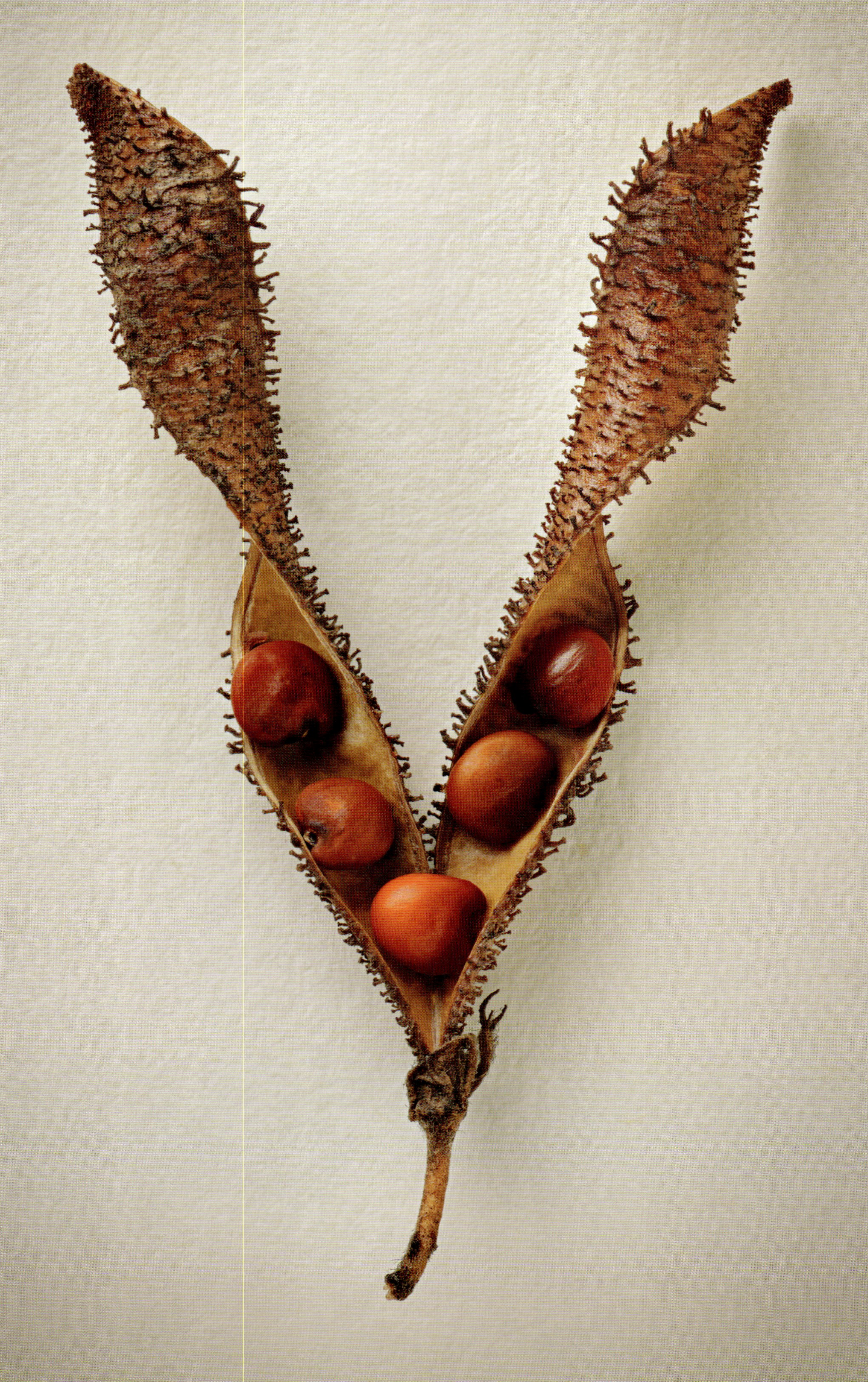

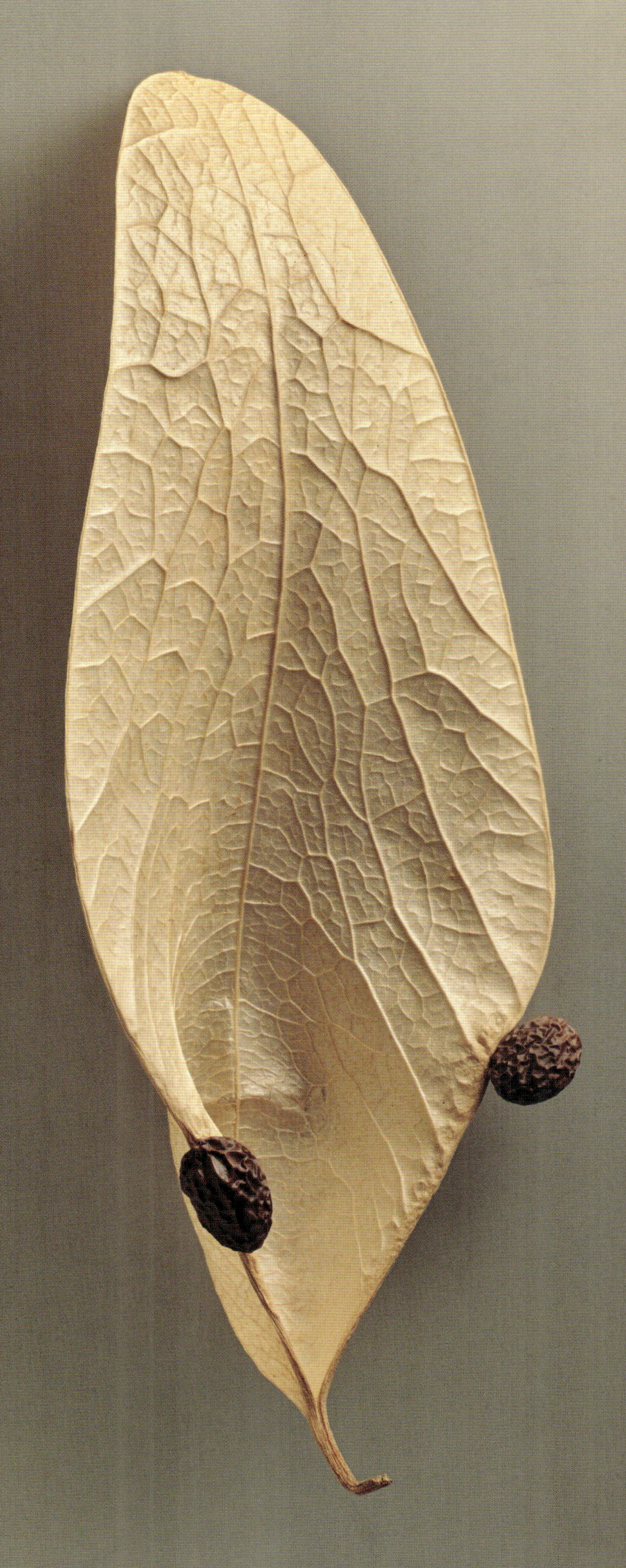

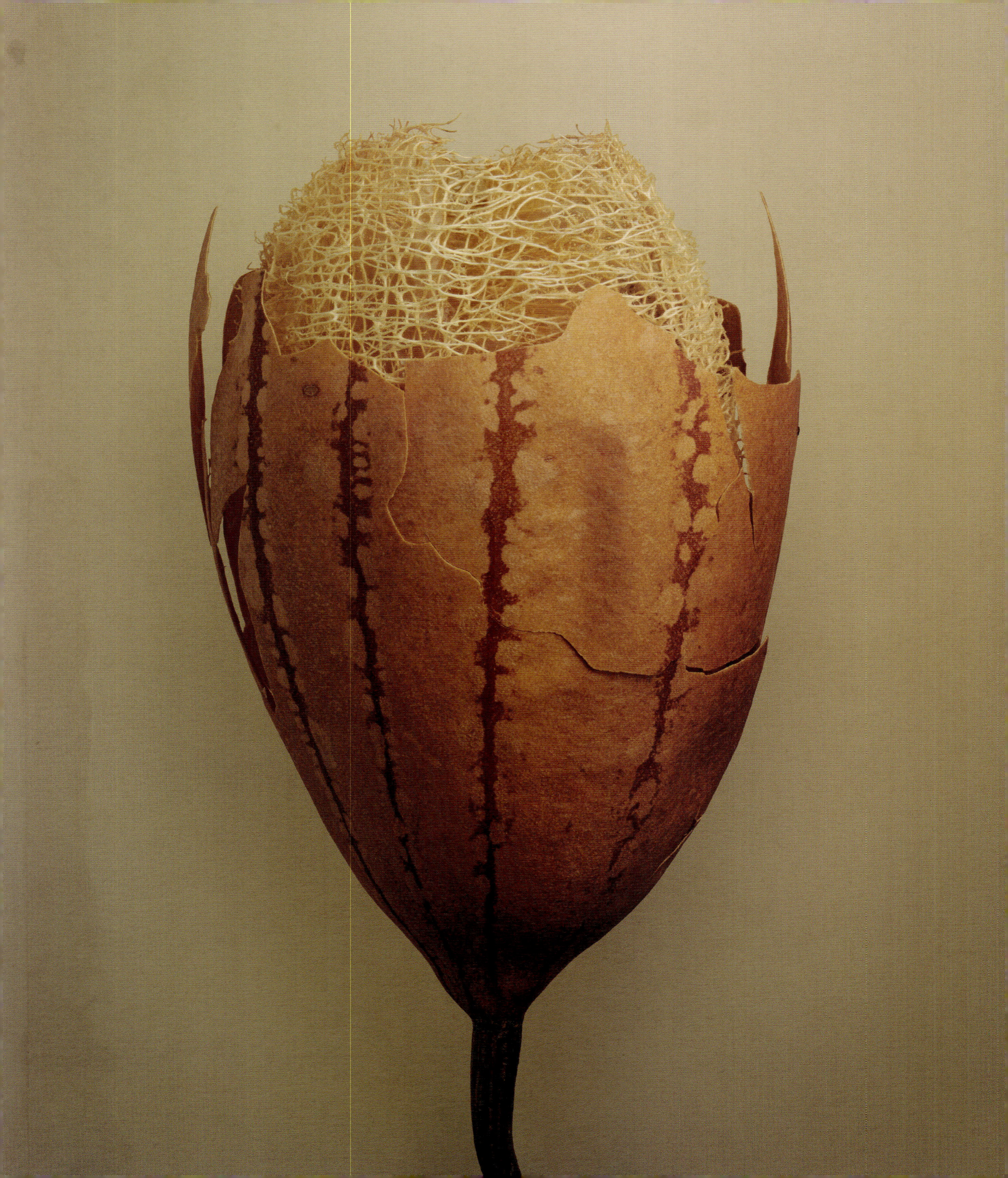

LUFFA

Luffa cylindrica (Cucurbitaceae)

OPPOSITE: Members of the genus *Luffa* are distributed across the tropics, where they are grown as a crop or found in the wild as a scrambling vine on shrubs or trees, often beside rivers. The young fruits can be eaten either raw, like those of their relative the cucumber (*Cucumis sativus*), or cooked. The older fruits are inedible. Left on the stem, the fruit dries and its exocarp (the outermost layer of the fruit wall) starts to fall away. All that is then left of the fruit is its inner network of fibers and its seeds. Dried gourds that have subsequently been rotted (by soaking in water) and peeled, and had their seeds removed, are used as luffa sponges. Their rough surface makes them an effective exfoliating tool.

BHUTAN

BUCKEYE

Aesculus glabra (Sapindaceae)

OVERLEAF LEFT: This tree species is found from southeast Canada south to Texas. Native Americans called it *hetuck*, which means "eye of the buck deer"; the name clearly derives from the appearance of the nut. This nut specimen was collected during the Challenger Expedition of 1872–1876, probably when the ship made landfall in eastern North America in 1873. This was a landmark oceanographic expedition. Its primary purposes were to take water samples and soundings to determine ocean currents, temperatures, and depths, and to carry out biological investigations. To this end, HMS *Challenger* was equipped with a laboratory and had a number of scientists on board in addition to the main crew.

EASTERN NORTH AMERICA

RED-FLESHED DURIAN

Durio graveolens (Malvaceae)

OVERLEAF RIGHT: This wild species of durian is closely related to the cultivated species, *Durio zibethinus*. It is a large tree (up to 164 feet/50 m), typically with steep buttresses, that grows in lowland rain forest, often along riverbanks and in swamps. The large, spiny fruit contains a glossy brown seed completely enveloped by a pungent fleshy layer. This is the edible flesh of the fruit; its sweet, cheesy taste is appreciated not only by humans but also by orangutans, hornbills, and sun bears. The flesh ranges in color from light yellow to orange or red, hence the other common names for this species: "yellow-fleshed durian" and "orange-fleshed durian." Although the specific epithet, *graveolens*, means "strong smelling," the fruit has a mild scent compared with other durians.

MALAYSIA

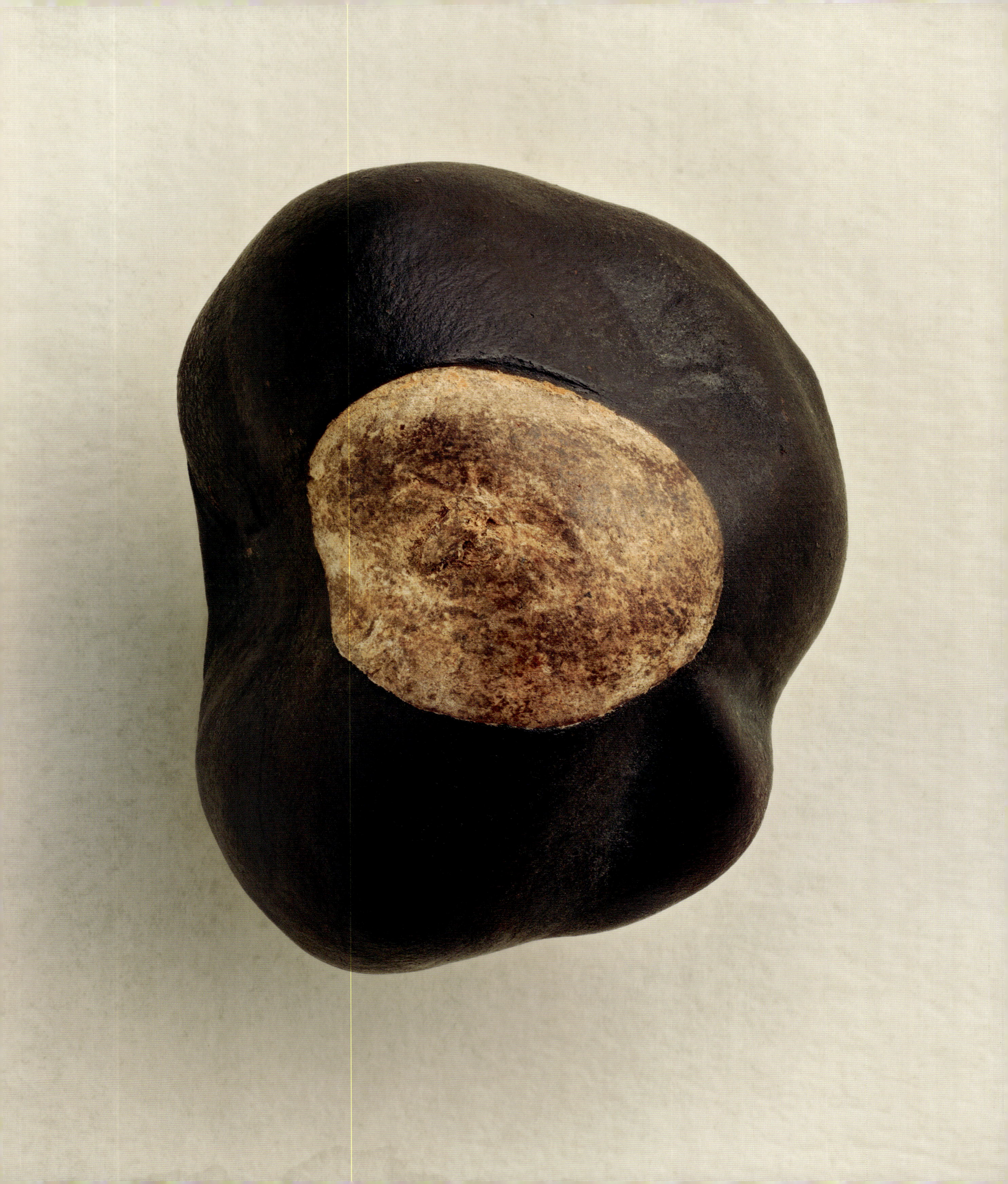

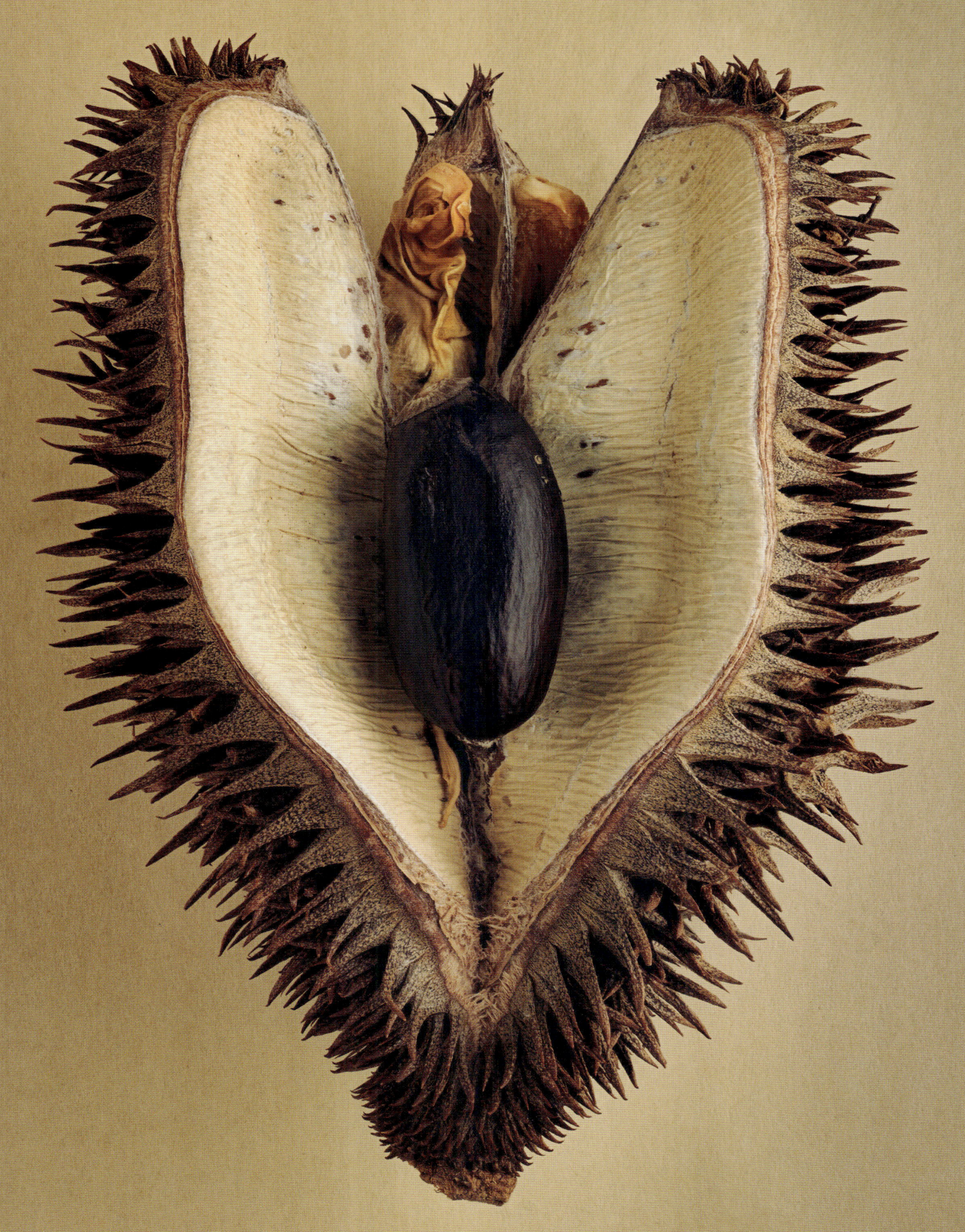

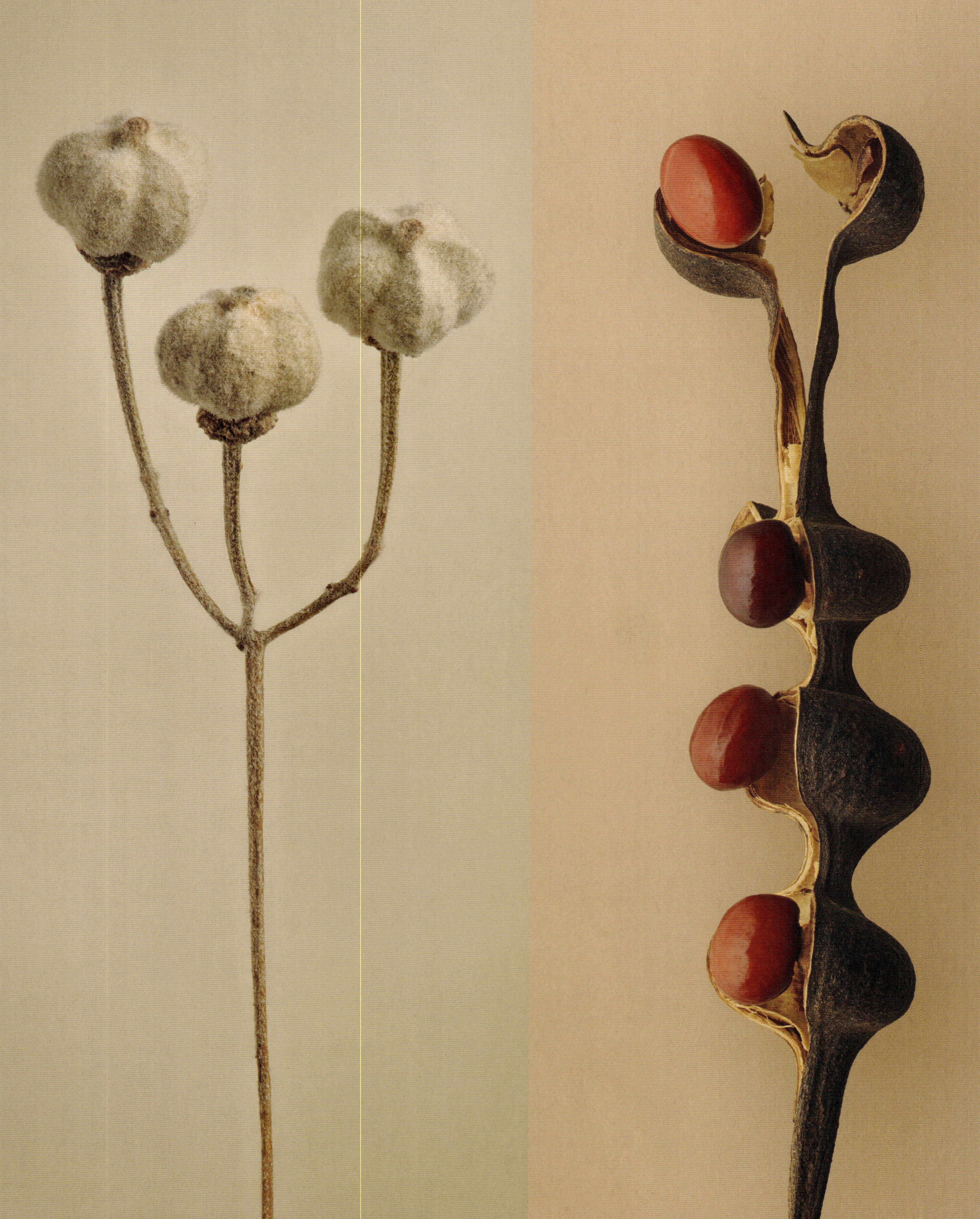

SILVER LIME

Tilia tomentosa (Malvaceae)

OPPOSITE LEFT: This species is native to Southeastern Europe. It is a graceful deciduous tree that provides ornament and shade in parks and gardens throughout the temperate world. In the Balkans, its sweetly scented flowers are much prized by beekeepers as a source of the nectar their bees use to produce a delicious and distinctive honey. In some countries outside its native range, however, its nectar has been considered toxic to bees. There is no experimental evidence to support this belief, and the mass bee deaths associated with *Tilia* are more likely to be a result of starvation due to an insufficiency of nectar late in flowering.

RBGE CULTIVATED

COMMON CORAL TREE

Erythrina lysistemon (Fabaceae)

OPPOSITE RIGHT: The bright red flowers of this tree appear before the leaves, thus creating a stunning sight on otherwise bare branches. In common with many other species with red flowers, it is pollinated by birds. In Africa, sunbirds are dominant in this role. They are dusted with pollen when they visit a flower to feed on its nectar, in the same way as the similarly specialized hummingbirds in the Americas. The seeds of *Erythrina lysistemon* are used as charms, hence one of its common names: "lucky bean tree." However, the seeds are poisonous and should not be eaten by people. The tree was traditionally planted at the graves of Zulu chiefs; now, it is commonly used as a street tree. It is distributed from South Africa to Zimbabwe and Angola.

SOUTH AFRICA

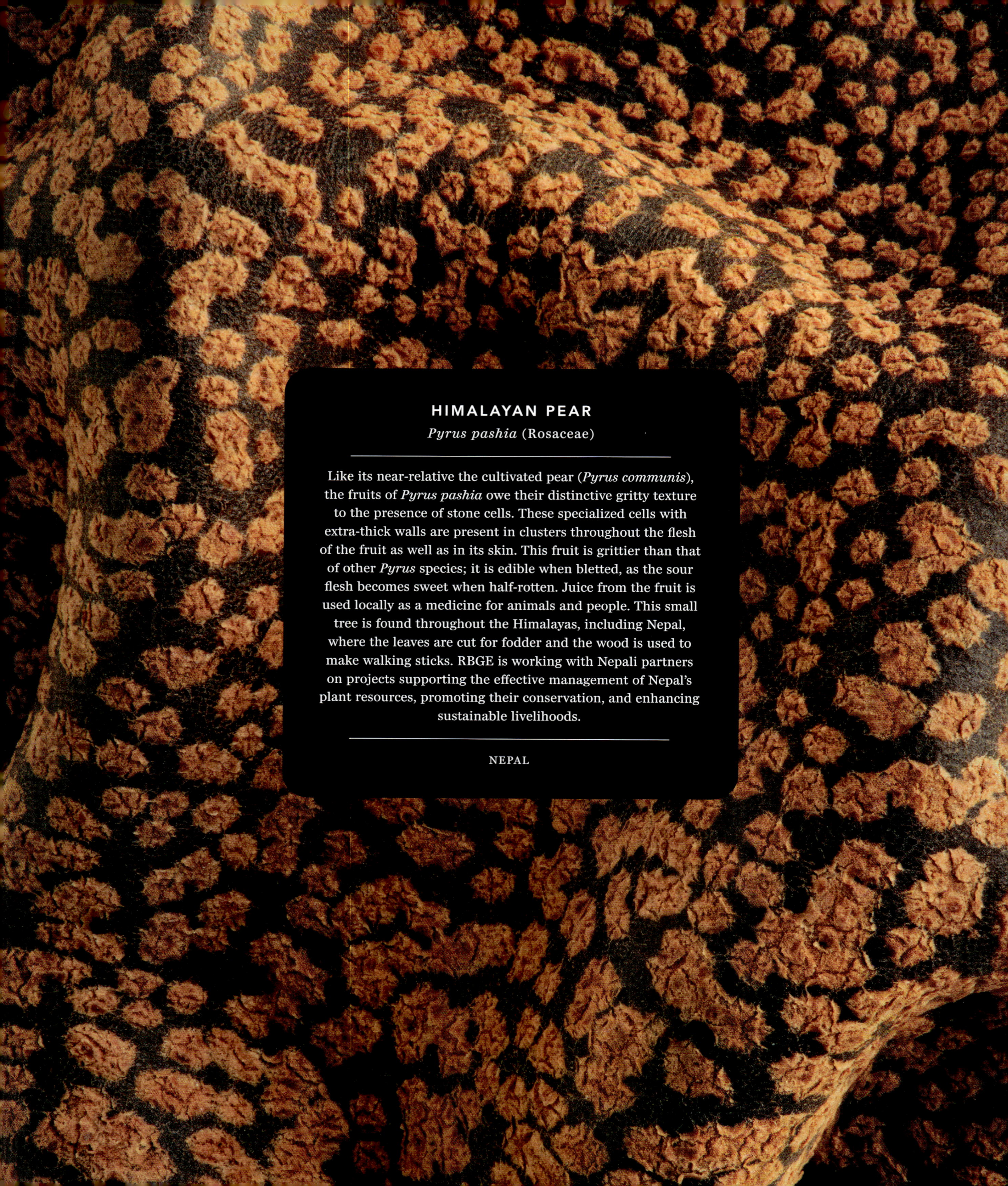

HIMALAYAN PEAR

Pyrus pashia (Rosaceae)

Like its near-relative the cultivated pear (*Pyrus communis*), the fruits of *Pyrus pashia* owe their distinctive gritty texture to the presence of stone cells. These specialized cells with extra-thick walls are present in clusters throughout the flesh of the fruit as well as in its skin. This fruit is grittier than that of other *Pyrus* species; it is edible when bletted, as the sour flesh becomes sweet when half-rotten. Juice from the fruit is used locally as a medicine for animals and people. This small tree is found throughout the Himalayas, including Nepal, where the leaves are cut for fodder and the wood is used to make walking sticks. RBGE is working with Nepali partners on projects supporting the effective management of Nepal's plant resources, promoting their conservation, and enhancing sustainable livelihoods.

NEPAL

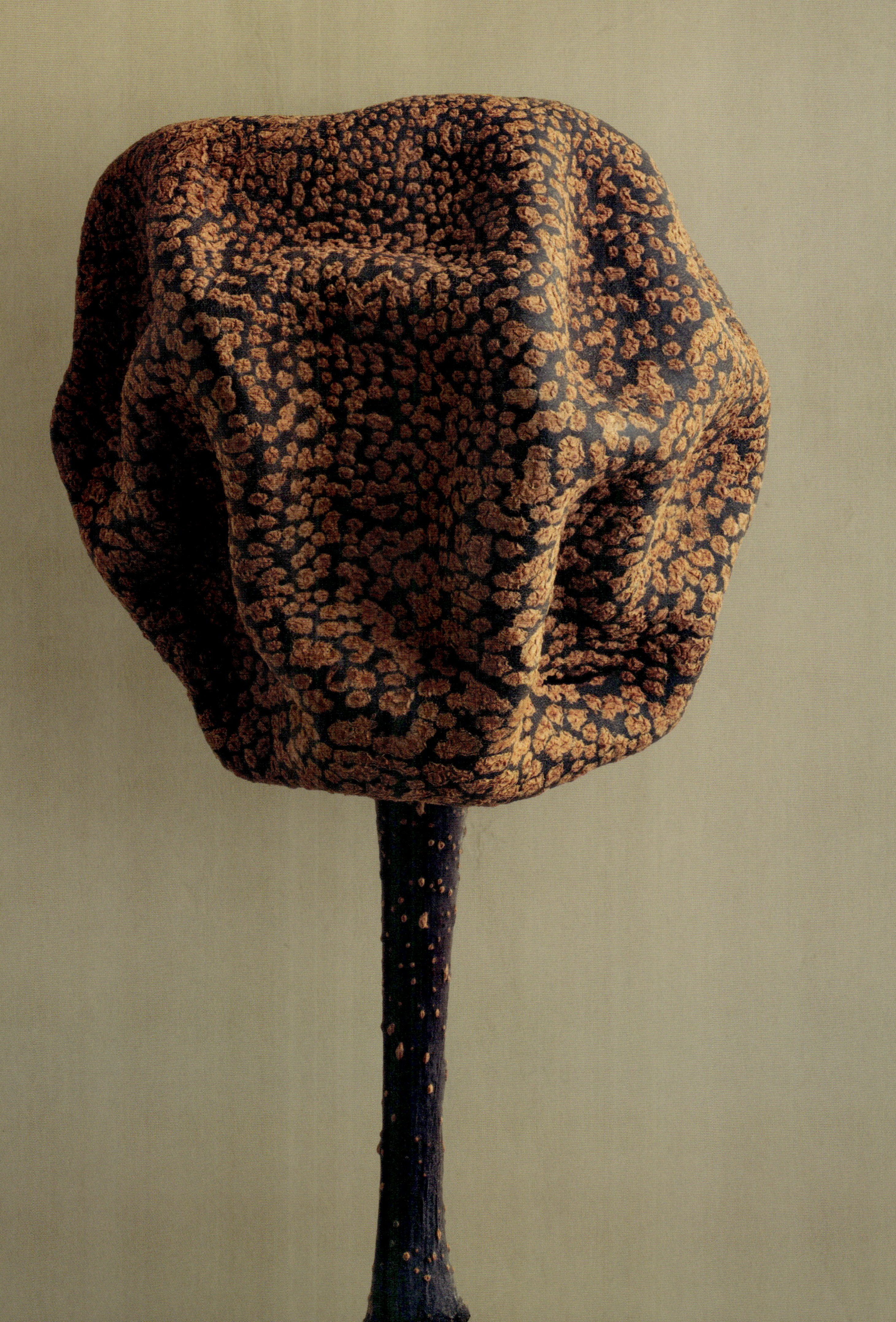

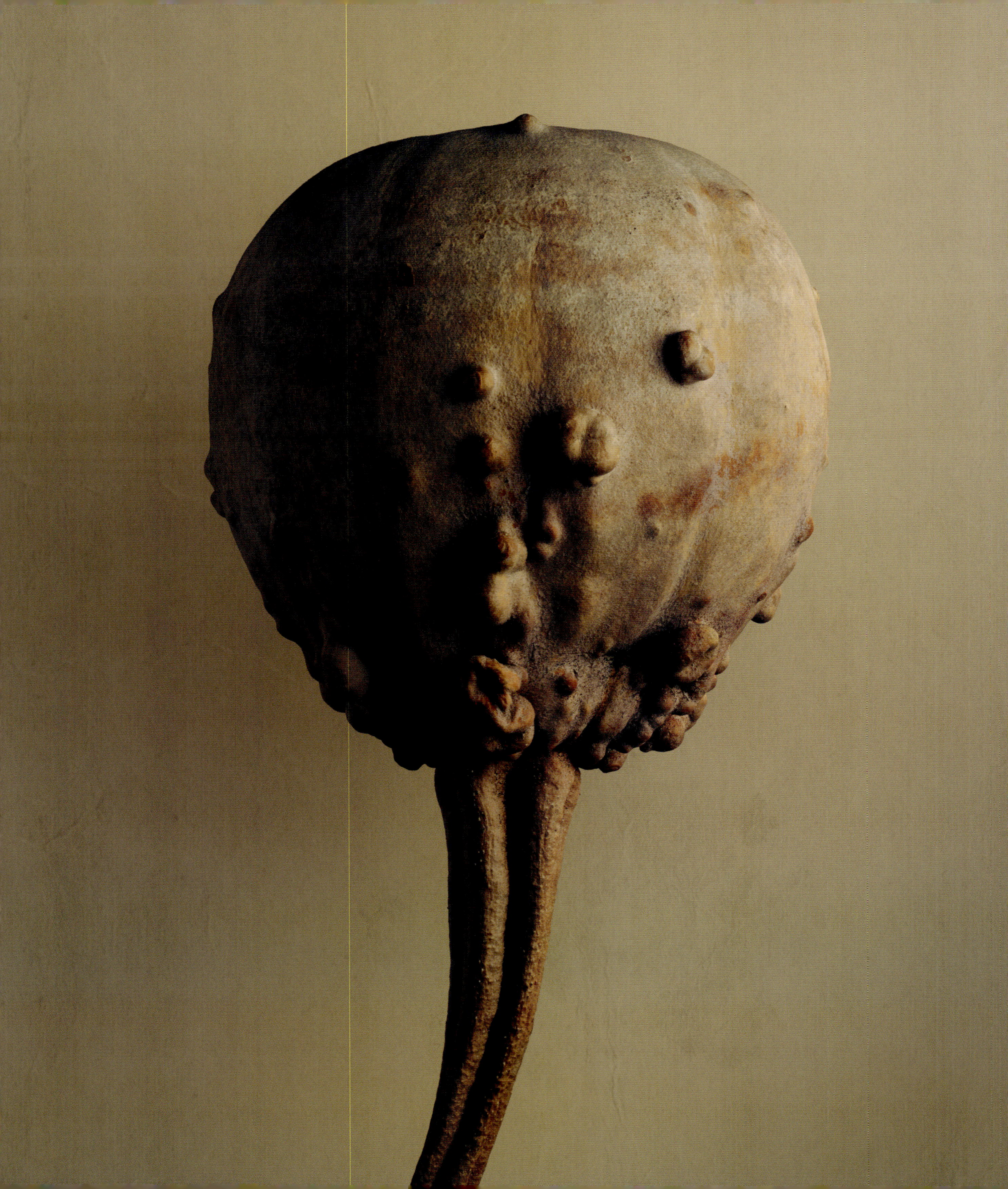

GOURD

Cucurbita sp. (Cucurbitaceae)

OPPOSITE: This genus contains squash, pumpkin, and zucchini (courgette). It also includes some of the gourds that are among the first plants to have been cultivated in the Americas. Part of the evidence for this comes from archaeological research, specifically phytolith analysis. Phytoliths (from "plant stone" in Greek) are the microscopic silica-containing structures produced by many plants. They are preserved in a plant's fossilized remains, and their shape can be used to identify the species or genus. Phytolith analysis has shown that *Cucurbita* species were being cultivated in northern South America as early as 5000 BCE. Phytoliths are found in the rind of fruits and may provide protection by making them more difficult to consume and digest, at least for smaller animals. Gourds considered inedible are often dried and made into ornamental items or musical instruments.

RBGE CULTIVATED

GIANT BANKSIA

Banksia grandis (Proteaceae)

OVERLEAF LEFT: The specific epithet for this tree (*grandis*, Latin for "great") refers to its leaves, which can grow up to almost 18 inches (half a meter) long and are the largest in the genus *Banksia*. They are arranged in a tight spiral at the base of each of the plant's flower spikes. The distinctive cone-like fruit head is what remains once the hundreds of tightly packed flowers borne by a single spike have fallen away. The genus was named after the naturalist Joseph Banks, who led the team of scientists aboard HMS *Endeavour* on the first scientific expedition to the Pacific under the command of James Cook. Banks and his Swedish friend and fellow naturalist Daniel Solander collected the first specimens of *Banksia* from the site where they made landfall in Australia in 1770, which Cook later named Botany Bay.

AUSTRALIA

JACQUEMONT'S HAZEL

Corylus jacquemontii (Betulaceae)

OVERLEAF RIGHT: This tree is endemic to the western Himalayas, where it occurs from Kashmir to western Nepal at altitudes between 4,900 and 11,490 feet (1,500 and 3,500 m). Each nut is cradled in a cupule with elaborate tentacle-like projections. The seeds within the nuts are edible, just like those of the commercial species, *Corylus avellana*. It is named after Victor Jacquemont, a French botanist who traveled to India in 1829 and made notable explorations of the Himalayan flora. He never returned from the trip, dying of cholera in Mumbai in 1832 at the age of thirty-one.

RBGE CULTIVATED

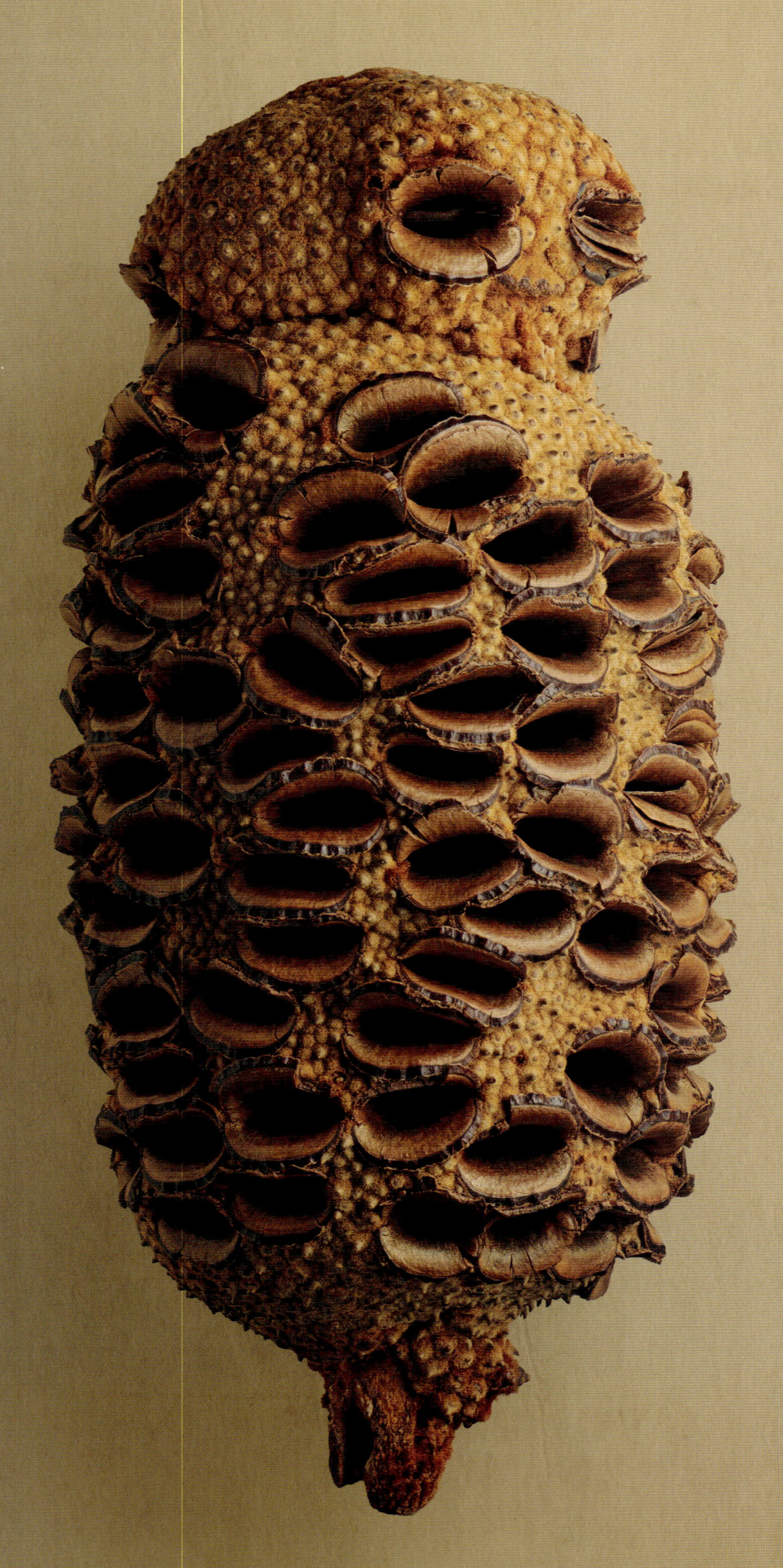

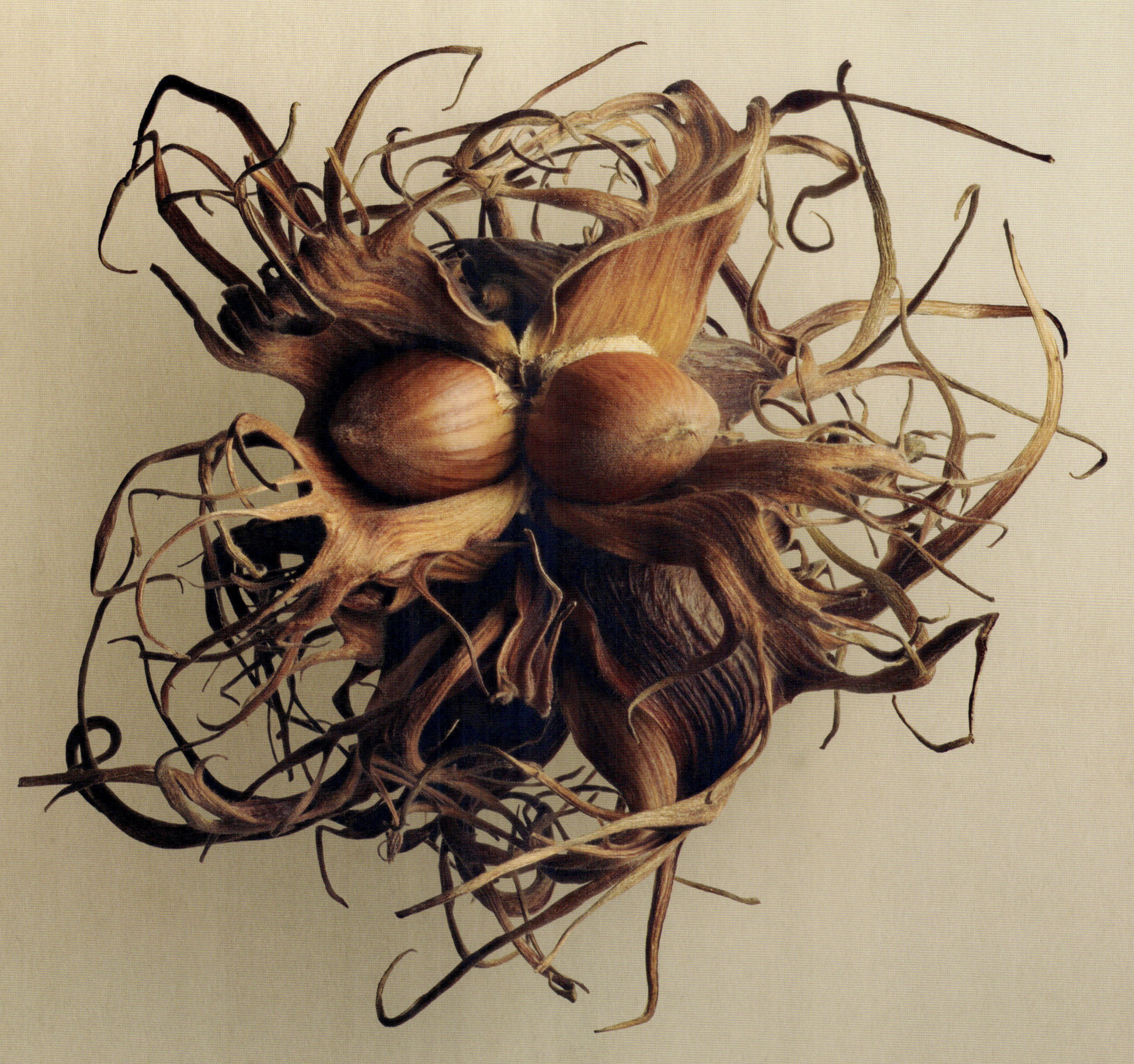

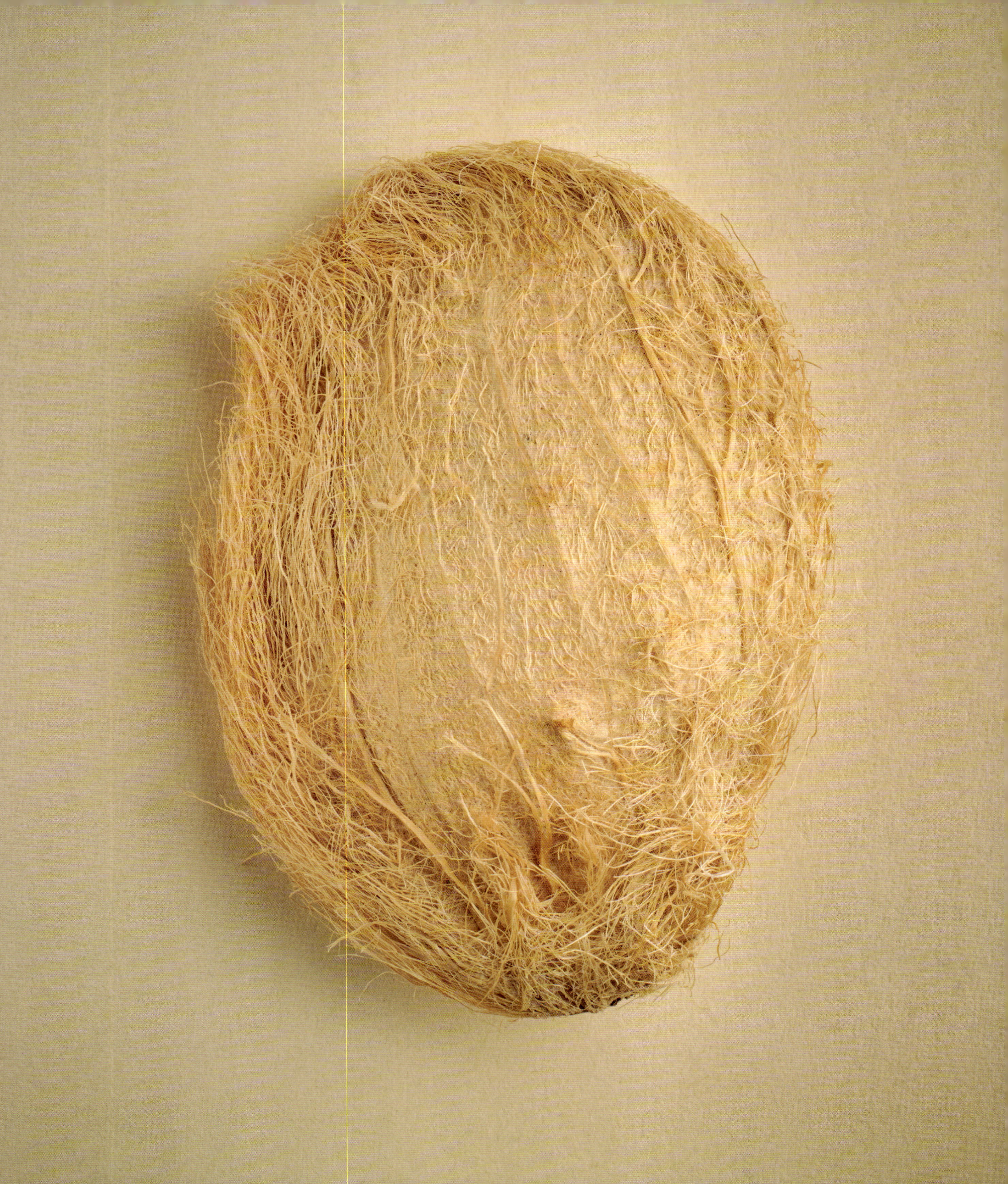

MANGO

Mangifera indica (Anacardiaceae)

OPPOSITE: This species is native to the Indian subcontinent and belongs to the poison ivy family. It is one of the oldest cultivated plants in the world, having been grown in India for over four thousand years. It is now grown throughout the tropics. Mango trees can reach a height of 148 feet (45 m) and usually take five to eight years to produce their first fruit. Flowering is irregular and fruit may appear only every three or four years—sometimes even longer. The fibrous stone with a large single seed, shown here, has astringent properties, which have traditionally been used to treat stomach complaints. Oil extracted from the seed is an ingredient in cosmetic products used to cleanse the skin and close the pores.

RBGE CULTIVATED

STONE OAK

Lithocarpus sp. (Fagaceae)

OVERLEAF LEFT: *Lithocarpus* comprises around 340 species of tree occurring predominantly in South and Southeast Asia. The fact that *Lithocarpus* (the stone oaks) is closely related to *Quercus* (the oaks) is reflected in the similar appearance of the fruit of the two genera. The image shows the densely aggregated, acorn-like fruit of an unidentified species of *Lithocarpus*. The bark of the majority of species is rich in tannins, which are used as a preservative for ropes and leather. The wood is a good fuel and is also suitable for making charcoal.

CHINA

KO PHUANG

Lithocarpus aggregatus (Fagaceae)

OVERLEAF RIGHT: Members of Fagaceae, comprising the oaks and beeches, are found in woods in several parts of the world but are particularly diverse in Asia and North America. They are most commonly found growing at altitudes greater than 1,640 feet (500 m). One curious feature of the seeds is that they do not store well. The trees evolved in habitats with a damp climate, where the seeds germinate almost immediately after falling from the parent tree. Seeds that behave in this way are called recalcitrant or desiccation-intolerant. *Lithocarpus* are ecologically important canopy trees, providing shelter and food for a host of rain-forest organisms, including many rodents and insects.

THAILAND

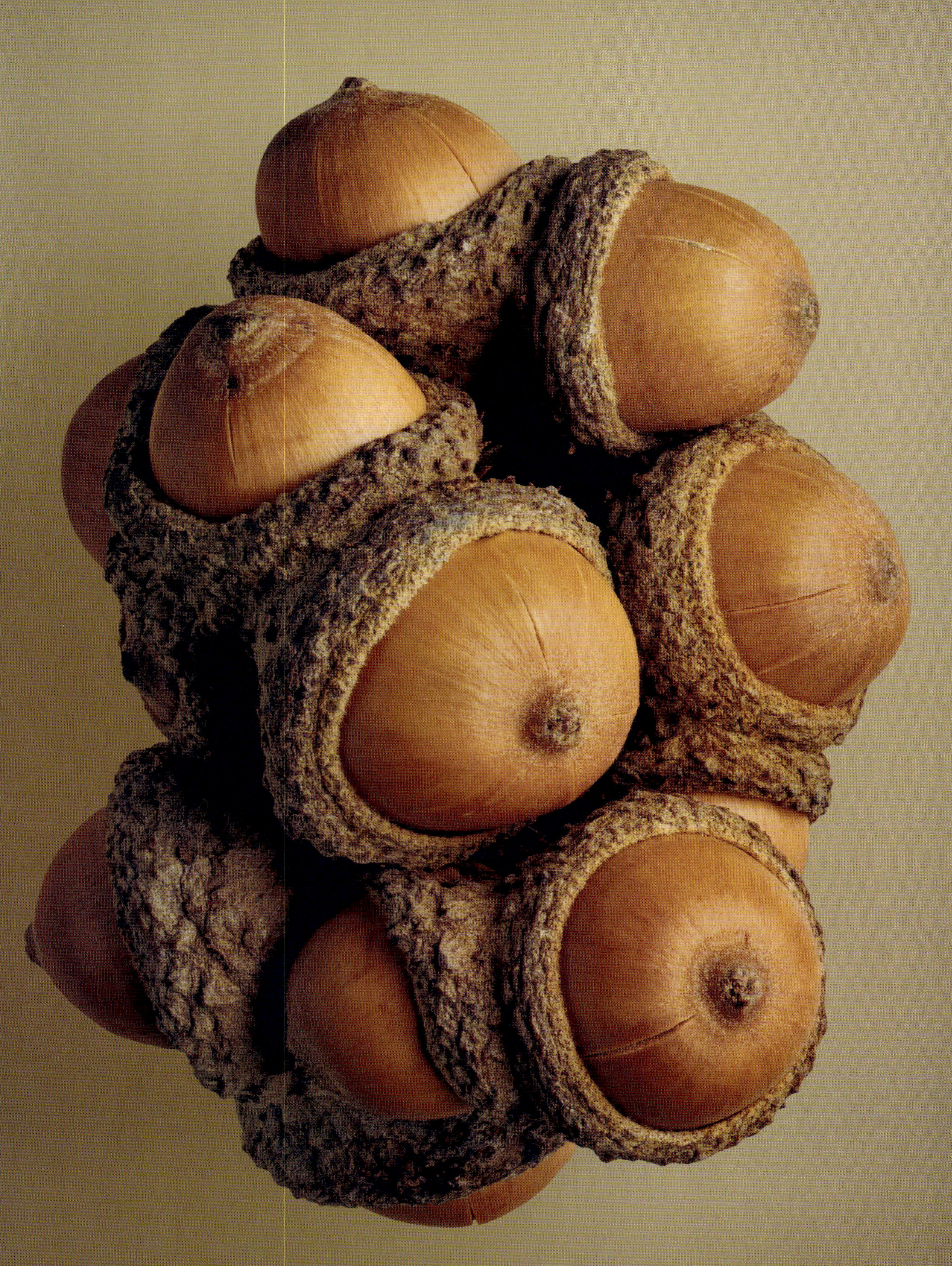

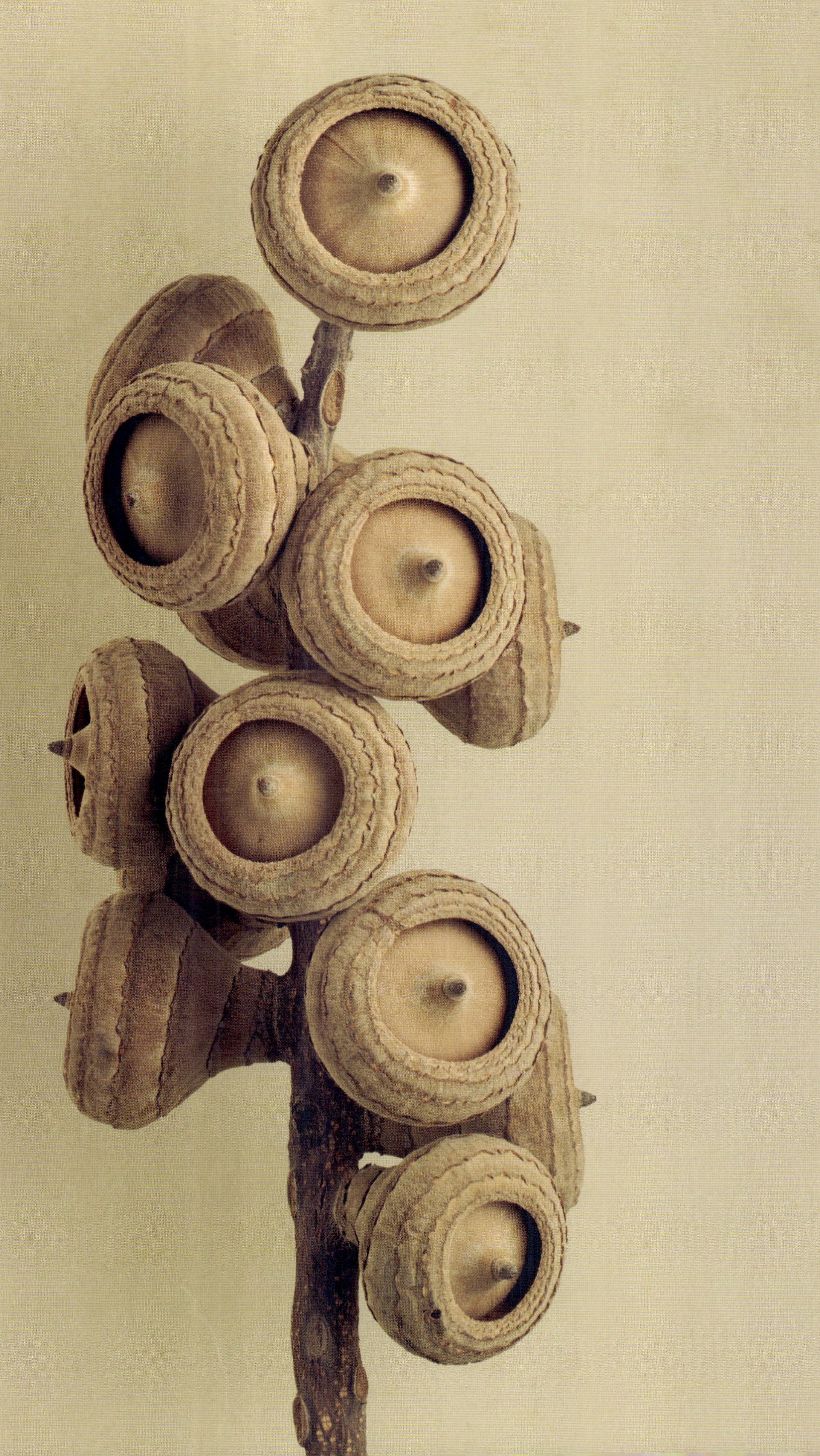

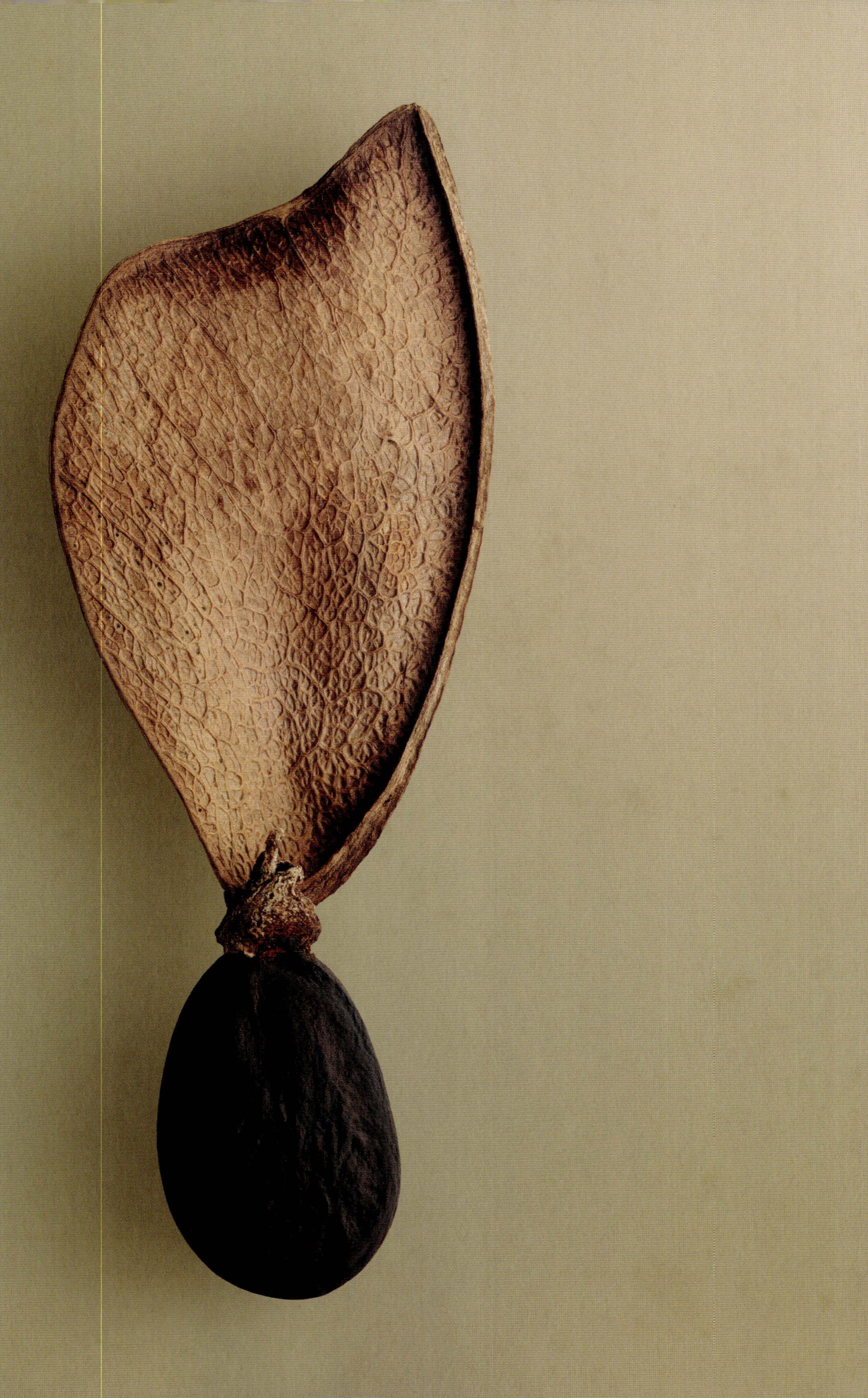

AXE BREAKER

Peltogyne confertiflora (Fabaceae)

OPPOSITE: This species is a shrub characteristic of the Cerrado, the savannas of central Brazil. Its trunks are so hard that it is known locally by its Portuguese name *quebra machado*, meaning "axe breaker." This specimen of its fruit was collected by legendary RBGE botanist Jimmy Ratter. His pioneering research on the Cerrado led to recognition of this ecosystem as a globally important biodiversity hot spot; it has inspired a generation of Brazilian researchers and earned him the Grand Cross of the National Order of Scientific Merit from the government of Brazil. The fact that expansion of industrial agriculture has, since 1970, destroyed more than eighty percent of the Cerrado makes the research being carried out by the RBGE and its partner organizations in Brazil even more pressingly important.

BRAZIL

WU CHI QING GANG

Quercus semiserrata (Fagaceae)

OVERLEAF LEFT: This medium-size subtropical tree in the oak and beech family is native to southern China and northeast India, south through Myanmar, Thailand, and Malaysia to the island of Sumatra. The specific epithet, *semiserrata*, describes the slightly saw-toothed edge to the leaves. Its fruits, like those of all *Quercus* species, are acorns. Each acorn develops in a cup-like structure called a cupule and grows up to 1.5 inches (4 cm) long. The surface of the cupule has six to nine concentric scaly rings, delineated by the distinctive dark markings at their edges. In the Indian state of Manipur, this species is a host for the oak tasar silkworm (*Antheraea proylei*), which is commercially exploited for the high-quality silk it produces. The local name in China where this specimen was collected is "wu chi qing gang."

CHINA

CANYON LIVE OAK

Quercus chrysolepis (Fagaceae)

OVERLEAF RIGHT: *Quercus chrysolepis* forms a large evergreen tree to 82 feet (25 m) tall. It has a native distribution from southwestern Oregon south to northern Baja California, Mexico. Typically occurring in extensive pure stands, it sometimes grows with other oak species and notably, the big cone pine (*Pinus coulteri*), which has the largest cone of any conifer in the world. Native Americans used the acorns as a staple food, and its roasted seeds to use in a similar way to coffee. The common name, "canyon live oak," comes from the tree's ability to readily regenerate from basal sprouts at the base of the tree after a fire. Other common names include "canyon oak" and "golden-cup oak."

USA

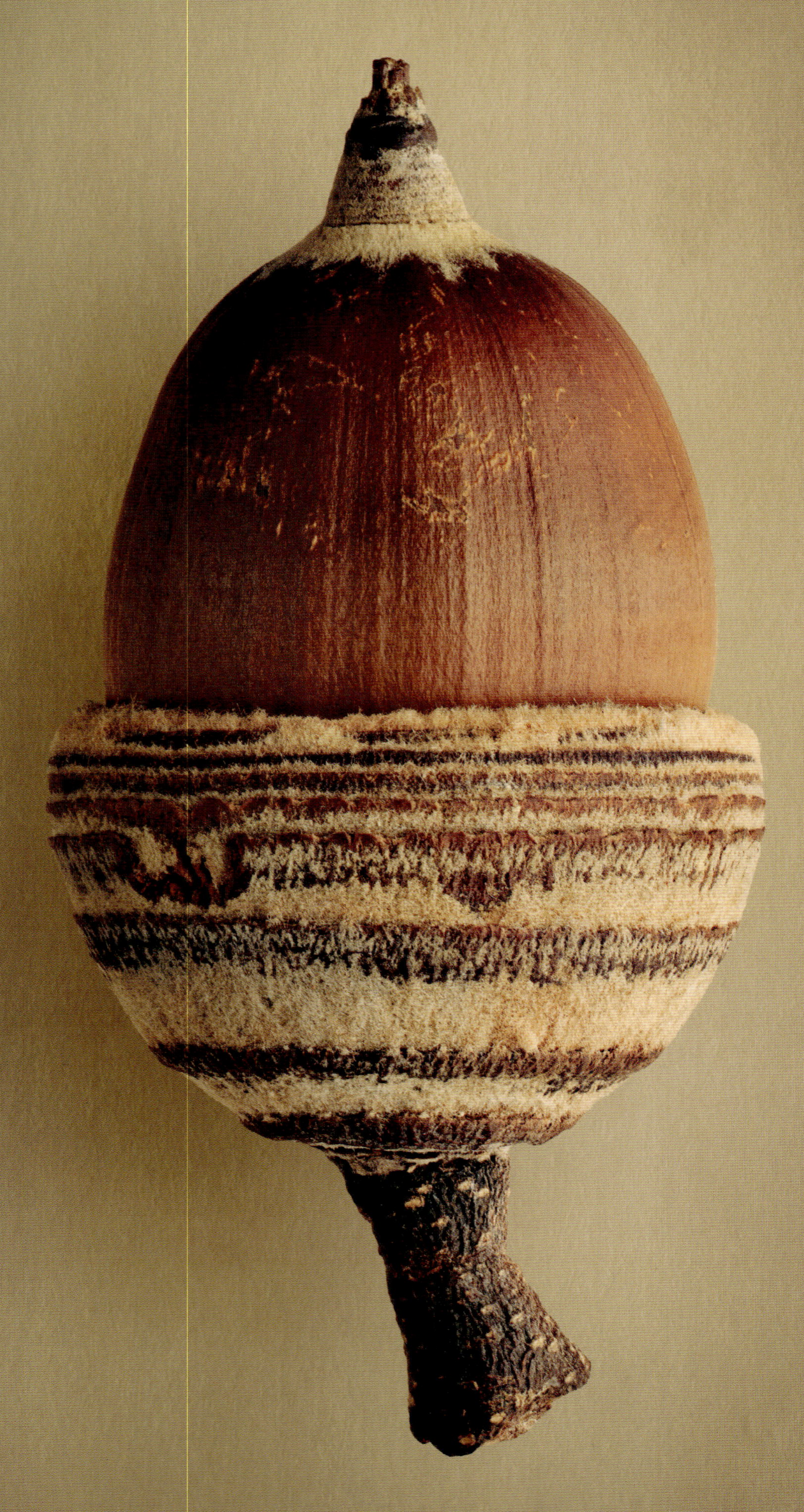

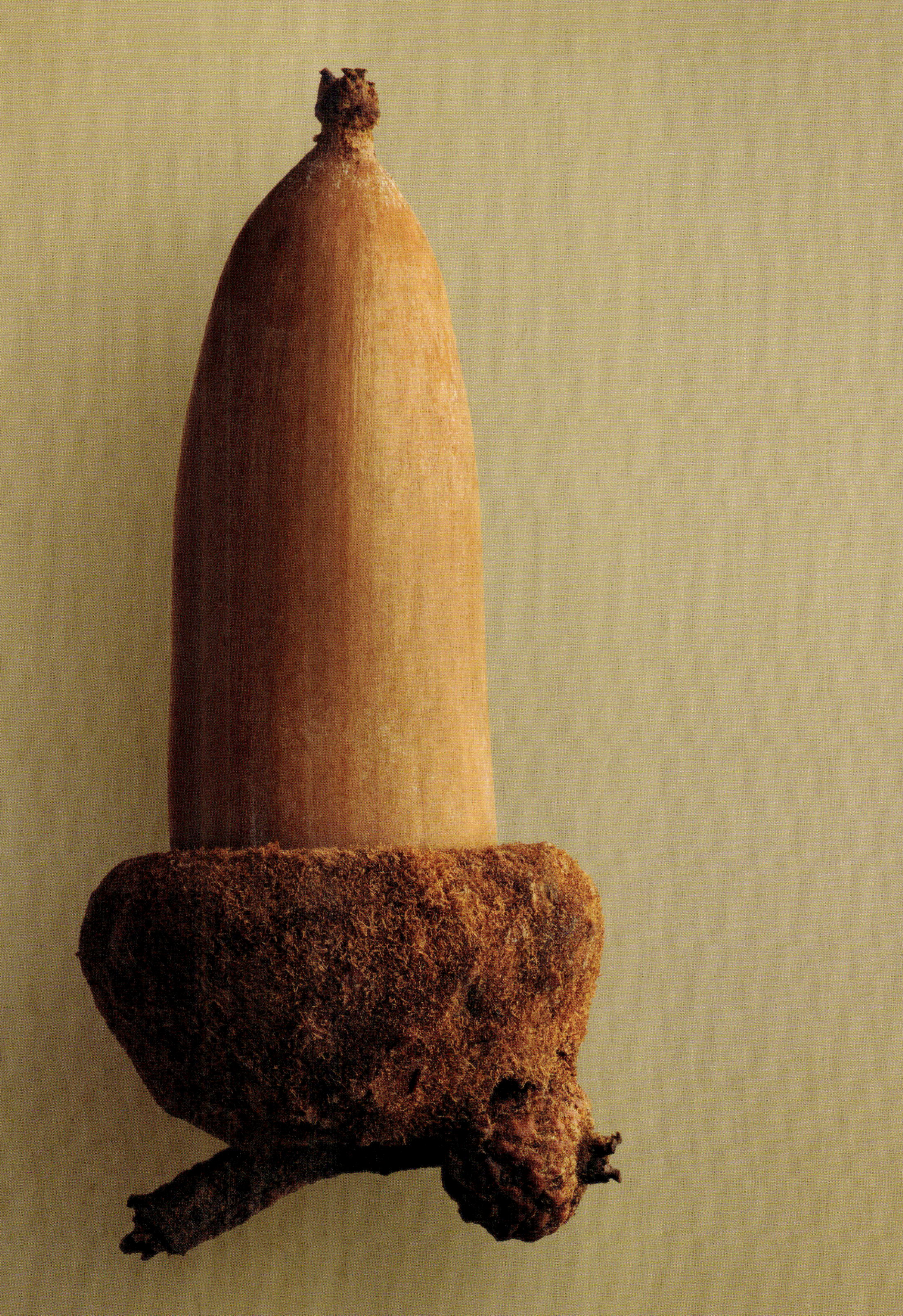

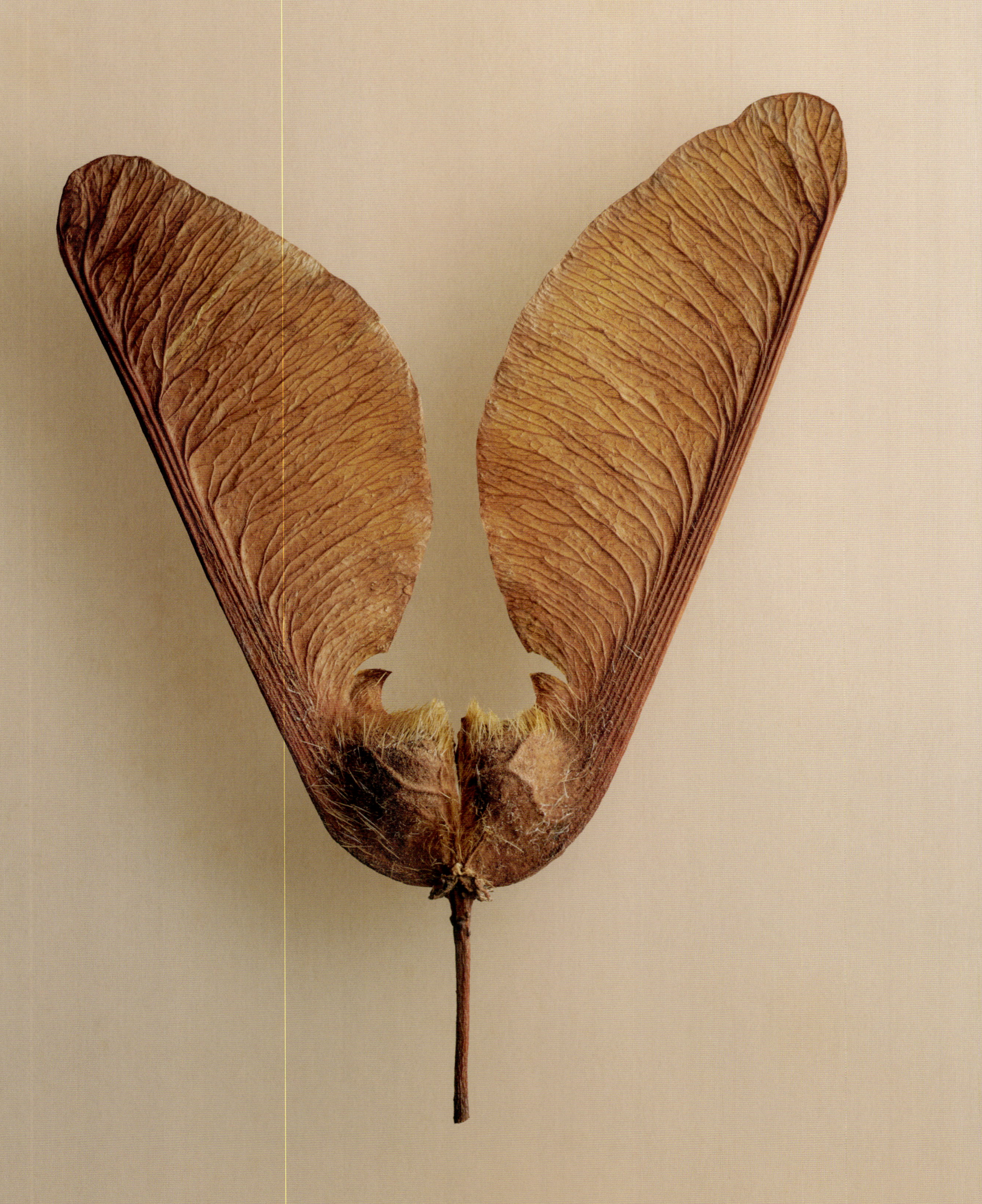

BIG LEAF MAPLE

Acer macrophyllum (Sapindaceae)

OPPOSITE: This tree can live up to three hundred years and is native to Alaska and south along the North American coast to California. The specific epithet *macrophyllum* refers to its large leaves, which can measure as much as 11.8 inches (30 cm) across and are the largest of any *Acer* species. As is typical for the genus, it produces a double samara: a pair of winged, single-seeded fruits joined at the base and remaining closed at maturity. When the double samara breaks apart, each fruit falls to the ground in a rotational motion. This ingenious mechanism allows the "helicopters" or "whirlybirds" to be carried a considerable distance from the parent tree. Those that are not eaten by birds and rodents germinate quickly the following spring.

USA

BEREMBANG

Sonneratia caseolaris (Lythraceae)

OVERLEAF LEFT: This species is a common tree of mangrove forests. A native of Southeast Asia, it is also found from India and southern China to Northern Australia and the Pacific islands. Its shiny, green, globular fruit ("mangrove apples") have a leathery texture and typically six horizontally spreading calyx lobes at their base. The buoyant seeds are embedded in the whitish, fleshy pulp. People from coastal communities occasionally eat the fruit, either raw or cooked, in savory dishes. Immature fruit have a sour taste that makes them ideal for flavoring curries, whereas ripe fruit taste like cheese. In traditional medicine, the fruit has been used to reduce hemorrhaging and soothe coughs.

INDONESIA

BLACK SHE-OAK

Allocasuarina littoralis (Casuarinaceae)

OVERLEAF RIGHT: This tree may look like a pine but is actually a completely unrelated species. The resemblance is due to convergent evolution: unrelated species independently developing similar solutions to the same environmental challenges. The morphologically analogous characters of she-oaks and pines—from the southern and northern hemispheres, respectively—are adaptations to the dry habitats in which they both grow. The slender branchlets of she-oaks and the needles of pines minimize water loss, and the tough, woody fruit heads of she-oaks and the cones of pines protect their seeds from destruction by forest fires. Only the female trees bear fruit, whose seeds are a favorite food of the glossy black cockatoo (*Calyptorhynchus lathami*). To access them, the birds crush the fruit heads with their large, powerful bills.

AUSTRALIA

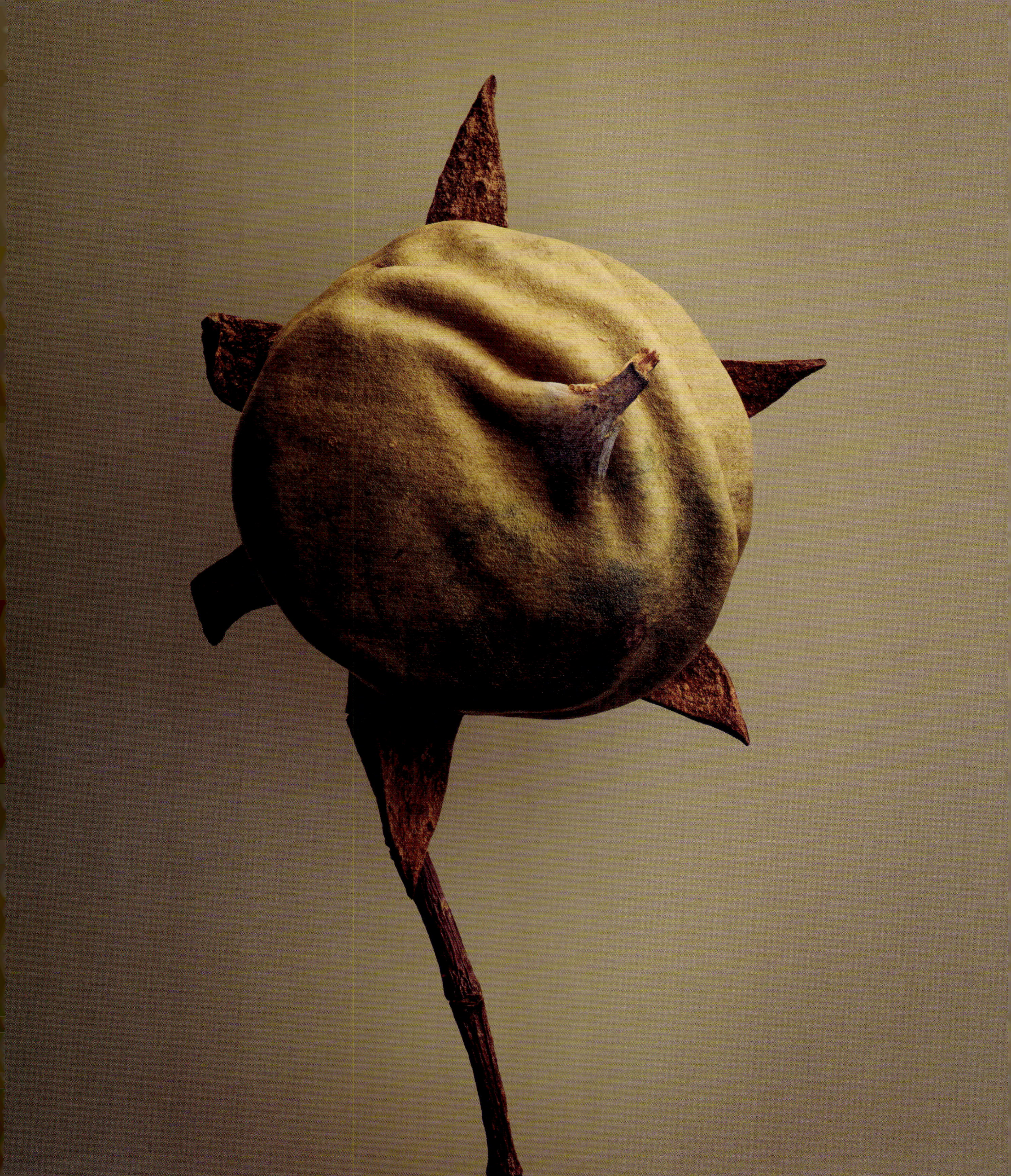

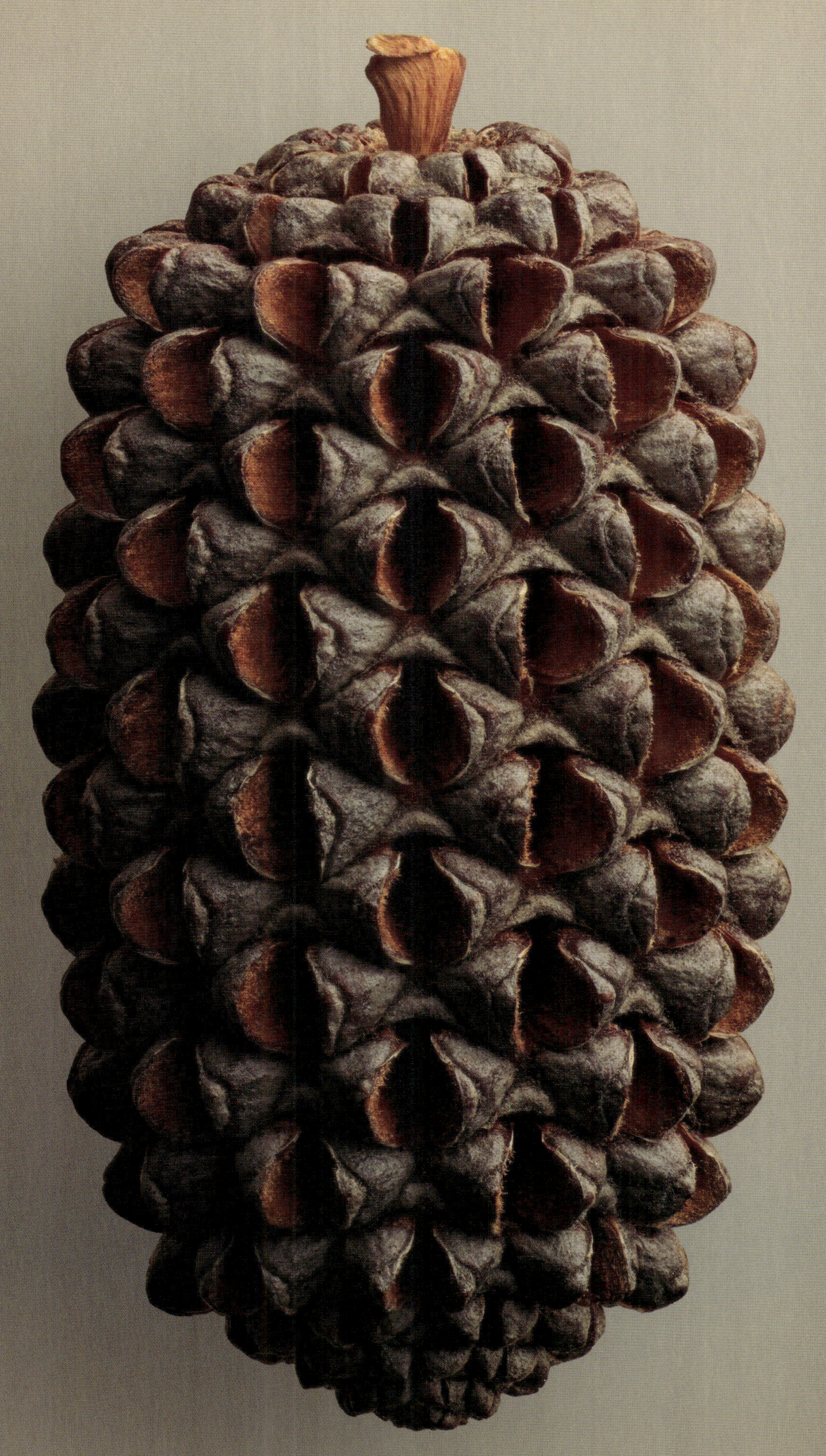

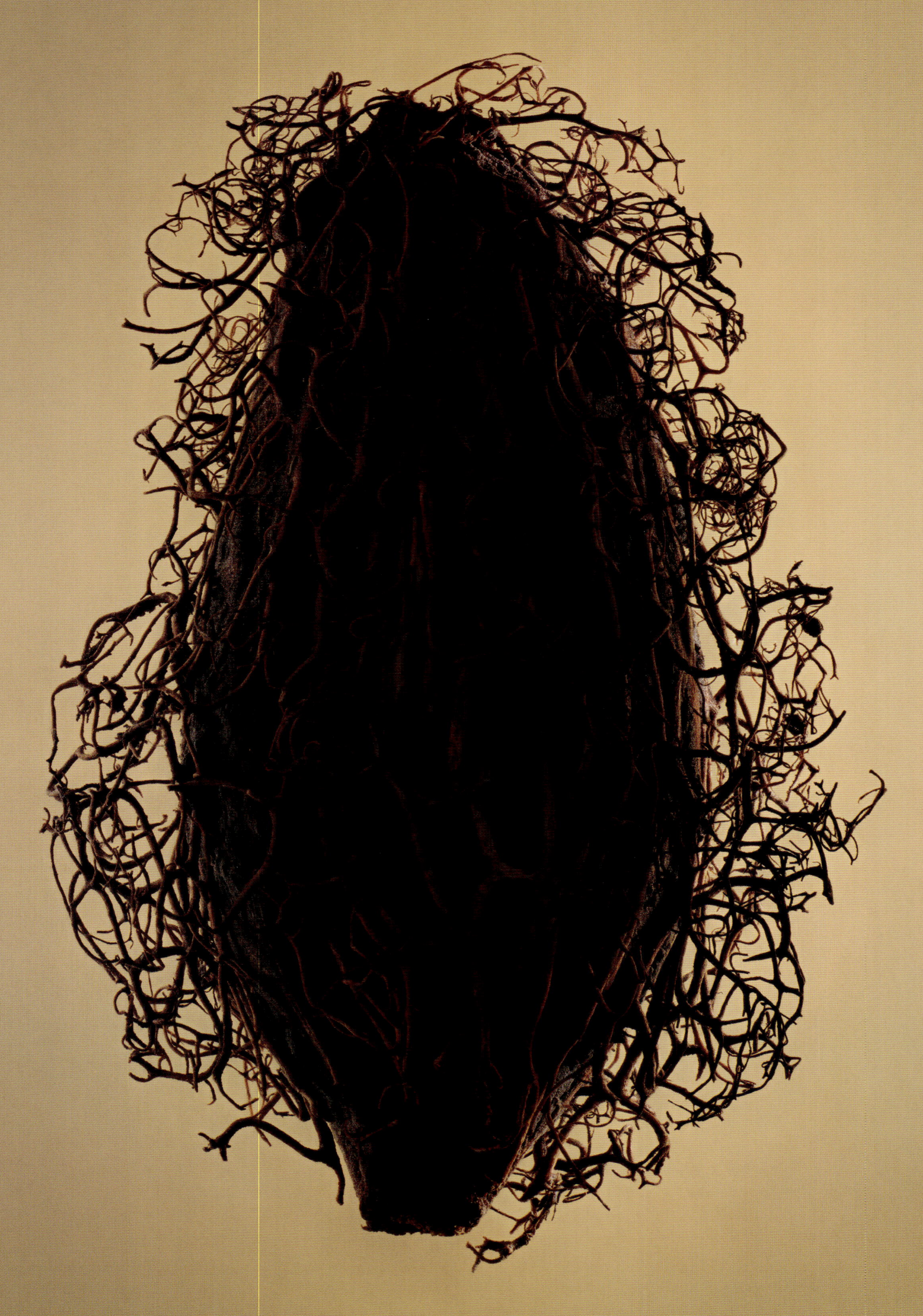

GREAT STIPULE TREE

Magnistipula butayei (Chrysobalanaceae)

OPPOSITE: This specimen was prepared from one of several ripe fruits found under a tree in dense forest close to the border between the Central African Republic and the Republic of the Congo. When he found the tree, the collector, David Harris, knew two things straightaway. First, that he had never seen this species before; and second, that the fruit must appeal to elephants. Its yeasty smell and mealy texture were reminiscent of other elephant-dispersed fruit, and he could think of no other animal able to ingest a stone of that size. Having taken the fruits back to camp to prepare dried specimens, he realized that their soft flesh would be unlikely to dry fully in the humidity of the rain forest. He decided instead to put one under a tap to wash away the pulp, which left behind this curious network of fibers.

REPUBLIC OF THE CONGO

YELLOW THISTLE

Tricholepis chaetolepis (Asteraceae)

OVERLEAF LEFT: This is a South Asian native species. It is most commonly found growing on sandy soils in semi-arid regions of Afghanistan, China, India, Pakistan, and Thailand. Collectors should be warned that it has vicious spines! Surprisingly, given the species' common name, this specimen was taken from a plant with rose-colored flowers. The "flower" of *Tricholepis chaetolepis* is actually a capitulum, that is, a composite of many tiny flowers. This is a diagnostic character for members of the daisy family and the reason they are sometimes known as the Compositae. Each of the flowers develops into a single-seeded fruit called an achene. These plants are widely sold in local markets for use in traditional medicine; all the aerial parts are dried and ground into a powder for treating various ailments (e.g. skin diseases), reducing fever, and "purifying" the blood.

AFGHANISTAN

UMKHALAPHANGA

Lichtensteinia interrupta (Apiaceae)

OVERLEAF RIGHT: This species is one of the Apiaceae (also known as the Umbelliferae), a family notable for its impressive number of edible species, including carrot, aniseed, celery, parsnips, fennel, dill, parsley, coriander, and angelica. It also includes a species that is definitely *not* edible: the hemlock (*Conium maculatum*) that ancient Greek philosopher Socrates was forced to drink. The great majority of the family are herbaceous plants with feathery leaves. When it comes to identifying the taxon (i.e. group) to which a member of the Apiaceae belongs, the leaves are arguably less helpful than the fruit. This specimen from *Lichtensteinia interrupta* is similar in character to the familiar coriander "seed" (technically a fruit): both fruits comprise two parts, with each part containing a single seed. The name "umkhalaphanga" is from the language of the Zulu people. The plant occurs naturally only in South Africa.

SOUTH AFRICA

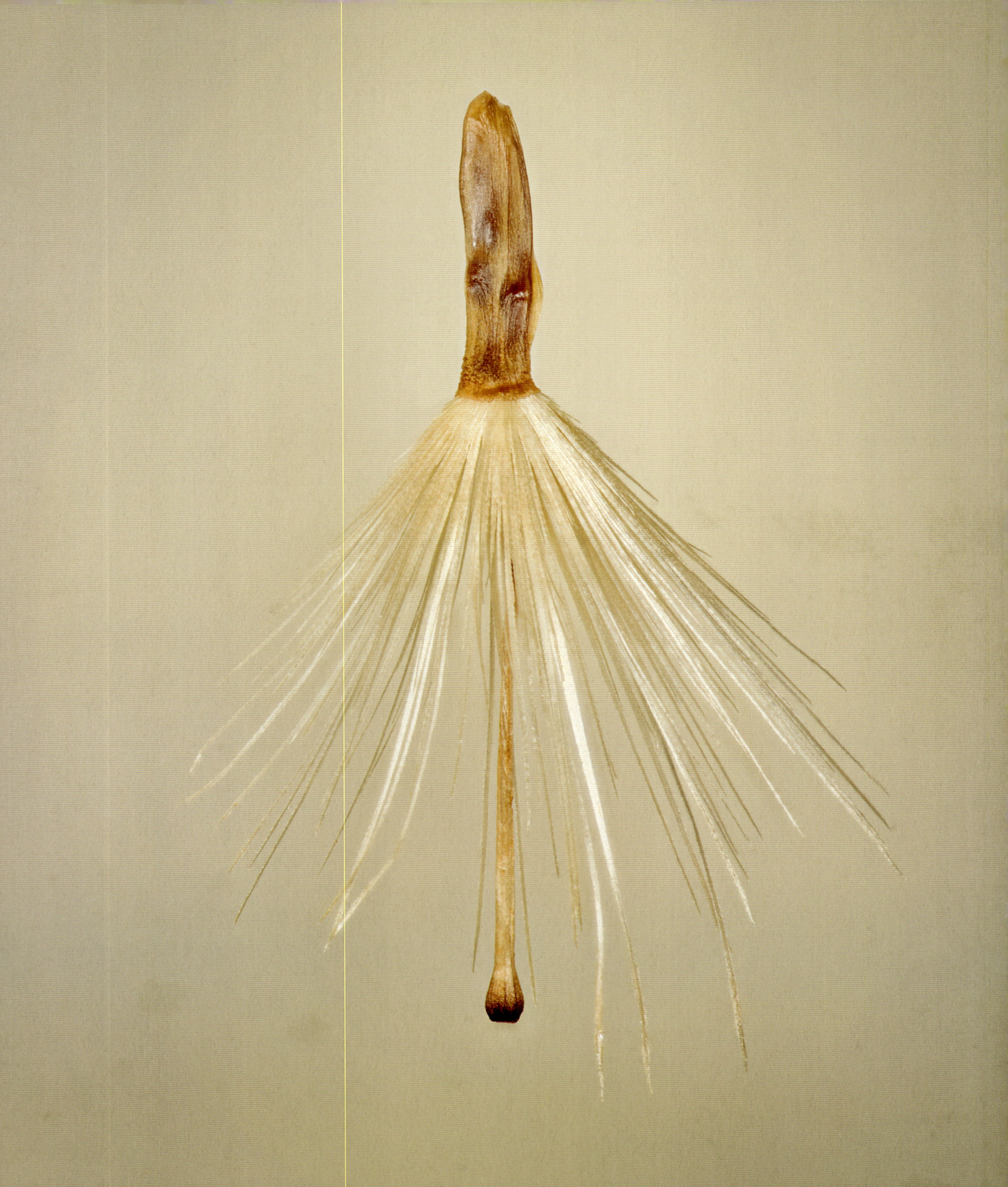

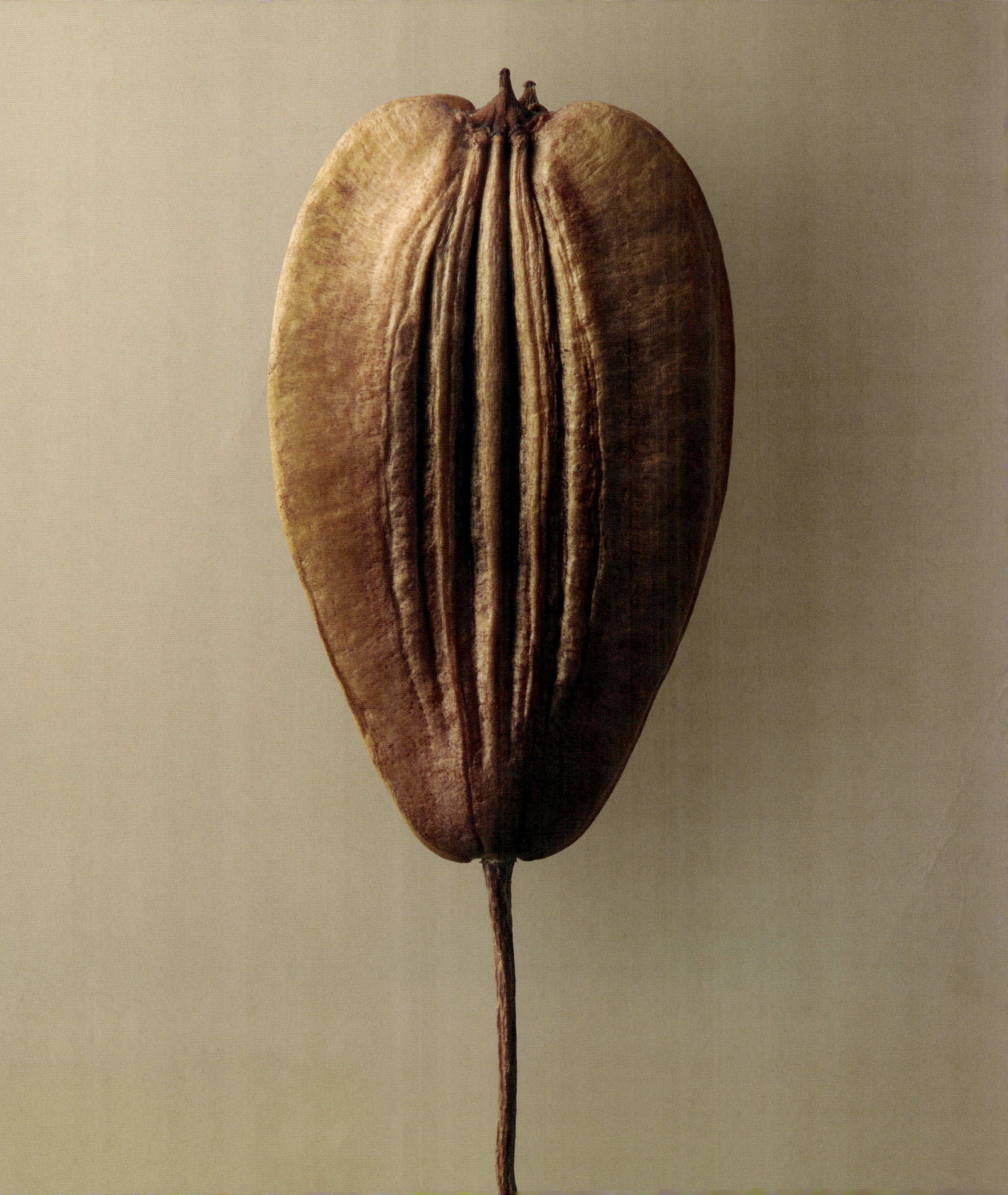

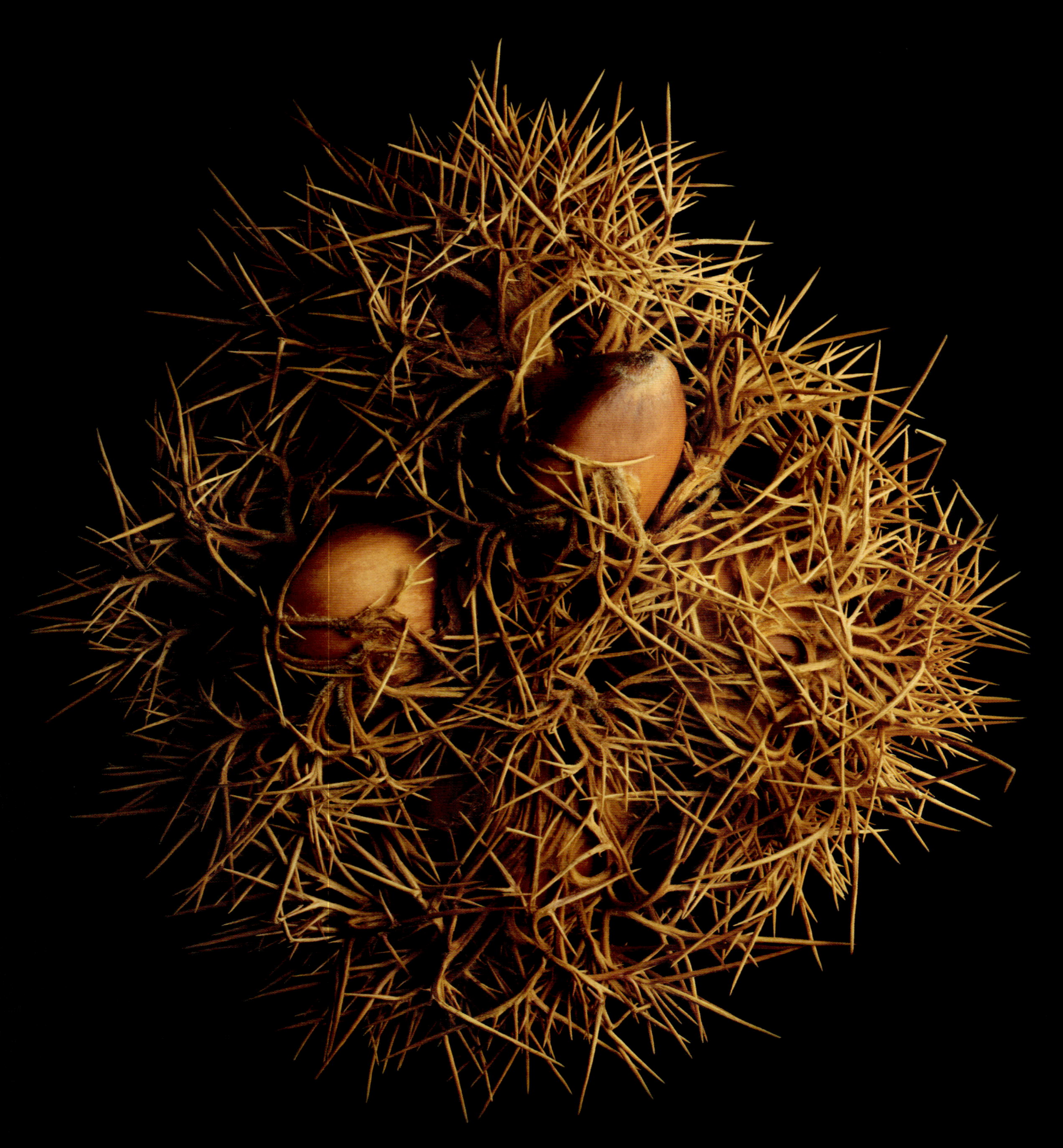

HIMALAYAN HAZELNUT

Corylus ferox (Betulaceae)

OPPOSITE: Native to the Himalayas, this is a medium-size tree growing at altitudes as high as 11,800 feet (3,600 m). This specimen was collected in Sichuan Province in China, from a plant within a broad-leaved, deciduous forest downstream from the Hailuogou glacier. The nuts are enclosed by a burr covered in sharp spines (hence the specific epithet *ferox*, Latin for "fierce"). The kernels within the nuts are edible; they can be eaten raw but are usually preferred roasted. The trees are rarely cultivated. Instead, local people gather nuts from wild populations and carry out different regimes of forest management to maintain them.

CHINA

ZANZIBAR COPAL

Hymenaea verrucosa (Fabaceae)

OVERLEAF LEFT: Many trees across the world produce resin, which people have put to various uses, including as lamp fuel, firelighters, incense, medicine, and varnish. The resin of *Hymenaea verrucosa* was heavily exploited in East Africa in the middle of the nineteenth century. Across Europe and North America at that time, the railway system was expanding and the resin was needed for the varnish applied to wooden train carriages. One of the common names for this species is "Zanzibar copal" because the sultan of Zanzibar historically controlled its trade. Copal is the name for hard, dried resin (amber is its fossilized equivalent). It occurs in coastal Tanzania, Kenya, Mozambique, islands in the Indian Ocean, and Madagascar.

MOZAMBIQUE

ZANZIBAR FIG

Ficus sansibarica (Moraceae)

OVERLEAF RIGHT: This plant is related to *Ficus carica*, cultivated in Mediterranean countries for its edible fruit. However, unlike that species, which is a small tree, *Ficus sansibarica* is a strangler; it attaches itself to a big tree and uses it for support. The ripe fruit is eaten by chimpanzees and the seeds are carried in their digestive system until being deposited at a distance from the parent plant. This specimen was collected by botanist and former RBGE student Sydney Ndolo Ebika, who observed chimpanzees feeding on it in the forest at Goualougo in the Republic of the Congo. The species is widespread across tropical Africa, but at this particular site individual plants are extremely rare. Therefore, primatologists suggest that chimpanzees are either very good at finding fruiting individuals or that they remember their location from previous visits.

REPUBLIC OF THE CONGO

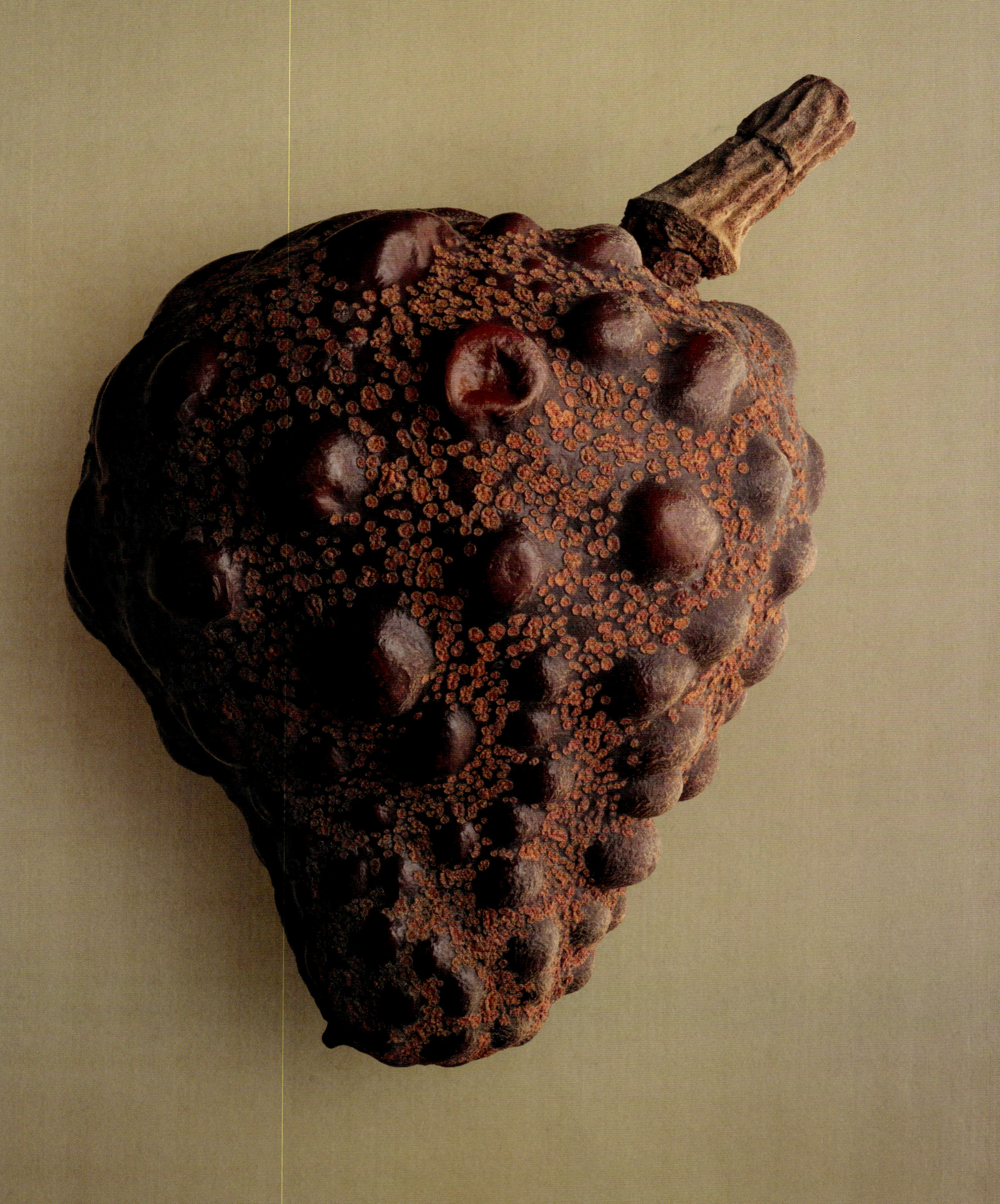

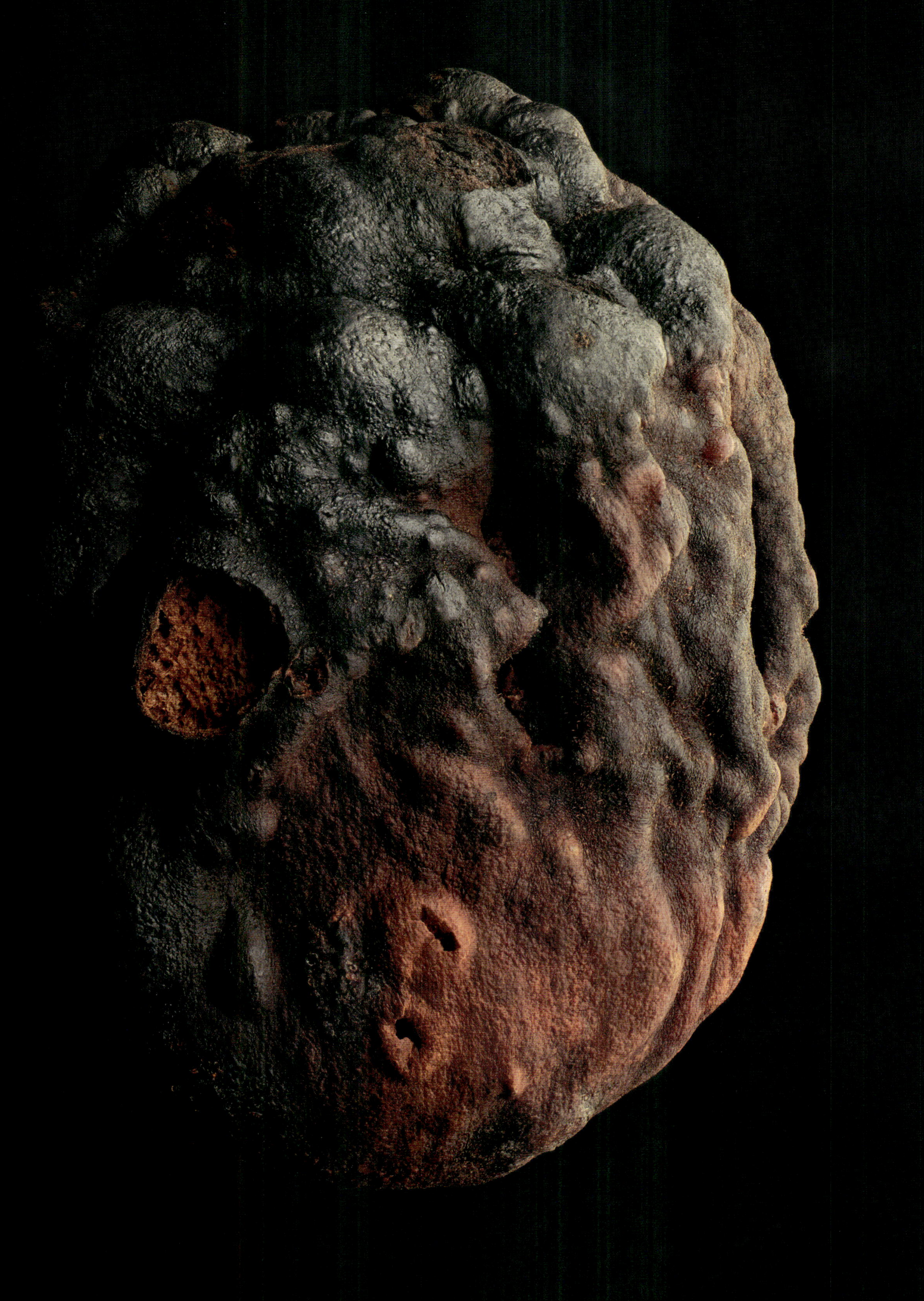

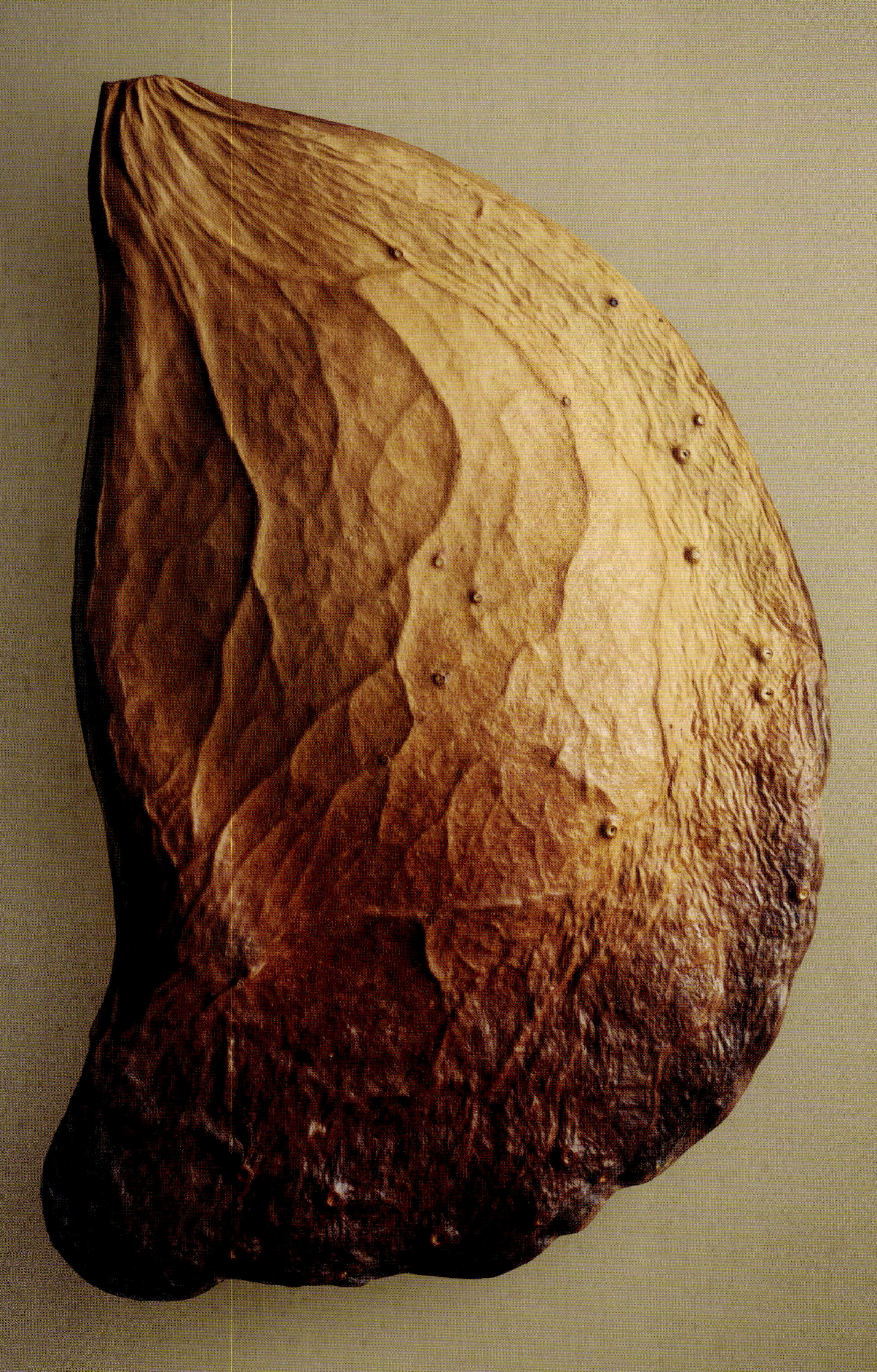

BITTER WOOD

Quassia borneensis (Simaroubaceae)

OPPOSITE: This small tree is found on the islands of Sumatra and Borneo, often in peat-swamp forest. Like other species in the genus, it produces bitter compounds known as quassinoids, which give its parts a bitter taste. In Peninsular Malaysia, it is known as *kayu pahit,* meaning "bitter wood." In traditional medicine, root infusions are drunk to treat a range of ailments, including hypertension and impotence. Extracts have been shown to have anti-inflammatory properties. The prune-shaped, slightly flattened ripe fruits are dark purple-red, becoming shiny-brown tan when dry.

MALAYSIA

LABLAB

Lablab purpureus (Fabaceae)

OVERLEAF LEFT: This twining vine is native to East Africa. Although its seeds are generally edible and it is grown as a pulse crop, certain varieties can cause cyanide poisoning. A surprising number of tropical food plants contain cyanogenic glycosides, which are converted to cyanide in the digestive tract. In some species, this is a natural trait that farmers have selected for in order to prevent pests from damaging their crops. Humans have come up with ways to prepare potentially poisonous seeds for safe consumption, for example by soaking pulses to leach out the toxins before cooking. Sadly, there have been cases of inexperienced cooks becoming seriously ill or even dying as a result of their ignorance of these methods. Lablab's resistance to drought makes it an ideal crop for low-rainfall areas.

NIGER

DISK TREFOIL

Anthyllis circinnata (Fabaceae)

OVERLEAF RIGHT: This is a sprawling herbaceous plant with multiple branched stems. It has a broadly Mediterranean distribution, occurring from France and Morocco all the way east to Iran and Iraq. Growing on open grassland and on abandoned terraces, it is a valued forage species. The yellow or orange flowers are reportedly visited by honeybees and mason bees. The characteristic circular fruits are easily recognized by their papery margins, which recall those of *Medicago* (the medicks and their relatives) and other closely related leguminous species. The specific epithet derives from the Latin word for "rounded," especially in the sense of a flat coil. This specimen was collected in Syria in 1908.

SYRIA

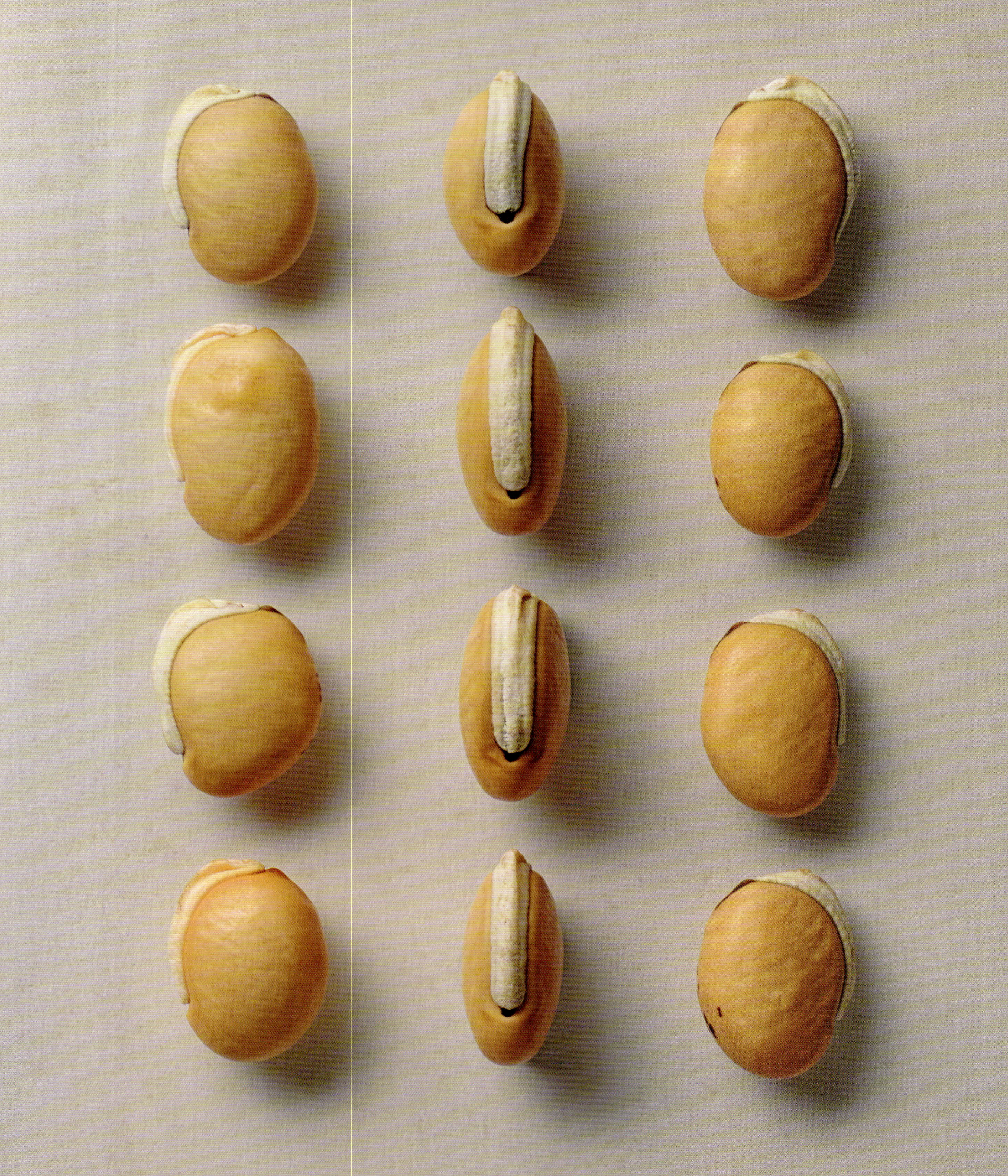

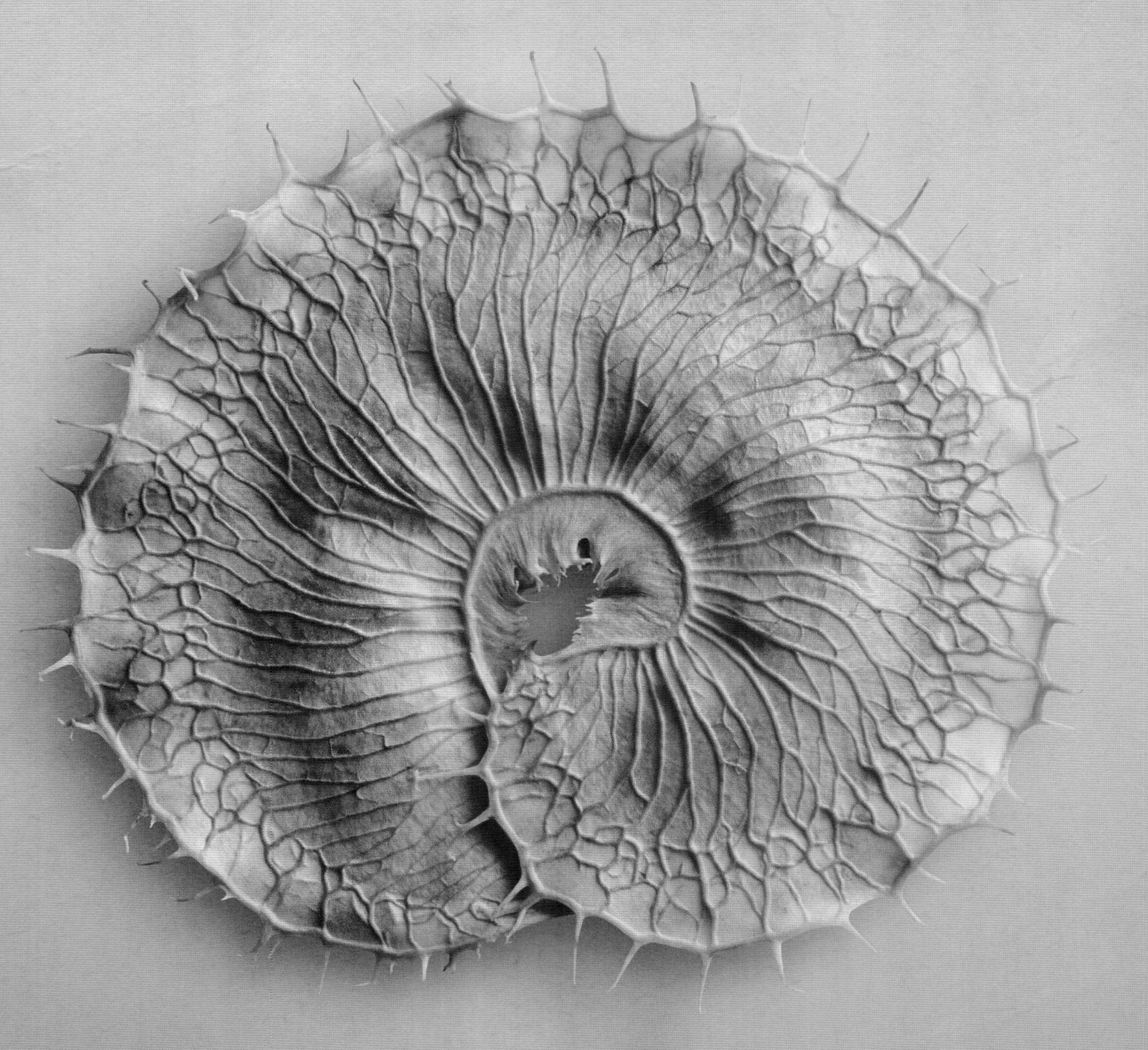

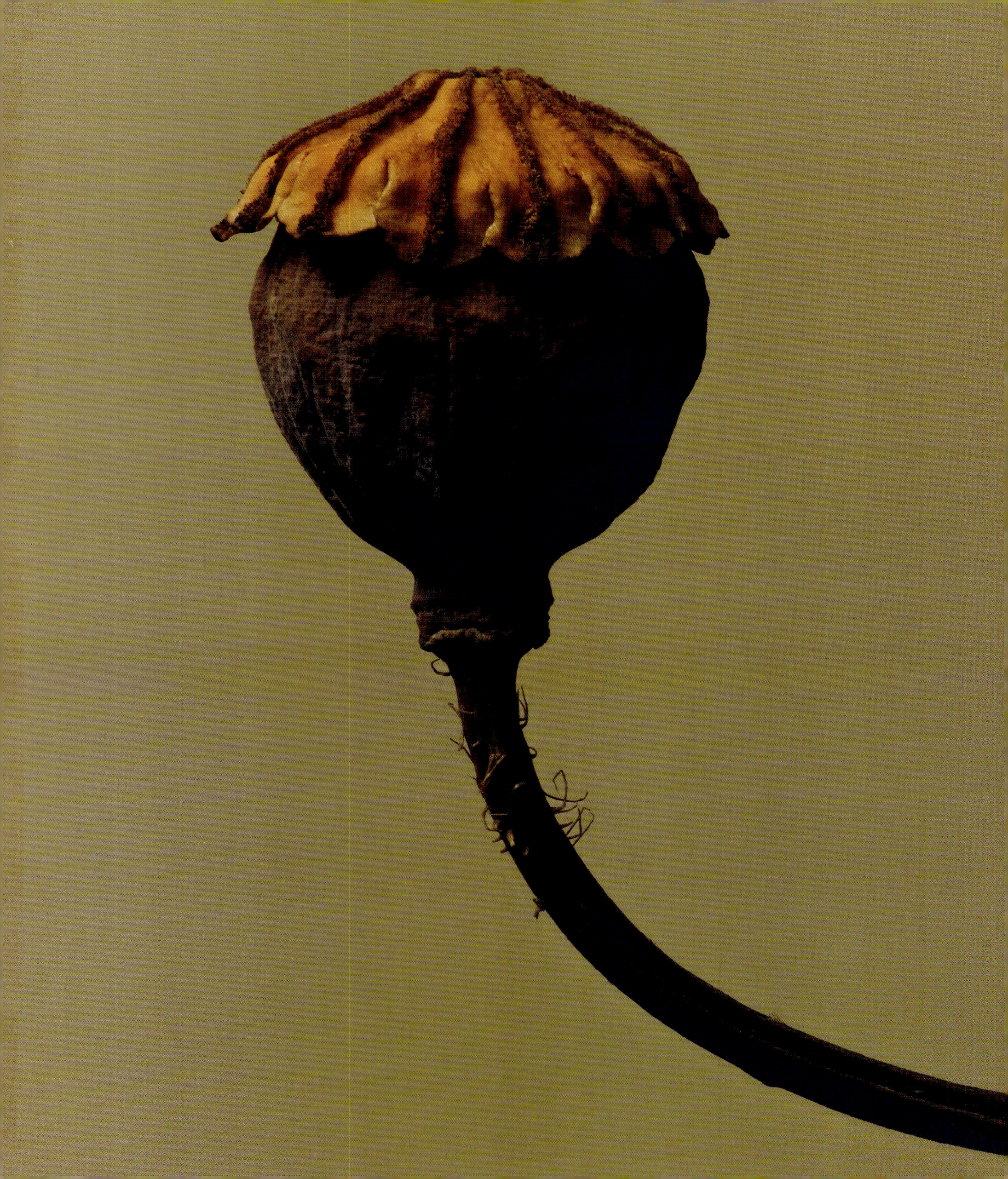

FLANDERS POPPY

Papaver rhoeas (Papaveraceae)

OPPOSITE: The flowers of this species have come to represent the loss of soldiers' lives in the First World War and subsequent armed conflicts. The extensive ground disturbance caused by battle allowed the plant to become established and bloom in the no-man's-lands between the trenches of the Western Front. Its flowers then came to be adopted as a symbol of remembrance after publication of the poem "In Flanders Fields" by Canadian officer and surgeon John McCrae, which referred to poppies growing over the graves of fallen soldiers. The black seeds are edible and are often used to add flavor and texture to bread and cakes.

RBGE CULTIVATED

SINGHARA NUT

Trapa natans var. *natans* (Lythraceae)

OVERLEAF LEFT: In this variety of the water chestnut, spines are developed from all four corners of the fruit, though with one pair longer than the other (in India it was therefore known to William Roxburgh as *Trapa quadrispinosa*). The fruit is "indehiscent," that is, its walls do not break open to release the seed, but gradually break down by decay or physical damage. The plant is a floating aquatic and the fruit sinks to the bottom of a pond, lake, or flooded field, where the seed within it can remain viable for up to twelve years.

INDIA

HEIRLOOM BEAN

Phaseolus vulgaris (Fabaceae)

OVERLEAF RIGHT: The genus *Phaseolus* was named in 1753 and comprises about seventy-five recognized species. Growth habits vary; some species are twining climbers, others have a more shrubby habit. Many have beautiful pea-like flowers, and all have the distinctive pod as a fruit. Their testae (seed coats) show great variation in color and pattern. *Phaseolus* is native to most countries in South and Central America, stretching as far as the southern states of the United States. Species have adapted or been bred over time to thrive in different climates. Consequently, domesticated species are cultivated extensively across the globe. *Phaseolus vulgaris* is also known as "common bean" and has many varieties, including the familiar kidney bean and pinto bean. These, along with other pulses (edible seeds of plants in the legume family), are key sources of proteins and starch. The specimens in this image are an heirloom variety, one which has not been widely domesticated and will grow true from seed.

RBGE CULTIVATED

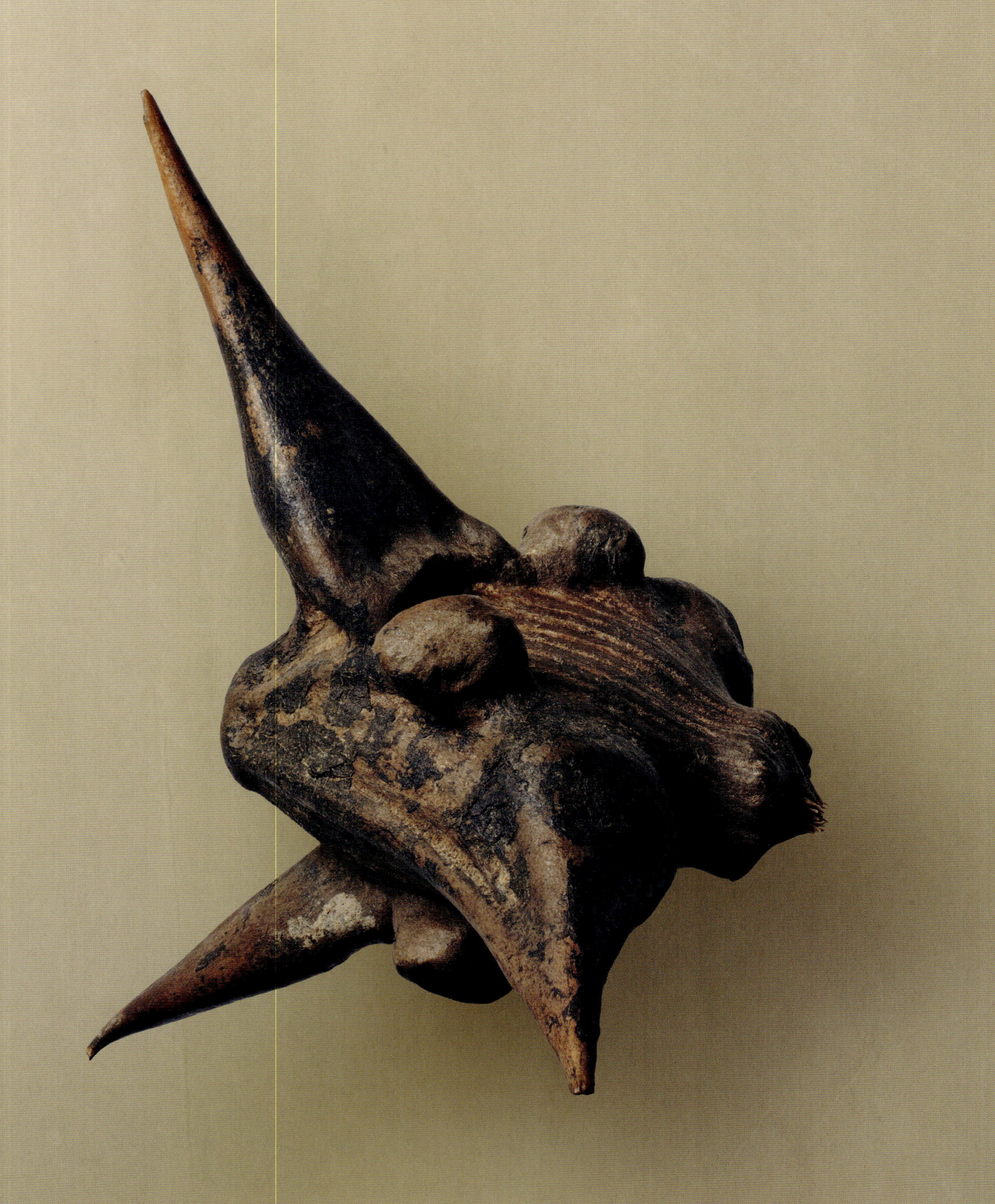

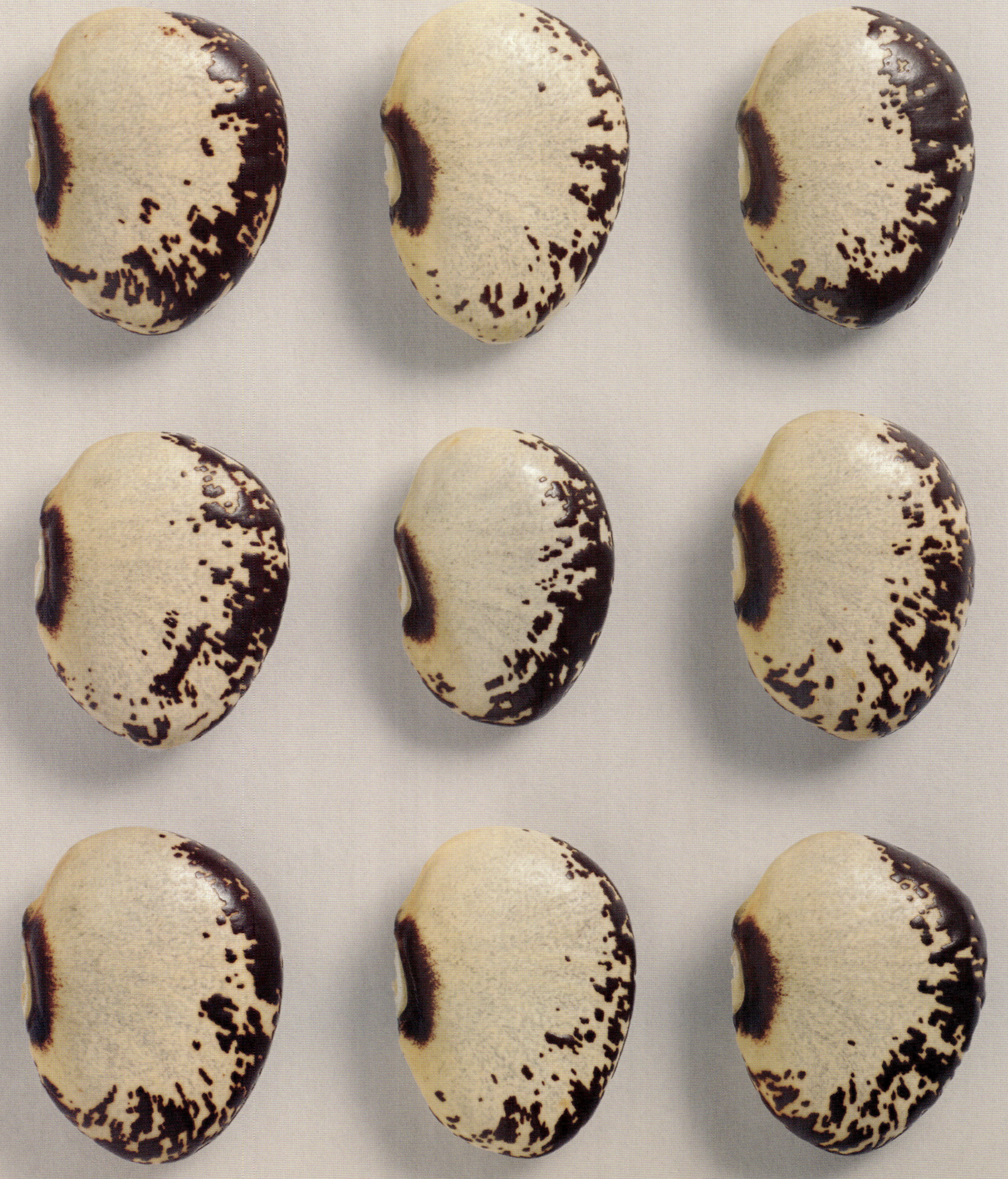

ACKNOWLEDGMENTS

The Hidden Beauty of Seeds & Fruits has been a hugely rewarding project to create, and it has opened my eyes further to the ingenuity and diversity of nature. I feel privileged to have had the opportunity to study the beautiful specimens within these pages, and I am hugely grateful to the Royal Botanic Garden Edinburgh for allowing me such open access to their collection. I hope you will be proud of this body of work, and I'll look forward to sharing your wonderful collections with a wide new audience.

My sincere thanks go to the following people for their contribution to the scientific text: Hannah Atkins, Alexandra Davey, Martin Gardner, Zoë Goodwin, David Harris, Kim Howell, Sabina Knees, Mark Newman, Henry Noltie, Lesley Scott, Mark Watson, and Peter Wilkie. Despite difficult circumstances due to the COVID-19 lockdown, you provided educational and entertaining text that I am sure will be enjoyed by many. I am especially grateful to Lesley Scott, whose enthusiasm and positivity for the project was a major help in bringing it to life. I feel very fortunate to have had you alongside me cabinet after cabinet.

Very special thanks go to Garrett McGrath and his publishing team at Abrams for their great work on this book. Following up *Microsculpture* was always going to be a big challenge, but once again you have produced a stunning publication, and I'll be looking forward to the next one.

As always though, big love goes to my wife Isla and children Seb and Elli. I am forever thankful for the support and freedom you give me to produce my work; it simply wouldn't be possible without you.

LIST OF CONTRIBUTORS TO THE TEXT

Hannah Atkins	Zoë Goodwin	Sabina Knees	Lesley Scott
Alexandra Davey	David Harris	Mark Newman	Mark Watson
Martin Gardner	Kim Howell	Henry Noltie	Peter Wilkie

ABOUT THE AUTHOR

Levon Biss is a British artist widely regarded as the leading macro photographer of his generation. His photography has been exhibited around the globe and is held in numerous public and private collections. Focusing on natural history, Levon's photography presents an unseen world to a wider audience, helping people enjoy and appreciate elements of nature that are normally invisible to the naked eye. He has worked with museum collections in the Middle East, Europe, and the United States, and his previous project *Microsculpture* has been exhibited in over twenty countries. Levon's TED talks have been viewed by millions, and his photography is now widely used in schools for engaging the next generation with nature. He continues to work from his studio in the English countryside.

Limited edition prints are available at www.levonbiss.com/prints.

DEVIL'S CLAW

Proboscidea louisianica subsp. *fragrans (Martyniaceae)*

HALF-TITLE: This herbaceous plant is named for the two curved horns on its fruit, one on each half. The genus name, *Proboscidea*, derives from the word *proboscis* and recalls the elongated mouthparts of certain species of insect; and the common name, "devil's claw," is self-explanatory. Each fruit contains about forty seeds, which are released gradually as it slowly dries and splits open. An example of a successful hitchhiker, this plant has developed a clever adaptation that takes advantage of large grazing animals to disperse its seeds. The claws attach readily to fur or get caught around fetlocks or hooves. The handwritten note on the label of this specimen says "Mule Grab," which is another of its common names.

USA

AIBIKA

Abelmoschus manihot var. *pungens (Malvaceae)*

FRONTISPIECE: This shrub is related to okra (*Abelmoschus esculentus*), but differs in that the leaves are edible, not the fruit. A fiber-like jute can be extracted from the stems. The species occurs in India eastwards to China but is also cultivated in West Africa and South America. This variety was first described as *Hibiscus pungens* by William Roxburgh, superintendent of the Calcutta Botanic Garden, based on specimens from Nepal. It occurs on the lower slopes of the Himalayas. The varietal name, *pungens* (Latin for "piercing"), refers to the bristly hairs that cover the plant and enter the skin like spines. This specimen was collected by George Henry Cave, probably in the Darjeeling District of West Bengal.

INDIA

KETEPUK

Claoxylon longifolium var. *rugifrux (Euphorbiaceae)*

FOREWORD: This small tree, growing to 33 feet (10 m) tall, is usually found along rivers or in secondary forest. It is found only on the island of Borneo, in Sarawak and Kalimantan. Each of its pendulous infructescences (fruit heads) bear many fruits, as seen in this specimen. The fruits are greenish-yellow, becoming red when ripe. The varietal name, *rugifrux*, means "rough-fruited." Each fruit comprises three parts and splits to expose three large seeds. The leaves are used to wrap fish for roasting.

INDONESIA

Editor: Garrett McGrath
Designer: Darilyn Lowe Carnes
Production Manager: Larry Pekarek

Library of Congress Control Number: 2020944093

ISBN: 978-1-4197-5215-5
eISBN: 978-1-64700-371-5

Printed and bound in China
10 9 8 7 6 5 4

Abrams® is a registered trademark of
Harry N. Abrams, Inc.

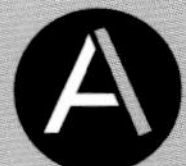

ABRAMS The Art of Books
195 Broadway, New York, NY 10007
abramsbooks.com

ABRAMS is represented in the UK and Europe by Abrams & Chronicle Books, 22-24 Ely Place, London EC1N 6TE and Média-Participations, 57 rue Gaston Tessier, 75166 Paris, France. abramsandchronicle.co.uk and media-participations.com
info@abramsandchronicle.co.uk